CHILDREN
IN THE
CROSSFIRE

CHILDREN IN THE CROSSFIRE

The Tragedy of
Parental Kidnaping

SALLY ABRAHMS

New York

ATHENEUM

1983

Strand M-21929 08-22-83 $14.95

Library of Congress Cataloging in Publication Data

Abrahms, Sally.
    Children in the crossfire.

    Bibliography: p.
    Includes index.
        1. Kidnapping, Parental—United States.   2. Custody
of children—United States.   3. Parent and child—
United States.   I. Title.
HV6598.A23   1983   362.8'2   82-73030
ISBN 0-689-11339-0

Published simultaneously in Canada by McClelland and Stewart Ltd.
Composition by Maryland Linotype Composition Co., Inc.
Manufactured by Fairfield Graphics, Fairfield, Pennsylvania
Designed by Kathleen Carey
First Edition

To little Annas everywhere

Contents

Contents

Contents

V
The Future

Preface

M Y C H I L D S N A T C H I N G "career" began two years ago when I wrote a magazine article on the subject. Friends and colleagues had never heard of the problem. "What do you mean, a parent kidnaps his or her child?" they gasped. "That's ridiculous. It doesn't happen. You're making it up." Even family law attorneys were confused when I consulted them. It was obvious that many of them, too, were unaware of the phenomenon. Only a couple of years have elapsed since I first explored the subject, but that short span is significant. No longer did I need to define *childsnatching* to lawyers and laymen while researching this book. In fact, today everyone seems to know an abducted youngster or a victimized parent. Childsnatching—or child stealing—is chic conversation on the cocktail party circuit and has even tainted some of the partygoers.

Sobering insights into the dimensions of the problem became apparent after I researched the topic for a national television program. Instead of finding a few ill-fated fathers and mothers,

I stumbled upon an epidemic of disturbing proportions. Some parents, themselves the victims of childsnatching, confessed that *they* had considered stealing their offspring. The head of one fathers' rights group told me: "Every divorced or divorcing man I know has thought of it as an option. Some of us do it. We all have our plane tickets in our back pockets, waiting for the right moment."

Anguished parents spoke of having their youngsters violently ripped from their arms, their feelings of pain and powerlessness when their children abruptly disappeared, the ceaseless agonizing: Are they safe? Are they happy? Are they alive? Parents told tales of giving up after frantic, financially draining chases, or realizing that their children would never be returned, or the euphoria of finding them—only to discover virtual strangers, often with new names, new hair colors, or foreign nationalities. I also interviewed the other side: parents who had stolen, claiming they had kidnaped "for love" when it was almost always for spite.

After speaking with snatchers and with parental victims, I wondered how the kids themselves—the objects of the feuding —were faring. Their quotations were curiously absent from newspaper and magazine pieces, which seemed to dwell on the parents' pain, paying mere lip service to the suffering of the children. Statements from psychiatrists and social workers testified to the destructive, sometimes irreversible effects of child stealing on the kids. Rather than rely on others to tell their stories, I wanted to learn about the experience firsthand, from the children. What did it feel like to be kidnaped by a parent? Was it as dreadful as family therapists contended? Or could running off with Mom or Dad ever be fun?

Childsnatching is so new a subject that no studies are available on how it affects kids. If I wanted to write a book that focused on the children, I had to do some sleuthing on my own. The trick was not only to track down these youngsters, but to get them to talk—if they could. So many were still so young that in-depth interviews were impossible. Nevertheless, a few barely past the toddler phase provided me with insights as revealing as any I had gathered from more grownup subjects. My most promising prospects, I discovered, were the eleven- to thirteen-year-olds. They were old enough to sort through the fantasy, yet young enough to remember their experiences vividly.

The problem proved to be twofold: not only to locate these children but, more important, to convince their parents to let them be interviewed. It is a telling fact that even though there are hundreds of thousands of children snatched each year, only a few will talk about their abductions. One West Coast therapist who had planned to study the effects of the crime on returned children abandoned her project when she couldn't find enough participants.

Over and over, parents apologized to me for bowing out of interviews. "My child is too disturbed. Perhaps some day when he gets better he can speak with you." "My son was in such bad shape when he came back. He is finally leading a more normal life. I can't risk a relapse." "You can't talk to my daughter because I have to protect her. Her father certainly never did. I am the only one left who can." Refusals came because some of the younger children had no idea they had been stolen and their parents did not want to tell them. Some said no because they were in hiding. Out of fear of a repeat snatch, they had gone underground, and thought I might betray them to their exes. Many parents were reluctant to introduce me, but consented, telling me, "If it will help others . . ." All agreed on the condition that I change their children's names—many were used to aliases anyway, from living on the run!

I interviewed a handful of youngsters in person, but most of my conversations were conducted by telephone. The kids, I found, were grateful for the anonymity the phone provided, and therefore were candid and cooperative. Of course I received my fair share of "I don't know" or "I can't remember" when I pumped them about their time away. Did they really not remember? Therapists whom I consulted assured me that the children recalled being stolen—perhaps too well—but simply could not bear to rehash the details of their ordeals.

Despite my difficulty in finding suitable subjects, I spoke with a variety of stolen children: those found as long ago as twelve years, or recovered only the day before; away for a decade or a few days; whisked to the next town or to another continent; snatched just once and back for keeps or taken more than once, interviewed "in between" abductions. (Two youngsters had been kidnaped six times, three by each parent.) I quizzed boys and girls returned to their parents and those on the run. I even managed to talk with kids left behind in a snatch, who described watching their fathers or mothers steal their siblings, but not choose them.

Whatever their situation, the message was the same: terror at being taken by a parent-turned-kidnaper. Being abducted by a stranger would have been less traumatic, they maintained, but by a *parent* . . .? They spoke of trusting and admiring that adult, but later feeling betrayed, cheated, and frightened. Most were too scared to bolt. Those who sneaked away to call home told how they got caught by their "captors" or tried to dial their deserted parents, only to find a different voice in a different state, because they were too young to know about area codes.

The children recalled feeling all alone, of having no support, no one in whom to confide, always running, hiding, being hunted, and of longing desperately to be caught and returned. They explained their anxiety even after being rescued, of having to disappear again, perpetually on the alert for yet another kidnaping.

Children cried when they relived their days away—even those abducted several years before. "What did I do wrong?" they'd ask me. "If only I had been a better child. If only my parents had not gotten a divorce. If only . . . if only . . ." they'd say.

I was naive. Like most of you reading this book, I assumed

that while it may be unpleasant to be stolen, at least a child is with a concerned parent. How bad could that be? It never occurred to me that a parent who went to the trouble of kidnaping a child and uprooting himself or herself would hurt that child.

I was wrong.

What I discovered was shocking. I uncovered rampant acts of child abuse—sexual, physical, and emotional. The sordid stories I heard repeatedly were not the innocent fantasies of young kids, but true-life accounts of mistreatment and, in some instances, outright torture. Child after child catalogued the devastating tales he and she had been told by "loving" parents: "Mommy is a whore"; "Your father is an alcoholic"; "Daddy is dead." Abductors did not mind hiring professional thugs to do their dirty work, or resorting to violence themselves, even if their children might be hurt, or killed, in the scuffle. These were confused, seriously sick adults, rather than nurturing parents.

From interviewing both snatchers-to-be and successful stealers, I unearthed an alarming profile—parents intent on satisfying their own selfish impulses at the expense of their kids, using their children as bargaining pawns in perverted reconciliation attempts, or simply as ways to torment a former mate. Some did not attempt to mask their motives, but confessed that all they wanted was to "get even." I spoke with children who did not even live with the parent who abducted them, but down the street, or in another state. Despite their one-upmanship, the snatchers found little glory. Like their victims, they said they were forced to change their names and jobs and give up all contact with family and friends. They were as desperate and lonely as their children.

Ironically, abductors were often easier to scout than parental victims. Eager to justify their kidnaping (to rescue their offspring from an unfit father or mother, they'd claim), most viewed themselves as Robin Hoods—naughty for breaking the law, but noble for taking the risk.

Like returned youngsters, custodial parents proved elusive.

When I tried to locate several I had interviewed in the past, I found they had vanished. Apparently my contacts had been reunited with their children and now *they* were on the run from their former spouses. I had called one woman in Pennsylvania several times when I was working at ABC News's *20/20* on a child-stealing segment. A year later, I dialed the number to get an update for this book. A man answered the telephone, told me tersely I had the wrong number, that he had never heard of the woman, and that he had had the same telephone number for thirty years. I called back twice, convinced I had dialed incorrectly. "Wrong number," he insisted. When this mother and I last spoke, she had just gotten her son back and had been terrified of a resnatch. Obviously the man was covering up for her. She was hiding.

One support group for parental victims warned me that adults whose kids had been returned might question my motives for contacting them. They were accustomed to all sorts of ruses from their ex-mates. How could they be sure I had not been hired to track them down? To prove I was legitimate, I wrote a letter explaining my book project to the members of this group, and instead of sending it directly to them, forwarded it to the head of the organization. She passed it on to the membership with her own note, confirming that I was really a reporter and not a spy. It didn't make much difference. Parents were still paranoid. One anonymous call came from a grandmother. "How did you get my daughter's name?" she pressed, even though the support group's letter explained her question. "How do I know you haven't duped the group and are only pretending to write a book, all the time on the payroll of my ex-son-in-law?"

An endless supply of rich research material came from parents whose kids were still missing. Most were referrals from ABC and *Ladies' Home Journal*, where I had worked on child-stealing pieces. Desperate parents had telephoned the television network and magazine after seeing these stories, looking for leads, and were told to call me. Day after day, parents would plead with me to help: "I'll do anything to get my baby back. *Anything!*" I was their mentor and their therapist, and for many, their last hope. They spoke of the indifference and arrogance of prosecutors and police, the incompetence of attorneys, and of being cheated by unscrupulous private investigators. It was quickly apparent that even those who wanted to act often did not know how. One call came from a Minnesota judge's clerk, who wanted information on child-stealing laws.

Parents phoned seeking advice, but also approval. "If I find my child, can I steal him back?" they'd ask. "Should I steal him back? Would you?" Or equally thorny problems: "My brother's wife just escaped from jail, broke into my brother's house, and grabbed their son. My brother went looking for them. He is carrying a loaded gun. I'm afraid if he finds her, he's going to kill her. What should I do?" Or another conversation: "My wife's ex-husband kidnaped their daughter. His brother is in touch with them. We want to intimidate the brother so he'll tell us where they're hiding. We're going to rough him up, and if he doesn't confess, tell him he's dead. What do you think of the plan?"

I was disturbed by my power. By my responsibility. People I had never met were trusting me. I listened to their stories and their schemes, offered what assistance I could, but never advocated illegal tactics. Yet I also knew that unless they resorted to them, it was unlikely they would ever see their children again. I became enraged at a "legal" system that encourages parents to break the law, even though the parents are more than willing to work through proper channels.

I built up a relationship with victimized parents across the country. At first they called for advice, but soon they began phoning with progress reports on their cases. Often they would call back to help *me,* supplying in-the-field tips on what agencies and procedures worked well, and which were guaranteed dead ends. We shared a bond. We became old friends.

I also cultivated a network of professional child stealers, some who commanded up to twenty thousand dollars per child. They would call from as far away as Europe, bragging of their latest kidnapings, trying to woo me with their yarns of muscle and derring-do, so that I would mention them in my book. While at ABC I watched a kingpin in the childsnatching business, who brags of a thousand successful recoveries, bungle an abduction from a schoolyard. With the rest of the ABC crew, I wound up in the principal's office, trying to explain the embarrassing episode.

Parents of missing children, wounded and desperate, are easy marks for aggressive detectives and lawyers. The problem with child stealing has been that no one, including experts like the Minnesota judge who called *me* for advice, has known how to act. A distraught mother told me: "If someone had given me a check for twenty-five thousand dollars and said 'Go find Michael,' I wouldn't know what to do." This book is a guide for parents like Michael's on what to do, where to go, whom to consult, even whom to avoid. Never do I suggest a parent should snatch a child whether it be legal or illegal, before or after a custody decree. The outcome is the same: damaged youngsters with lingering psychological, sometimes physical, scars.

My work is intended for mothers and fathers, sons and daughters—both victims and victimizers—who have been affected by parental abductions. It should help them cope more competently with their experiences by illustrating how the kidnapings have, and will, affect their lives. But my book has an even greater audience: children; detectives; attorneys; teachers; therapists; police; and all parents, divorced or with troubled marriages, who have youngsters.

Like a disease, there is no way to prevent it and no way to predict whom it may strike. Child stealing may occur after lots of warning or with none at all. No one is immune. "I'm no different from other women," moans one mother whose child has been missing for five years. "I met my ex-husband in college. We weren't weirdos. We were normal, average people."

In this pitiful war between the parents, it is the kids who are caught in the crossfire. Child stealing is the heartbreak of the Eighties.

Acknowledgments

I WOULD LIKE to thank the following people for their generous time, support, and candor: Gloria Yerkovich of Child Find; Professor Henry Foster, Jr.; Dr. Eugene Evans; Detective Ian Withers; Helen Hombosky of United Parents Against Child Stealing; my editor at Atheneum, Neil Nyren; Barbara Lowenstein, my agent; David Meyer, formerly of ABC: Patricia Hoff of the American Bar Association's Child Custody Project; Gerald A. Silver of Fathers' Rights of America; and Jan Harayda.

I am truly grateful to David Rosenthal for being a superb coach, counselor, and confidante.

Many thanks, too, to all of the stolen children who consented to being interviewed, even though they would have preferred to forget their experiences. I am especially appreciative of "Peter," "Ted," "Cliff," "Amy," "Rick," "Judy," "Laura," "Peggy," and "Jaime."

CHILDREN
IN THE
CROSSFIRE

Introduction

THEY ARE upper-crust or underprivileged, living off trust funds or on welfare. Snatchers scoop up their youngsters and vanish abroad, or live out of suitcases and station wagons, dragging their "spoils" from one seedy hotel to the next. Child stealing cuts across class lines, from billionaire bankers to maintenance men. Marital woes spare no ethnic or social group. When relationships dissolve, the custody battle is waged ostensibly to protect "the best interests of the child." Parents chant this phrase like the chorus in a Greek tragedy; it often turns into a classical tragedy when they play out their anger through their offspring. Emotions explode and children become easy tools for inflicting pain.

Childsnatching has a variety of definitions. Some consider it any abduction or concealment of a child by one parent, regardless of who has been awarded custody, and even when a custody decree has not been granted. Included is "restraint," where one parent denies the other access, but does not actually kidnap

3

the child. Based on the language of state and federal statutes, purists confine their definition to the theft by a noncustodial parent (or grandparent or other relatives) or their agents (such as detectives) from the custodial parent. Since both parents have an equal right to their child, no crime is committed if the father or mother runs away with the youngster before there is a custody decision—if they are still married, for instance, or are separated or divorced and have not filed for custody, or had their papers finalized.

The majority of snatchings do not fit this legal definition, however. Most occur before a court has awarded custody. One former national clearinghouse for child-stealing information, Children's Rights, Inc., in Washington, D.C., estimates that 70 to 80 percent of all parental abductions take place in this pre-decree period. Another study, conducted by Courtney Elliott for his Ph.D. dissertation at Catholic University, confirms that the majority of parents who steal their kids are not legally divorced. Elliott surveyed 243 members of Children's Rights and discovered that only 42 percent were divorced when their children were taken. Ten percent were married and living with their spouses at the time of the snatch, and 5 to 7 percent were never married but were still under the same roof with a mate when their kids disappeared.

Sometimes it is the custodial parent who vanishes with the child, but strictly speaking, this is not snatching, because the court has given the child to that parent. The lawful guardian is usually free to pick up stakes, provided a court has not conditioned its custody award on the parent's remaining within the jurisdiction. What frequently happens, too, is that the custodial parent stays put but refuses to allow an ex-spouse to see the child during visiting periods.

It is unrealistic to restrict the definition of child stealing to any one of these situations. Regardless of which parent does the snatching or the legal status of custody, the child is de-

4

prived of one of his or her parents, and a parent is deprived of her or his child. "One thing we always say in Fathers United for Equal Justice," claims Barry Sandrew of the Massachusetts men's rights group, "is that for every illegal kidnaping there are thousands of legal ones. We consider it child stealing even when a parent moves away. To kids it makes no difference if it is legal or illegal. It still affects them the same way."

Snatchers' styles vary; so do the names given to their crime: "child stealing"; "legalized kidnaping"; "childnapping"; "parental abduction"; "childsnatching"; "child rustling." One fathers' rights leader calls it "growing wings." Whatever the semantics or the modus operandi, the number of child thefts is soaring. No reliable statistics exist on how many children are snatched each year. One Library of Congress study estimates twenty-five thousand cases annually, while Children's Rights places the figure closer to a hundred thousand—or one abduction for every twenty-two divorces. Tucson, Arizona's United Parents Against Child Stealing, Inc. (UPACS) calculates three hundred thousand, and Michael Agopian, author of *Parental Child-Stealing,* contends the toll could be as high as four hundred thousand a year. The number of cases has more than doubled in the last five years, UPACS believes. In one California county, kids disappear at a rate of more than two a week.

Statistics vary startlingly, depending upon how the record keeper defines the act. Compiling accurate figures is practically impossible. There is no national reporting bureau, nor do all police keep track. No legal complaint can be filed without a custody decree. Even with a valid legal document in hand, some parents do not report an incident, knowing they will be turned away. They realize that child stealing of the 1980s is what wife and child abuse were to the 1960s and 1970s: a taboo topic, regarded as a domestic dispute rather than a serious social and legal problem.

Who are these missing youngsters? Most victims are between

the ages of three and seven, although many as old as twelve are taken. Children under three are too tough for a working parent to care for alone, while teens can phone home or run away. Even kids in elementary school, like those in third, fourth, and fifth grade, are grownup enough to understand what has happened and to take action, if they choose.

The number of childsnatchings is not surprising, considering today's staggering divorce statistics. Whenever a marriage is in jeopardy, child stealing is an option for one or both of the mates. In 1980, 1.2 million divorces were granted—67 percent more than in 1970, and triple the figure for 1960. In some parts of the country, one out of every two marriages dissolves; nationwide, the figure is one-third. Separations are also abundant. Each year, divorce affects more than 1 million children. In total, 12 million Americans under the age of eighteen are victims of split-ups, and 45 percent of all children born today will live with only one parent. In the past ten years, the number of single parent households leaped 80 percent.

After a separation or divorce, there are two parents, two separate homes, but only one child. A struggle often ensues over ownership of the offspring, and only one side can win. The loser seethes, furious at the judge and frustrated with his diminished role in parenting his child. Noncustodial mothers and fathers feel shut out, often convinced that their former spouses are unfit, or are disparaging them to the kids. Unable to shed their scheming partners, they are forced to keep in contact with each other "for the kid's sake," scheduling drop-offs and pickups so that Dad or Mom can have his or her all-too-brief time with the children. When a warring couple is unable to break off a bitter relationship, hostility escalates. For modern feuding parents, the children become the ultimate instrument of pain. "I've handled a lot of matrimonial cases," says one New York City attorney, herself the victim of child stealing, "and in the past, money and the division of the house and the car were the big issues. Now that both parents usually work and people generally have more, money is not the weapon it used to be, so couples use the kids."

Youngsters have always gotten a bad deal, even as far back as the Middle Ages, when they were viewed as nothing more than property to be passed between parents. Six hundred years later, this children-as-chattel attitude still prevails—only the management has changed hands, from the father to the mother. It used to be that men had total control over their offspring, including the right to sell them or condemn them to death. Those as young as seven were frequently shipped off to service, valued for the labor they could provide for their masters. Not until the sixteenth century were they appreciated as people, rather than potential purses, although the paternal right to the children remained undisputed until 1817. That is the date that poet Percy Bysshe Shelley became the first male-custody casualty, denied his children on the grounds that he was a "vicious and immoral" atheist. Soon after, in 1835, the Talfourd's Act gave courts the discretion to decide between parents for children under the age of seven. (Today the "tender years" doctrine still dictates, but judges now seem to favor Mom over Dad for the youngsters.) In the early 1900s, men no longer won automatic awards. In fact, by 1925, when England passed the Guardianship of Infants Act, it was a pretty even male/female race.

Custody decisions in America reflected English Common Law. The father-right entitlement triumphed throughout the last century, in part because of finances. Courts reasoned that since men were responsible for supporting their children, they should get to keep what they paid for, as with any other piece of property. Logically, when a father was denied custody, judges ruled he had no obligation to support his youngster.

Only when the treatment of children developed into a social and political issue in the early 1900s did their welfare outweigh monetary considerations. The new yardstick in custody decisions became "the child's best interests." Jurists decreed that because of their ability to breast-feed—and their availability to baby-sit—mothers were best qualified to nurture. Fathers, on the other hand, were out earning a living. How could they be expected to raise their children?

Mothers work away from the home, too, these days, but it does not seem to matter. Fathers are so out of favor in the courtroom that they are denied custody 92 percent of the time, qualifications notwithstanding. Recently a pediatrician lost custody to his ex-wife, and so did a man in charge of an elementary school. In a private conference with a New York State judge, another father recited a domestic relation law which states that neither parent has a superior right to custody. "Don't quote law to me," the judge snapped. "I would never allow a little girl to be in the custody of her father. Little girls belong with their mothers." Though usually unspoken, the "tender years" doctrine of the 1830s still prevails.

The word is out on sexist judges, and disapproving or discouraged attorneys who don't believe their male clients have a chance in court. Because of the maternal bias, fathers fed up with the unfavorable custody ratio are stealing their kids. Some abduct after they have lost an action; others avoid the courts completely, unwilling to take the risk they will be one of the lucky 8 percent.

But lately fathers have been making out a bit better in the custody contest. "The courts are now being a little more even-handed about it," says attorney Daniel Molinoff. "The trend is that if the mother is somewhat unfit, then the judge will give custody to the father, whereas years ago she had to be a real mad-bomber Communist prostitute."

Slowly the tide is turning. Disgruntled fathers are beginning to make waves, refusing to become "zoo daddies" relegated to the status of weekend visitors, instead of round-the-clock parents. They are organizing men's rights groups to legislate for more equitable custody laws and to fight for their children.

It is fast becoming acceptable for men to do the mothering. The 1980 Census reports that fathers raised more than a million children, a 65 percent increase over the past decade. Large numbers of single fathers make it easier for men to get away with child stealing. Full-time dads no longer look suspicious or conspicuous the way they would have even five years ago, so they are likely to hide undetected, no one wondering where Mrs. Jones may be.

Snatching is also on the rise because fathers are rejecting the once popular notion that men who divorce their mates must divorce their children. The abundance of single fathers has shown them that they need not be dismissed as parents simply because they have stopped being husbands. Men expect to be true dads. They spend thousands of dollars in order to hold onto their kids, battling through nasty custody contests. When they are denied their right to parent, these frustrated fathers may run off with their offspring.

Sex roles are changing, in part for financial reasons. A treacherous economy has made the two-paycheck family almost essential. According to a recent study conducted by the marketing research firm of Yankelovich, Skelly & White, only 16 percent of all households fit the traditional concept of mother, father and two children, with dad the breadwinner and mother staying home to care for the family. Today nearly 60 percent of the nation's mothers with children under the age of eighteen work outside the home. Twice as many women worked full-time in 1980 as in 1970, and by the year 2000, most mothers will be in the labor force.

Sharing child care is the inevitable consequence of this employment revolution. One General Mills survey of 1,500 U.S. families found eight out of ten men agreed that when both parents have jobs, mothers and fathers should split the child-rearing chores. Wellesley College psychologist Joseph Pleck's research confirms that in two-career families, husbands and wives do, in fact, spend equal time tending to the kids.

If both parents minister to the children while the marriage is "on," why should this arrangement change simply because the marriage is "off"? Fathers most likely to lose out on parenting have begun to request joint custody, where both spouses share the care of their child. Until recently, judges have dismissed joint custody, arguing it is too disruptive for kids. While it is still not a standard custody option, behaviorists are beginning to convince these traditionalists that children need continued contact with both parents and that joint custody is one method of providing it.

Many mothers, however, balk at the idea of joint parenting. Having exclusive custody may make them feel superior to their ex-mates. Withholding the child is a way of punishing their former partners, and for many, a source of power over them. It took one New York father two years to convince his ex-wife to sign a joint custody agreement. Today the woman admits: "Giving up sole custody was like giving up some sort of trophy, the power and the control that came with the role of being Mother."

Custody struggles—whether for sole or joint status—are increasing. More suits promise more bitterness and more stealing. A slow, expensive decision-making process—which can take up to two years and cost close to $40,000—is too long and too steep for impatient, modest-income parents. Lately fathers are finishing first more frequently, and noncustodial mothers are doing much of the snatching. Child Find, Inc., a Westchester, New York, support group for parental kidnaping victims, claims that 35 percent of its registrants are fathers.

This shift from men to women is due, in part, to the increase in working mothers. In the past, fathers did most of the stealing because, as the money-makers, they had the means to flee. These days, career mothers can just as easily afford to relocate as their male counterparts and find jobs in secret cities. Housewives and unemployed husbands get hit the hardest. Without an income, they cannot fight back and are unable to hire detectives or attorneys, or even do the searching themselves.

Money does not always matter. Parents robbed of their offspring invest their savings to scour the country. They look endlessly, sometimes forever. Figures vary, but the American Bar Association estimates that seven out of ten victims will never see their children again; another statistic often cited is one out of five. Unless children are found within the first six months, maintains Washington, D.C.'s Children's Rights, they probably won't be found for years, if ever.

The grim divorce rate has spawned a slew of abductions. So, too, has our winner-take-all custody system. Antiquated though the courts may be, they are not the only culprit. Plain old spite, vengeance, and selfishness have conspired to carry out the crime. Snatching, however, would never be an option were it not for the pervasiveness of the "Me Generation" and the self-centered attitude of the Seventies: "I'll do whatever I want; the other fellow be damned."

Ironically, the greatest incentive to steal comes from the law itself. Kidnaping is practically a risk-free crime. Parents know that the worst penalty many judges will dole out is a simple wrist-slapping for the record—if the thieves are unlucky enough to get caught.

I

THE CHILDREN

· 1 ·

Life on the Run

My name is Ray. I was abducted from my Mom when I was three years old. My father took me to live with his brother. I didn't live with my father. He didn't say why— I don't think he really wanted me. I used to think about Mommy a lot. I asked my father to help me find her, but he wouldn't do anything. I went to different schools and used to fight, maybe to get attention. I was hit many times with a belt by my uncle and not fed meals the right way. Sometimes I ate raw food. When my birthdays came, nobody celebrated them. I was forgotten. The time I was away was the loneliest and worst of my life.

RAY'S DEGRADATION was seven years long. Carla's was shorter, but equally grim. Remembers her mother: "We were driving to see some friends eight months after I found my daughter. Carla was sitting in the back seat. All of a sudden she said, 'Daddy was always fooling around with me.' I stopped the car on the highway and said, 'What do you mean?' 'He'd start to play with my stomach and work down,' she said. Once it got out, she never stopped talking about it. They had intercourse. She was only nine years old, and she was afraid of him. Carla saw him beat his women, and as long as she didn't question him, she was okay."

The unnatural charade fugitive children are forced to play out is most poignantly described by Rochester, New York, psychologist Jeannette Minkoff. As Family Services Coordinator for the Monroe County Probation Department, Minkoff has treated abducted children for almost twenty years, perhaps longer than any other therapist in the country. "A father entered his stolen son, my patient, in school under a false name. The man didn't bring the boy's school transcripts, and made up the name of a private school in New York, which he claimed his son had recently attended. The principal asked the child about the other school. The boy said, 'I don't know about that school,' so the principal said, 'Then where did you go to school?' and then the boy caught himself. When he did his work in school he would often write down his given name on papers and then would have to erase that and replace it with his fake name.

"Teachers began to become concerned about his behavior. Finally, he was called into the principal's office and asked why he kept erasing and why the names he kept writing were different. He went home that day and informed his father he had spoken with the principal, and then he began to cry. His father asked him what he had told the principal, and he said, 'I told him what my real name is.' That very night the father and son took off for another city. The boy was in and out of school, always with the same fictitious story.

"Kids would invite him to parties and he was never permitted to go. His father wouldn't allow him to identify with other kids out of fear that someone would catch on. They

16

moved a lot—from New York to Oregon to California to Utah to Massachusetts. They finally got a room which they shared with another man in a roominghouse. This man had a girlfriend who would cook for them once in a while. Other than that, they had no money for food or clothing, since the father didn't work. He took his son to a Salvation Army barrel in the street and got him sneakers that were too small. The child started to get blisters, and when his mother finally tracked him down, he had a horrible infection in his feet."

The experiences of these wounded waifs may seem extreme, but unfortunately they are all too typical of abducted children. A myth prevails that kidnapers do not hurt their offspring because they are their parents. The leader of a men's rights group confirms this notion: "If a father cares enough to steal a child, then I think that child will have a good life."

Practically all youngsters on the run would dispute that claim. The psychological and physical scars inflicted by "loving" abductors are commonplace, rather than rare. Sexual or physical abuse is standard fallout from the war between the parents. Child Find, Inc., a New York support group for victims of child stealing, maintains that the majority of snatched youngsters are beaten, sexually molested, or neglected, with fathers more likely to be violent and mothers neglectful. The group contends that these parents do love their children, but that love under pressure creates violence. Another organization in California surveyed five hundred snatchers and found that 90 percent had a history of physical or emotional abuse.

"You don't know how many times I heard 'Your son is okay, he is with his father,'" winces a mother recalling her conversations with law-enforcement officials. "They'd say, 'Your ex-husband should not have taken the child, and we can understand your wanting him, but at least the boy is not with a stranger.' But no one is stranger than a childsnatcher, and no one is safer with a childsnatcher than with a stranger." When she finally found her son—without police assistance—he had been dragged to five states, and whipped. His father even tried to dye his hair.

Even parents who have never abused their kids may be pushed to the point of violence or perversion on the run. They transfer their frustration and fury to their only companions, the children. "Often the youngsters are stand-ins for spouses," declares Dr. Mel Roman, a New York City family therapist who has treated abductors, "so that a lot of anger meant for a mate can be displaced on the children. A parent who steals is under tremendous internal pressure and fear, and has a very low frustration tolerance." Youth and dependence can also irritate a restless father or mother. Asserts Dr. Minkoff: "A snatcher resents the child. He resents the fact that he had to steal the kid to get even. Now he is sorry he did it, and realizes the child is a pretty big responsibility, and he has lost all of his freedom. He doesn't have an opportunity to interact with other adults, because he is too afraid to share his life."

Not having contact with women their age can cause parental kidnapers to turn on their little girls and treat them as surrogate spouses. "There are a lot of theories about why men who have stolen their daughters sexually abuse them," says Dr. Minkoff, "and some of my colleagues and I believe it is because they don't have an opportunity to identify with women. Most of the time they have left their jobs and have to hustle to make a buck, and don't have money for baby-sitters, and won't hire them anyway. These people have physical needs and go a little berserk and begin to put the children in love relationships."

While common in snatching situations, sexual abuse is peaking in the general population, too. Incest experts estimate that one out of every hundred American women was sexually molested as a child by her father; some scholars say that figure is low. Since the mean age of a first assault is around eight years, these victims are too young to sort out love. An absent mother cannot set them straight, so stolen children are prime targets for misplaced lust.

For physical abuse, too. Some kidnaped youngsters die from mistreatment. "God forgive me for what I'm about to do," implored a sick father in a note he wrote before he murdered his daughter. Another child almost wound up a fatal statistic. Swearing he'd steal his kids if his wife walked out, the unhappy father hauled his three sons from state to state, unable to support them or stand their wild, pubescent pranks. "Steve was getting whipped and whipped, and my dad wouldn't stop," the youngest child remembers, his voice still quaking two years after the episode. "My father slugged him as hard as he could and there was blood. He made Steve take off all his clothes and told him to hold onto the sheets. He was given such a bad beating that he tore the sheets off the bed. My brother still has scars."

Kids are also abused by stepparents who resent having to hide with their new spouses' children. They may view these boys and girls as uninvited guests with hefty appetites and whiny dispositions. Their mates' problems turn into *their* problems, and often they take out their hostility on these hapless pawns, the children. When her little boy was recovered after two and a half years, a horrified mother spotted scratchmark scars on his neck and arms, meted out by the child's stepmother for "being a pest."

Children shunted off to indifferent relatives tend to fare poorly, too. These new "mothers" and "fathers" may not have a special feeling toward the kids. Dumped at his aunt and uncle's by his father, Peter still cringes when remembering how he and his brother were treated. "They'd beat me, force me to eat my vomit, and dress me up as a girl. In third grade I got back my report card with all F's. I couldn't concentrate in school because I missed my mom, and was kept out of classes a lot since we moved around so much. My uncle decided to teach me a lesson for getting bad grades, but instead hurt my brother. He wanted to show Jim that if he didn't do well in school, he'd be in trouble, too. He took us down to his dark basement and whispered to me, 'Peter, you better play along with this if you know what is good for you.' I was petrified of him and felt I better not cross him. Then he said, 'Jim, I'm going to kill your brother for getting bad grades.' He took his ax from a shelf and lunged for me, missing intentionally. But Jim was behind a post so it looked as if my uncle had gotten me. He made me shriek as if I were being mutilated. Jim thought I was dead and screamed hysterically."

Injuries may be more subtle. Those who are not hit or fondled are still scarred. Stolen youngsters almost always suffer from insecurity, triggered by their perpetual pick-up-and-go lifestyle. Like prisoners of war, they are forced into endless marches from place to place, always on the alert for a midnight move to yet another secret retreat. Even children who stay put in one town are still uprooted from their familiar communities. They ache for absent parents, grandparents, and pals. "I was so miserable," recounts a San Francisco boy about his four months in captivity, "that I dreamed of being with kids back home I didn't even like that much."

Racing around the country takes its toll. When there is no "home, sweet home," but only a succession of transient addresses, kids lose their confidence and their sense of identity. Children need to feel that they belong someplace, but usually are scooped up without their favorite blankets or prized Paddington Bears—often without even their clothes. All children have one object that is special to them and makes them feel good about themselves. If they are always moving around, they won't have a chance to identify with anything.

But youngsters on the run do have time to think. Over and over they replay the original kidnaping. Most psychologically damaged are those who witness violence between their parents, and then are abruptly removed—sometimes forever—as their injured mother or father lies limply in the road or on a blood-stained bed. Tormented, these youngsters think back on the brawl, wondering if the custodial parent has ever recovered from, or even lived through, the fight. Laurie is probably still haunted by what happened to her. One minute her parents were having a friendly chat on the patio, the next she was heaved into a truck by her father. She screamed as her mother ran to the truck, clutching frantically at the door. The child watched her mom being dragged down the street and then letting go of the door handle when she could no longer hold on. The distraught woman staggered and fell in the road while the truck sped down an otherwise quiet residential street.

Not only are they traumatized by their first experiences, but children are terrified of being resnatched, too—even if they long to be reunited with their custodial parents. Explains Judith Nadeau, a social worker with the Douglas A. Thom Clinic for Children in Boston: "There is still the immediate fear of 'Oh God, I have to go through that again to get back there.' They ponder, 'How will I be stolen again?' and 'Will it be anything like what happened before?' "

Their terror may be justified. In fact, the original snatch may be minor-league compared to the second time a parent strikes. Hit men may capture them, or violent struggles may ensue between Mom and Dad. A cruel father, for instance, told his daughters that their mother was dead. When she finally fetched them, the girls were shocked to see her alive and were startled by her entrance. Police cars with sirens shrieking accompanied the woman to her husband's hideout. The father's mother held onto one tiny hand of the two-year-old, while his ex-wife yanked the other and made off with the baby. Then the woman pursued daughter number two, who was at a nearby day-care center. The combination of a coterie of uniformed police and the reappearance of her "dead" mother haunted the four-year-old long after the reunion.

Most hostage children fret about their missing parents. "Does

Mom think I ran away from home or was kidnaped by a stranger?" "Is Dad trying to find me, or does he know where I am, and just doesn't want me back?" "How are they coping without me?" many kids question. "Are they eating and sleeping all right?" Some youngsters are tormented by the specifics of the search, such as the amount of money it must be costing custodial parents to find them. In fact, experts agree that often stolen children are more anxious about their deserted parents than about themselves.

If that is possible. Separation is like death to children who don't understand the concept of time. Many youngsters interpret a father's or mother's absence as a sign that he or she has died. Abductors often nurse this illusion by stating that Mommy or Daddy has mysteriously expired. A kidnaping can be more frightening and more isolating than a death. The child has no one with whom to share his or her grief—surely not with the snatcher—the way things would have been had there been a full-fledged fatality, with loving relatives to give comfort.

Children who have suffered the death of a family member and have also been stolen contend that both are equally traumatic. Ted's brother had just succumbed to a battle with brain cancer when the boy was kidnaped by his estranged father. Ted had not yet adjusted to life without his big brother and was terrified to leave home, let alone his mother. "It was just as bad to be taken by my father as to go through Bill's death," muses Ted. "At least I knew I would be with Mom for a while after Bill died, but then"—he hesitates—"I got stolen." "It is the inability to reach the other parent that is the biggest problem," claims Santa Ana, California, social worker Peg Edwards, who has treated more than fifty abducted children. "If a parent is not there, you can't tell a stolen child Mom or Dad is three states and a six-hour drive away. That doesn't mean anything to a young child. If that person is not there, he or she does not live for the child."

Short spans of time away from a parent can permanently

scar a youngster or cause a transfer of loyalties. Continuity in relationships is essential for a child's normal growth. Kids do not have that consistent care when they are taken away from a parent. Dr. Albert J. Solnit, Director of Yale University's Child Study Center and professor of pediatrics and psychiatry at its medical school, states: "A young child cannot hold on too long to the knowledge and memory of the original parent, and since a youngster needs an adult to take care of him, he may form a strong attachment to the abducting parent, provided that parent is at all nurturing and protective and affectionate. If the child is abducted by a parent who hasn't seen much of him, and he has a strong attachment to the custodial parent, the child usually goes through a period of terrible sadness and fear, because the person on whom he had counted is no longer there. It's like breaking a part of his psyche. He tends to give up the relationship to the original parent and tries to form a new attachment, one in which the new parent will take care of him and be someone to be counted on. It takes much longer to form that relationship, though, because the child has already had one such relationship broken. Children have a different sense of time when they are older than when they are younger. To young ones, a small amount of time seems like a long period of time."

In *Beyond the Best Interests of the Child*, Dr. Solnit, along with Dr. Anna Freud and Joseph Goldstein, charts a child's inner waiting clock vis-à-vis placement in foster homes. Their timetable also applies to parental kidnapings, since the child is still deprived of Mom or Dad. The authors maintain that infants and toddlers are overwhelmed by a parent's absence after only a few days. Adults who tend youngsters under two years of age may become their psychological parents, but cannot replace the feeling of devastation brought on by the initial loss. Children under five, the authors believe, may be permanently traumatized if a parent is not around after two months; six months is the maximum for younger school-age kids.

Child authorities say that youngsters absent awhile eventually settle into their surroundings. "After long periods of time," asserts Peg Edwards, "snatched children will adjust to their environment. Initially they may be rebellious and have temper tantrums, but then they will give up. They don't forget, but on the outside it looks as if they have. They learn early to cover up their pain when they can't do anything about it, because they have to survive day to day. It's a mechanism we all have." Six-year-old Sandy, stolen twice, best describes the on again/off again grieving process: "Sometimes I wanted my mommy and sometimes I forgot about her."

Other children become exhausted by, and indifferent to, the custody chase. Taken and retaken six times in a year and a half, an Ohio youngster claims it makes no difference who "wins" her, because, "if my mom gets us, then my dad will get us, then my mom, then my dad. It just keeps going on like that. I can't believe this is really happening. I keep thinking I'll wake up and it will be a dream. When I'm with one parent, I always worry that my other parent will come and disrupt my life again. When I was with my mom, we would worry about which day my father would come and get us. My dad is so scared now that my mother will take us again that he watches us every minute, and whenever I go somewhere, my brother has to stay because my dad doesn't want both of us out at the same time. I go to school and wonder if one of my parents is going to steal me. My father got me the first time that way. A boy came up to me in class and said to go to a certain side of the school. I was supposed to walk home with a friend and thought, 'That's where she wants to meet me.' My dad was there instead, and he pulled me into the car and took off."

New friends would help—if only these lonely victims had any. They might replace those left behind and give a child some security and "roots" in the new hometown. Thieving parents, however, discourage their kids from cultivating peer relationships, afraid they will confess their plights. The youngsters, too, shy away from strangers, unsure they can trust themselves to keep quiet. Friendships are crucial to a child's development, especially from the ages of five to twelve, say child psychiatrists and psychologists. Asserts Dr. Minkoff: "I have never seen a stolen child who had a good friend. When normal kids get to be around eight to twelve years old, a friend becomes everything to them. They can share different changes in their physical appearances, sex, and other special things they can't talk about with their parents. Can you imagine not even being able to play with other kids during recess, because your feelings are so ready to burst that you can't trust yourself to keep quiet about what has happened to you? Who could live like that without getting a little screwed up?"

Children whose names are changed have additional woes. They must live a lie, unable to develop relationships or share their secret past for fear of slipping up. Many older youngsters feel guilty for keeping up the pretense, not only about fake names, but about fabricated life histories. Steve, a devout Catholic, brought up never to lie, was ordered by his father to tell teachers and playmates his mother had been killed in a car crash. His father's directive—that it was okay, even essential, to lie—was contradictory to what his mother had taught him—to tell the truth. Because he complied, he was ridden with remorse. Another snatcher instructed his ten-year-old son to say he was living with his father, when "home" was actually elsewhere. A solicitous probation officer coaxed the boy into admitting he had never slept at his father's in all the six years he had been stolen.

Abducted children who cannot bear to lie may escape their phony existence through fantasy—and often by more lying. A Michigan girl, perpetually on the move with her kidnaping father, pretended she was the daughter of a show-business tycoon to justify her abnormal lifestyle. Every time they packed up and fled, she'd graciously bid adieu to her recently acquired friends. "We've got to leave now, but it was so nice meeting you," she'd say. "The only reason we're on the road is because my father is an entertainer. It's a wonderful, exciting life for me." It couldn't have been too wonderful. She attempted suicide in yet another two-bit town.

Kids may daydream out loud, or keep the fantasy to themselves. A youngster whisked away to Idaho from Oregon played a mental game to transcend his misery. "When I was with my father," the sixth-grader explains, "I'd imagine myself at my mom's house hanging around. I didn't want to think it was happening to me, so I'd pretend it was happening to someone else."

Fibs and fancy ease the bewilderment stolen children suffer. They can't comprehend why they have been kidnaped, and often wind up blaming themselves. Explains one confused victim: "I felt, 'Why me? Something must be wrong with me.' " Not having confidants to refute this notion reinforces their sense of guilt. Youngsters who attempt to discuss their plights find snatchers unsympathetic and are told never to mention the other parent. "Never think about your mother," one father warned his homesick son. "Never mention her name. Just shut up."

It is not only the lying and the loneliness that devastate the victim, but the unnatural and often cruel circumstances under which abducted youngsters are forced to live. These conditions stem from the peculiarities of life as a fugitive. It took ten trips to London before Zygmunt Bejnarowicz, a Chicago oral surgeon, located his six-year-old boy in a secret "safe" house. The mother had managed to elude British authorities by shutting away her son inside an apartment for five years. The boy had never been to school, nor did he know what a playground swing was until his father introduced him to the outdoors. Another lad was found with his father in the hills of South Carolina in a tent, which they left only occasionally for food. A nine-month-old baby boy was locked in a car by himself. For four months, the infant and his father had been living off garbage behind a supermarket.

Cars are common living quarters for outlaws—a guarantee the kids won't make friends and the means for a speedy getaway. A six-year-old told his mother the best part about being back was having a bed. For seven months he had subsisted on ketchup with rice, and ingenuously exclaimed to his mother: "Gee, you must be rich because you have a refrigerator!" One abducting father of four alternated between his car and motels. "When we'd drive there would be no place to go," remembers his son Henry, eight years old at the time. "Motels were an adventure compared to sleeping in the car. It gave us a destination, and the rooms would all be different. We went from motel to motel for six months." The kids were eventually abandoned.

A parent who has given up a job to disappear with the child often finds it difficult to make ends meet in strange surroundings. Again, it is the kids who suffer. One seven-year-old boy played "mother" to his brothers while his real mom was a madam, part of a profitable prostitution ring. She would hustle from eight P.M. to six A.M., and turn a few tricks on the side, too. While she was busy, abusive boyfriends lolled around the house.

Little Mike had twenty built-in baby-sitters—bikers from one of the meanest motorcycle gangs in California who "took care" of the child while his mother worked. Even though he was only four years old, Mike sensed they were thugs. He was right; one was the president of a local hoodlum chapter. "My uncle almost ran me over with his motorcycle," says Mike, back with his dad in New Hampshire. "The others weren't nice. My mommy locked me in a room and went to Disneyland."

Kids are usually astute enough to notice when they are not valued. This second-rate treatment makes them both sad and angry. "He'd go off for weekends and spend all his money on his girlfriends," says a child from Nebraska, who eventually escaped, "yet he'd never have enough money to buy me or my brother clothes." Snatchers often skip necessary doctor and dentist appointments for their children, too, and serious medical problems may be ignored. Rush surgery was ordered for a California toddler with a tic when his father grabbed the boy and fled to Yugoslavia. The mother retrieved her son two years later, only to find his neurological disorder had worsened and his face was distorted.

Parents may suspect their children are not getting tip-top care, but are rarely prepared to find them groveling in gutters or physically or sexually abused. "I was shocked," says a mother who located her filthy daughter after a two-and-a-half-year hunt. "I knew there was something wrong when I saw her. Sarah's clothes were two sizes too large, and she was wearing a blouse my husband had picked out of someone's garbage. She was covered with blackheads. Her hair was matted from not being combed or washed. It took months before her face cleared up. Sarah had a fetish once she got home. All day she took one shower after another, and changed her clothes continually, because she hadn't been able to do that when she was hiding." A Massachusetts mother, elated after spotting her kids stowed away on a primitive island in Samoa, became distraught when she discovered boils all over her son's body and head lice on her daughter. Their temporary shelter had no electricity or hot water, so they never bathed. Horrified parents have wept at the sight of their offspring covered with flea bites or serious infections. "I've had youngsters come back with broken arms and limbs," attests a child psychologist.

Much appears in print about the offspring of divorce: their devastation by the split-up, and their conflicts of divided loyalty. Very little has been written, however, about how these same children fare when they are abruptly uprooted, often violently, from one parent and forced on the road by the other. What happens when they are deprived of the custodial parent's love, as well as other supports so crucial for proper maturity—doting aunts and uncles, best friends, and beloved pets? Most veterans of custody battles claim that traumatic though a breakup may be, it does not rival the terror of being held hostage. The kids agree: "Being stolen was a lot worse than when Mom and Dad got divorced," affirms Margo, whisked twenty-five hundred miles away from home by her father. "I was gone for two years and wasn't allowed to see my mom. When my parents broke up, I was living with my mother and could see her anytime."

Divorce is traumatic, even in the best of circumstances. Usually youngsters are still coming to terms with their parents' separation when they are abducted. Most social scientists believe that it takes at least a year or two for kids to adjust to a single-parent setup. Studies indicate that children suffer long after their parents part, and that how kids cope is often directly influenced by Mother's and Father's continued interactions. Researchers Judith Wallerstein and Joan Kelly tracked 131 children from sixty divorcing Marin County, California, families for five years. They discovered that the offspring still suffered hurt and pain a year later. Many, in fact, fared worse than they had at the time of the split. Thirty-five of eighty-nine youngsters under ten, for example, were diagnosed as having deteriorated—a startling statistic, since they had seemed to be functioning well the year before. Twenty-nine percent were muddling through, and 34 percent were resilient. The thrivers and survivors, they found, were children who had meaningful and loving relationships with both parents. Those not visited by their noncustodial parents were plagued by a variety of emotions: guilt for the parent's absence; loneliness; anger; sorrow; a sense of powerlessness; and a lack of self-esteem. Delinquent behavior, like temper tantrums, drug abuse, and stealing, also was evident in single-parent households.

Participants at a 1978 National Institute of Mental Health conference on the consequences of divorce on children echo the thesis that continuous, close contact with the noncustodial parent is a major factor in a child's post-divorce adjustment. So, too, says the Foundation for Child Development in New York, which conducted a study of twenty-two hundred kids ages seven to eleven, and their parents. In a child-stealing situation, all the ingredients for a difficult adjustment are present: the child is cut off entirely from one parent, usually after the bitterest of breakups and breakdowns in communications between parents.

Problems exist not merely because one parent is gone, says Dr. Daniel O'Leary, a noted authority on childsnatching and a professor of psychology at the State University of New York at Stony Brook. Key are the circumstances behind the disappearing act. O'Leary points to the results of a study comparing children of divorce with those abandoned through a parent's death. "There is some evidence," states O'Leary, "that children who are fatherless from a death have a better adjustment than children who are the products of divorce, where discord remains an issue between the parents. It is not the parent's absence per se which makes a kid cope poorly, but the absence of a parent under what condition, like death or divorce (or child stealing). Research reveals that adolescent girls build up the image of the father when he is no longer alive. The father who dies is often painted positively by the surviving mate, while a divorced spouse may describe the former partner in negative terms to the kids. Child stealing and divorce are similar because the remaining parent usually speaks disparagingly about a former spouse."

Even if a parent does not deprecate an ex-partner, children denied a mother or father may be permanently scarred. "They grow up thinking that one parent is all bad or all marvelous," says family therapist Mel Roman. "The child doesn't see the parent and internalizes those images and has no way of having an objective, realistic view of the parent, or the parent's good and bad qualities."

Kids on the run and children of divorce share other likenesses, too, including almost identical physical and psychological reactions. They suffer from headaches, nausea, stomachaches, insomnia, bed-wetting, and crying jags. Worried sick with uncertainty and apprehension, some develop serious health problems. Symptoms can surface as many as three times for stolen kids: when their mothers and fathers separate; when their parents steal them; and again when they are brought back home. Young kids are the most maimed, for they do not understand what is happening. "Why did Mom leave?" they wonder, or "Why did Dad run away with me?" Children of all ages think that if one parent left, maybe the other will desert them as well.

Between the ages of two and four, toilet-trained toddlers often revert to diapers and insist on being fed rather than on feeding themselves. Victims of divorce and parental abductions may be finicky eaters, or stuff their stomachs without pleasure. Fear dominates the four-to-eight-year-old bracket. School may haunt them or the thought that no one will be home to greet them. Older kids may have trouble concentrating in school, and are furious at the parent they perceive as the home-wrecker.

Teenagers are wrenched apart by loyalty conflicts and weakened by a loss of self-confidence. Often they try to compensate for feelings of inadequacy through power plays, like shoplifting, sex, or drugs. Boys especially act out. University of Virginia psychologist E. Mavis Hetherington studied the impact of divorce on seventy-two middle-class families and found that boys are harder hit than girls, because more is expected of them and they receive less support. Often boys pick on their peers, slugging out of frustration and disappointment, not out of conviction. Abducted males also frequently find a false sense of importance through their fists. They threaten and thieve, break bones and break laws, because they are broken as well. So, too, are the kidnaped girls who are sexually abused.

Siblings left behind in a snatch also suffer. Deprived of giggles and gossip and "knuckle sandwiches," they mourn their missing brothers and sisters. "Two nights ago," attests a

woman whose older daughter was kidnaped seven years ago,
"my younger girl said, 'Mommy, it just isn't right. I'm supposed
to have a sister with me. I wouldn't be scared in my bed at
night if my sister were here.' " Another child who shared a
room with his brothers could not bear even to enter their
quarters the eight months the boys were away. Glenn insisted
on sleeping in a window seat in his mother's room. At his
third birthday party, while playmates sang "Happy Birthday,"
he ran from the room and screamed "I want my brothers."

Stay-at-home siblings yearn for a reunion with abducted kin,
but also resent them for being stolen. They feel rejected and
insignificant for not making the kidnaping "cut." Over and over
the children ask themselves, "Why them, not me? Wasn't I good
enough? What did I do wrong?" Jessie is still baffled by her
sister's abduction. "We were outside at my friend's house playing jump rope. My dad drove up and grabbed Kate and locked
all the doors and took off. I remember running after them, but
my father didn't take me. I don't know why he left me. Still to
this day [eleven years later], I wonder why he didn't want me. I
was his first born, his little princess. I thought he adored me."

Jealousy resumed when Kate returned at the age of twelve.
Fumes Jessie: "I thought, 'Why is she getting all this attention?
If Dad had taken me, I would have called home. If Kate had
wanted to leave, all she had to do was pick up the telephone.' "

Jessie's father was fond of the straightforward approach to
selecting siblings—nab one and leave the other standing in the
road. Other snatchers prefer to dupe the child left behind. Take
a calculating California stepfather, for example. Shortly after
breaking up with his wife, he coaxed her two daughters from a
previous marriage into spending the day with him at Disneyland. He promised their only child together, a son, time alone
with Dad, too. The girls had always viewed him as a father and
were delighted by his offer. The trip was terrific. They returned
to their mother in radiant spirits. Since the girls had such fun,
the father pledged to stage a Disneyland repeat the following

week with his son. He never returned the boy. The girls were devastated when they realized their special outing had been a setup for an abduction.

Those not "elite" enough to be stolen may feel left out and let down. Grieve though they may, kidnaped children would swap places with their siblings any day. For they know the grim facts of life on the run: the moving, the hiding, the beatings, the loneliness, the lying.

· 2 ·

Calling Home

I T I S O D D , even eerie: stolen kids often can call home, but don't. Many are old enough to have mastered area codes and operators, or to consult an outsider for help. They aren't chained to their beds, either. Instead, kidnapers muzzle their subjects with fear.

Convincing strongmen, they whip their children into submission and complicity through threats of force or fantastic falsehoods about the absent parent. "Better watch your step," the abductor bellows. "Better not call home. Better believe what I tell you. Better behave. Or else . . ."

Or else what? Like professional interrogators, child stealers brainwash their offspring, wearing them down so the kids will come over to their "side." Their goal: vilify the missing father or mother, and make him or her look uncaring or even dangerous. Get the youngsters to be dependent upon—even grateful to—their captors. "Squeal on me, and you'll be left

34

stranded," they threaten. "Mother does not want you, and if I get arrested, she won't take you back, and you'll be all alone." Or, "You'll be sent to jail for being a tattletale." Or, "Dad knows where you are. If he *really* loved you, then he would have come to claim you." Or, "You'll never reach your mother if you phone—she moved." Or, "How can you call Daddy if he's dead?"

The threat of force, explicit or implied, also makes children button up. Many kids have been beaten in the past and are reluctant to bring on another attack if they get caught sneaking to a telephone. Some never before hit are slugged once they broach the subject of going home. Others merely suspect they will be roughed up for contacting their custodial parents. "If my dad found me calling, he'd do something about it. I don't know what," trembles a New Jersey youngster who speaks for many. Size differences between a parent and a child reinforce this notion. Says Stuart, who was nabbed from a schoolyard: "My father was six foot two and I was five foot one. This guy I hadn't seen in four years started doing all this crazy stuff and I wasn't going to question him."

Quickly, kids turn into cooperative hostages. They can't bear to be punished, and ponder the consequences of resistance. Twelve-year-old Tommy, dragged to seven states, explains this intimidation technique: "I told my stepmom I wanted to go back to my real mom. My stepmother told me to wait until my father came home, and then he whipped me with a belt and said he didn't want me talking about Mom. It made me scared, so I stopped."

Stolen children also get a glimpse of their abductors' tempers by watching parents tangle. Seeing them spar convinces kids that if they don't keep quiet, they may be the next victims in line. Quakes Bennett: "My dad used to beat up on my mom. One Christmas he picked up our Christmas tree and threw it through the window. He broke the window, and made

35

me go to my room. I could hear him hitting my mother. I opened my window and called our neighbor and he came over. There is no way I was going to make my dad mad at me."

Dr. Eugene Evans, a Tucson, Arizona, psychologist with expertise in childsnatching, offers an intriguing theory about why some youngsters may not get in touch with their missing parents: "Children may be willing to refrain from doing a lot of things, such as complaining or dialing home or running away, because it could bring their parents back for another confrontation. They are deathly afraid of what the two people will do to each other, that one could literally kill the other. So they think about what they have to do to avoid having Daddy hurt Mommy, or vice versa. The sacrifice may just be that they are willing to be stolen, or to stay stolen, so they don't see one of these confrontations."

Not all children have a choice, though, of calling or keeping quiet. In fact, many kidnaped children would gladly risk fisticuffs between Mom and Dad for a chance to be reunited with the parent left behind. They are either too young to know how to make contact or to hop a bus home, or they are trapped. Paranoid parents frequently escort their stolen "cargo" to and from school and do not allow them to play outside alone. Like the most dangerous criminals in a full-security prison, they are under twenty-four-hour surveillance. "There was someone with me at all times," says Cliff of his month-long abduction. "Even when I went to the bathroom, they'd wait outside the door. My father's new wife and sister-in-law followed me around the house when my dad went to work. I wasn't allowed outside. They kept the phones up high so I couldn't reach them—the one in the kitchen was placed in a tall cupboard, and another was near my dad's bed. He enrolled me in a private school and a teacher stayed with me constantly, walking me from class to class. I had no money to make a phone call. My father said if I needed anything, to ask a teacher. I later found out that my dad had told the school to watch me every minute, claiming my *mom* planned to steal me!"

Snatchers have even more insidious ways of keeping their kids in line. Frequently, conniving kidnapers convince their offspring that the absent parent is dangerous and will harm them if she or he returns. Children are told they must hide from Mom or Dad, or else they will be found and mistreated. One terrified girl reports that her mother said her father would sell her to cannibals if he got his hands on her. Sure he would be shot if his mother tracked him down, another youngster lived in fear because his dad had told him she toted a gun in her pocketbook, waiting to blow the boy away.

Ruthlessly, snatchers prevaricate. Declares a distraught father: "My son was told I had molested him, and the only reason I wanted him back was so I could put him in a foster home." Taken at the age of three, one boy was repeatedly told his mother was a tramp. "Did you know what that meant?" the straitlaced woman asked her son when he was returned seven years later. "I didn't know when I was younger," he answered, "but when I got older, I knew."

Stating that the other parent is unfit is a popular tactic. Abductors concoct outrageous yarns in order to convince their offspring not to call home, or to explain why they must keep the kidnaper company. For the unconvinced, snatchers draw on their trump card—maintaining that the missing parent is dead. It is a winning play, because it will silence even the most inquisitive of children. An easy out for abductors, it gives them less reason to explain their actions, and more chance of gaining the children's loyalty. After all, youngsters are led to believe that no one else, besides the kidnaper, is left for them. One sick San Francisco snatcher who had not seen his four-year-old daughter in two years barged into her day-care center. He said that her mother had been killed five months earlier by narcotics agents, and she believed him, even though the child

37

had seen her mother that very morning. The father also warned that if they did not flee immediately, the dealers would murder them both. He topped off his tale by claiming he was a CIA agent. Although the little girl did not understand either "dealer" or "CIA," she was sufficiently horrified.

Young kids rarely question their captors. Maintains Boston social worker Judith Nadeau: "Little children do not have the capacity to reason, to say that the parent can't be dead, I just saw him." Therapists agree that kids under ten years of age are often not sure what to believe, but will usually go along with what they are told. One girl, fed preposterous falsehoods, sums up the attitude of many stolen children: "I never contacted my father because it is your mother, and you think she's always right." "It's not too hard to create stories that are untrue," asserts child-stealing specialist Dr. Daniel O'Leary, "especially if there has already been some instability in the family. Clearly that is the case in most of these instances. From the beginning, the parents were not getting along, so the kid probably heard a lot of deriding of the other parent. The seeds are already planted for one parent to be critical of the other."

Unless abductors trip up, young children usually do not doubt the veracity of a story. Nine-year-old Adam eventually caught on, however. "For three weeks, I thought I was on vacation and would go home soon. Then as we were driving up the coast of Oregon my father said my stepdad and my mom had died, and my little brother Jim was in a foster home. I couldn't stop crying when he told me, but after a while, I knew my mom wasn't dead. I sent Jim a birthday card, and saw my dad address one envelope to our house, and then put that letter into another envelope to his girlfriend. It didn't make sense that he addressed the card to my house if Jim was living in a foster home. I was confused. But then I knew. It was sad because I had thought he was telling the truth, but I was also happy because my family wasn't dead."

It may be years before youngsters discover that the stories they have been fed are lies. It took Emily three years to get the facts: "I was seven when I was stolen by my father. He had visitation rights and told my brother and me we were going camping, so we should bring a lot of clothes. After we got in the car he said, 'It's time for you to come live with me in our own house.' He took us from Michigan to Indiana where he bought a farmhouse. He would talk about how awful my mother was and say she would beat us with sticks and go out all night to parties. He also said she used to lock us in our rooms for long periods. When my mom finally found us, she showed me there never were any locks on the bedroom doors. But I had believed my dad because my older brother said, 'Yes, it's true. Mom used to lock us in our rooms. I remember it.' "

What makes Emily's account so illuminating is not the fantastic lies, but the fact that her brother substantiated the stories, even though he knew they were false, in order to stay in his captor's favor.

Cruel but clever abductors often use sophisticated psychology to beguile their trusting children. "One time my brother and I had a fight," recalls a still baffled youngster. "My father said, 'You're such a bother, I may as well send you back to your mother.' I was confused. I was dying to go back to my mom, yet he was saying, 'Your punishment for acting up is going home.' I started to think if that was what I got for being bad, Mom mustn't be so great."

The left-behind parent is transformed into the bad guy by an architect who masterminds a perverted plan. Snatchers may tell homesick children that their missing mother or father knows where they are, and is not interested in retrieving them, or that their parent has a new husband or wife and children, and no longer needs them. Not showing up is proof that the parent does not love the child. The rejection can be unbearable. One child was despondent because she was convinced her mother wasn't interested in fetching her. "I asked Dad if he was going to call Mom and tell her where we were and he said he already had, so I thought she knew."

Older children are less gullible. They may initially accept an explanation but upon reflection, usually can figure out they have been conned. "Every day my dad would say, 'Your mother doesn't want you, your mother doesn't want you,'" confides a now more sophisticated boy. "Finally I asked myself, 'Why is he saying this to me all the time?'" Craig, too, caught on to his father's lies. The abduction was especially traumatic for him, since he had not seen his father for years before the kidnaping. "I was confused about why my father took me, because he had never even sent me a birthday card. Then he pops up and says, 'It's about time I get to see you,' and, 'I love you, and that's why I want you with me.' I kept thinking, how can this be true? What is this guy trying to pull? Why does he grab me violently and throw me in a car? Why won't he let me go home?"

Curiously enough, even when they realize they have been deceived, kids usually stay put. They may toy with the idea of calling home, but they rarely ever dial the number. Social observers believe that fear is not the only factor that scares away youngsters; feeling dependent upon the parent also controls their behavior. Cut off from old friends and relatives, in new towns and schools, they have no one to turn to but the snatcher. It would seem that if a homesick kid did not contact her custodial parent, she might, at least, confide in a friend or a teacher. But she doesn't. Explains Judith Nadeau: "Children know there is only one person on whom they can count, so that even if that person is not treating them well, they won't say anything. Kidnaped children have only one person to care for them, and are absolutely terrified of doing anything to make that person unhappy."

Like abused children, abducted youngsters, out of fear and dependence, rarely confess their plights. Instead, they cling to their spanking/snatching parents. "They form a loyalty to whoever is in control," contends Barry Sandrew, a psychotherapist and leader in the men's rights movement. "I see this also in normal custody situations. The children have experienced such an upheaval, that to go against the parent who has control would continue the disruption. They have to have some semblance of structure, so they align themselves with the kidnaping parent."

In fact, stolen boys and girls try to ingratiate themselves with their captors, perhaps to convince themselves that the Mom or Dad they're with isn't so cruel. Child psychiatrist Albert J. Solnit comments on kids' unconscious conduct: "Out of a deep fear of being hurt or of being killed, or never again seeing the other parent, children may make an intuitive effort to form an alliance with the abductor. Without realizing it, they try and bribe their kidnaping parents into liking them and taking care of them. They try to reduce that terrible feeling that they are going to be hurt or destroyed. They make this alliance as a matter of survival, but they don't know they are doing this. It seems to them that they have suddenly discovered their parents are not villains, but Robin Hood in disguise."

While it is the exception, a few kids don't call home because they want to stay with the snatcher. Occasionally they are grateful for being stolen and prefer the abducting parent. At least initially, many childsnatchers lavish attention and goodies on their offspring in an attempt to "buy" their loyalty. They lure them with Pac-Man and pizza, tricycles and teddy bears. This "anything-your-little-heart-desires" attitude makes kids feel pampered and important. Recalls Amy, grabbed at the age of nine: "My father used to build everything up, so that going away would be a beautiful fantasy. I would be the princess, and he would be the king. He said we'd come into a ton of money, and I'd get everything I wanted and he wouldn't have to work. I believed him. I looked up to him a lot, and went along with him, thinking, 'He's the greatest, he knows what is best for me.' As I grew older, I began to despise my father. I looked around and saw what he had done, and I didn't think it was right." Too young to understand the motives of her father, a six-year-old gushed about her life on the run. "I went to the circus a lot, and to the San Diego zoo. Daddy took me to Disneyland, where I saw Mickey Mouse and Snow White and the Seven Dwarfs walking down the street. We went to a Japanese restaurant where I took off my shoes, and out to dinner where they play music. Every day I ran under the sprinkler and swam."

Although it may assuage the terror of being snatched, such treatment is destructive in the long run, claims psychologist Mel Roman. "It's a totally unrealistic way of living. Part of a child's positive development depends upon being able to have some objective perception of reality, and of his or her family. You can't be a recreational parent all the time; that's not what life is all about. So kids grow up with a false notion of their own worth. They become very self-centered and preoccupied, unable to have relationships where they are expected to give, and don't see that people can't give them everything they want all the time."

These children may balk at going back to their lawful guardians. "I wanted to stay with my mom. I had fun with her," laments a girl recently reunited with her father. Eleven-year-old Lucy went so far as to dial home and wait for her missing mother to pick up the phone and say hello before she hung up the receiver. She wanted to make sure her mother had not moved, but refused to speak with her. "I was scared she'd want me back," the girl reasoned, "and I liked living with my dad." Two boys never contacted their father, even though they read an article in a national magazine about his frantic search for them. Instead, the boys were proud their dad was trying to locate them, and would brag about him to their school friends.

Child-stealing experts maintain that certain aspects of the abduction may be exciting for a child, but that kids practically never regard the overall experience as enjoyable. If the other parent had given them permission to leave, it might be different. But it is an occurrence too scary for even the most adventurous youngster. "Even small kids are savvy enough to know being stolen isn't fun," attests clinical psychologist Dr. Daniel O'Leary. "I've never met an abducted child who considered it to be a lark."

Youngsters who want to extricate themselves from the clutches of a kidnaper usually dream about leaving, rather than act. It does not occur to some that calling home is an option. Small and sheltered, they do not know how to phone home or mail a letter. Almost always taken out of town, and often out of state, young children are ignorant of area codes and first-class stamps. If they dare call "home," an unfamiliar voice on the other end of the line jolts them. Right number, wrong city. The logistics of dialing are even more difficult for boys and girls stowed away abroad. They might know their number in America, but not the international code. A foreign-speaking operator overwhelms them even more. The inability to contact a missing parent is confirmation to many kids that, indeed, Mom or Dad has moved, and has abandoned them.

Confused by custody arrangements, some children assume they are supposed to be with the snatcher, either by court decree or by private agreement between the parents. "My mother had permanent custody of us in Virginia," explains a twelve-year-old girl who was tricked, "and then my father took us away. He said he was a good friend of the judge, and the judge told him to come get us. He said my mom really only had temporary custody, but that he was supposed to have us full-time." Says another boy: "I didn't think of myself as being stolen. I thought, 'My parents are divorced and I have to choose between them or else one of my parents will decide for me.' I thought that's what happened, that my dad had decided for me."

Children may never know they have been abducted. Plucked

from a parent at infancy, they believe a stepmother or father is a biological relative. Only a custodial parent's sudden appearance will set them straight. Tragically, a youngster whose name is changed may never know the missing parent's real name—or that he or she ever had a different name. Such a child is probably lost forever, unless a searching parent does some sophisticated sleuthing. One forty-year-old woman contacted a parental kidnaping support group after she found out she had been grabbed when she was a toddler. Eventually the woman tracked down her mother. At their reunion, her mom broke out the baby pictures she still carried in her wallet, and displayed the stacks of detectives' receipts and court records accrued from her massive, unsuccessful hunt. When kids discover they have been taken, there is another hitch: it is sometimes impossible to locate an absent mother who has remarried and changed her name.

The reality of being kidnaped can make even the most frightened charges rebel. Desperate to be released, children may plead with their captors for freedom. One boy worked at being so offensive and insolent that his father eventually sent him packing. "I bugged my dad a lot and did everything so he wouldn't want me," says Oliver. "I would refuse to do things, and wake up early and turn on the TV full blast. Once I ran a tractor through a wall on the property. Every night I'd beg him to let me go back to Mom. I was such a pest that finally he said, 'Okay, leave if you really want.'" Oliver's sister also entreated her father to send her home. At first he agreed. As she was gathering her belongings, he hurled down her bag and huffed, "You're not going anywhere." The snatcher let Oliver off, but apparently the girl had not irritated him enough. She was forced to stay.

When pleading does not work, children consider running away. In fact, practically all kidnaped youngsters plot their escapes. One four-year-old asked his mother to buy him a kite so he could "hold onto the string and fly home to Daddy."

Whisked away to Rhodesia, Dennis yearned to call his father in Virginia. The boy did not know how to dial across continents, so he wrote his dad a letter and hid it under his bed. His suspicious mother discovered the communiqué during one of her daily searches of Dennis's room. She threatened to banish him to an uninhabited island if he wrote his father again. That warning was enough to keep Dennis in line.

Abducted children concoct elaborate getaways, but rarely carry them out. Running away, like calling home, is too risky, most of them decide. "We'd wait for my dad and his wife to go to sleep, and then, late at night," recalls a boy from Louisiana, "my brothers and I would talk about escaping. We planned to go to a store and call our mother. We didn't know our number, but we knew the area code, and how to spell my stepfather's last name. My oldest brother said we'd never make it, though. We were too scared to try." Another child chickened out, too: "My grandma had once given my brother and me a hundred dollars each, so I thought, 'When my dad falls asleep, I'll go to his wallet and steal the two hundred dollars, then wake up my little brother and run right out the door to the airport.' I didn't do it because I was afraid I'd get caught."

Bolder, more desperate youngsters hazard a try. Virtually a prisoner, a Colorado girl was able to sneak a message to her mother, telling her where she was being hidden. The woman slipped a bus ticket home in the mail, but the snatcher's sharp-eyed sisters intercepted the letter and ripped up the ticket. Life was so intolerable with her father that the girl marched into a store and stole an item in plain view of a security guard, praying she would get handed over to the police and sent back to her mother. Her plot backfired. The manager of the store called her father, and she was given back to him. Peggy and Greg R. also attempted to flee from their father. They vaulted over their backyard fence and dashed down the street. Peggy spotted a policeman on the next block and flagged him down, pleading with him to return them to their mother. The Minnesota cop did just the opposite: he escorted them back to their father and filed a runaway report. At the house, Mr. R. flashed his custody papers at the policeman. (Mrs. R. also had custody, but in a different state.) The officer summoned an attorney, who quizzed the kids about their life with Dad. Remembers Peggy: "My father was in the next room listening to our conversation. We were so scared of him we said everything was great. So the lawyer and the policeman both left."

Not all schemes backfire. Charles, spirited away to Iran at the age of eight, conned government officials into allowing him to leave the country by telling them he planned to attend college in France. His real destination, however, was Tecumseh, Oklahoma, where the eighteen-year-old promptly flew for a reunion with his mother, whom he had not seen for a decade.

What makes kids like Peggy, Greg, and Charles actually break loose, while others only escape through their imaginations? Much of the way children act depends upon how they view their captors. If a youngster feels he is not in control, he is likely to be scared and submissive. When he no longer fears his kidnaping parent, either physically or psychologically, he may risk calling home or running away.

Still, only a few ever feel comfortable enough to contact a missing parent. Take the case of Jaime. It took her three years before she could act independently. One May morning, when her father and brother were out weeding their vegetable garden, nine-year-old Jaime tiptoed to the telephone and spoke with her estranged mother. Over the next month, they hatched Jaime's escape plan. Every time her brother and father would leave the house, she would call her mother, who had taught her how to dial collect. The initial call home was a potential problem, since Jaime had charged it to her father. Afraid he would find the telephone bill and catch on, she would run to the mailbox at the end of her Indiana country road every day to see if the bill had arrived. When it finally appeared, Jaime tore it up, knowing that the next month, when the phone company requested the overdue check, she would be gone.

Here is Jaime's story: "For a while I hated my mother because I thought all the stuff my dad was saying was true. He'd say my mother used to go out and get drunk, which is impossible because she is allergic to alcohol and gets sick if she drinks. He said she was a pig and had me waiting on her. As I got older, I realized it was my father who had me waiting on him. He made me wake up at five A.M. to bring him orange juice, but when I came home from school, I would see it hadn't been touched. One day my older brother hit me and I went to my father and he said, 'You should have told me about it when it was happening,' but he hadn't been around then. He didn't make sense and I was losing my respect for him. I ran upstairs to my room and started thinking about my mom and decided I'd try to get ahold of her. I found her number in my dad's phone book. But it took me awhile to get up the nerve to call her, because I didn't know if she would be angry that I had waited three years to call. I thought she might hang up and say, 'I don't have a daughter anymore, my daughter left me.' But I called and said, 'Hi, Mom,' and at first she wasn't sure it was me, and thought it was a prank. We both started to cry. I asked her if she would come and pick me up. It was about a month before school was over, and she told me to hold on until school was over, so I wouldn't have to repeat the grade. We decided not to say anything to my brother. He wasn't interested in leaving, and would probably tell my dad. I sent my mother a map I had drawn so she would know how to get to my school. The last day of class, she and my grandmother waited outside the school. I met them and we drove off. I was free."

· 3 ·

Great Expectations

It was early morning. I had parked my car near the entrance to my daughter's school. I spotted her walking into the courtyard with a friend, and moved so I was standing right in front of her. She looked me over from head to toe, threw her books to the ground, and her arms around me. We were both crying, and I said, "I've been searching for you for more than three years. Would you like to come home with me?" She wept, "Oh, yes, Mommy, yes!" We hugged each other all the way back, and it has been beautiful ever since.

FOR A WHILE, perhaps. But the fairytale ending faded fast for this mother from Maryland. The aftermath of the reunion resembled more of an O. Henry finish than one from Hans Christian Andersen. No one lived happily ever after, since the twice-stolen twelve-year-old was ordered back to her father by a judge a short time later.

Just because children are returned does not mean the story is over. In fact, being back may just be the first chapter of a wrenching saga. Part of the problem is expectations. Father or Mother assumes that the child will be delighted to see him or her, and that the relationship will be as loving as it was before. Wrong. Frequently, parents are disappointed by the reception they receive from their offspring. Kids gone a long time may not recognize the missing parent, or worse, may recognize and then reject. Still under the spell of the snatcher, they may be angry with the absent parent and confused by her or his sudden appearance. They may even cling to their kidnapers. Grownups are devastated and unprepared; after all, they have suffered, too. "I missed my sons so badly," sobs one woman, "and thought that when they returned they'd be so full of love. Instead, these kids came home broken. They haven't put their arms around me or kissed me yet in the year they've been back. And that hurts." Says the psychologist who has treated her children: "She thought everything would be wonderful when the kids got back, but there is a grand illusion. She still has to raise three teenage boys."

Of course some youngsters are thrilled to be home, and make a terrific adjustment. They may even become stronger from the experience. Sadly, they are the exception. The majority return with an array of serious problems that would discourage even the most patient parent. Chicago child psychiatrist Ner Littner once estimated that as many as 40 percent of kidnap victims may return scarred, and that figure is probably conservative. Even the "normal" ones are deceptive. Kids may seem to be unaffected by the steal, but signs of disturbance can surface several months later. Or the damage may not be evident for years.

Most parents and experts have discovered that after the reunion, there is usually a "honeymoon" period of approximately two weeks to one month, and then after that, the offspring want a "divorce." During the lovey-dovey stage, kids are

49

affectionate with their long-lost parents and excited to be home. Adults overwhelm them with attention. Children try to please, too, being on their best behavior.

But make way for Phase II, where the kids are back and blue. The abduction has finally hit them, and the reality of the act is devastating. For the first time, youngsters may realize they were not stolen for love, but for spite; not because their captor wanted them, but because he didn't want the custodial parent to have them. Often they figure out what's what when the snatcher neglects to visit. They feel used and confused. Curiously enough, this revelation causes them to punish the "good" parents. Kids test them constantly, pushing them to proclaim their love during the most trying of temper tantrums. If a parent has remarried while the child was away, the victim may not like vying for attention with a stranger in the house. Children often resent the fact that life has gone on without them. How could Mom have suffered if she was able to date, kids reason, or even make more babies? Manipulative, too, children pit Mommy against Daddy, bargaining for more privileges and more goods by comparing now to the days of captivity. "But Dad would let me . . ." is a familiar line custodial parents are fed, or, "If you don't give me that, I'm going back to Mom." Never mind that Mom used to beat them or that she does not want them back. Overcome by emotion, the kids stew and suffer.

Being stolen is frightening. So is being recovered. Children may be torn literally between parents. Even if they aren't physically yanked back and forth, they are still victims of divided loyalty. "My mother grabbed for me," says one ambivalent boy, "and my father grabbed for me. I felt like a piece of meat, so I broke loose and ran as fast as I could away from them both." A Cincinnati father cringes when he recalls how his wife tried to turn their child against him as she was being led to the paddy wagon. "The police allowed my ex-wife to carry Rachael to the car, and every time she would look in my direction, my ex-wife would turn my child's head into her chest, and push her down so she couldn't see me."

Detective Ian Withers, responsible for retrieving more than two hundred stolen children, observes how these little people react: "Children up to the age of ten suffer an immediate shock that can last two or three days. But their first response is usually to run to the reunited parent and hug him. Kids are so busy talking, they agree to go off with that adult. Not until an hour later do these youngsters realize what has happened—they have been stolen again—and get upset and cry and scream, or beg the parent not to take them."

Not all kids leap into their absent parents' arms. Brought up to believe a thieving parent's mate is "Mommy" or "Daddy," they are confused when the real thing reappears. Sometimes the offspring were so young when they were kidnaped, they don't remember another grownup in their lives. Often these kids play their own version of *To Tell the Truth*: Will the real parent please stand up? Children may not be able to accept reality when the relationship of Mother versus Stepmother is explained. This is true, too, when kids whose names are changed discover they are not "Sally" or "Sam," but really "Mary" or "Michael." Out of disbelief, they lash out at their reunited parents. Patricia recalls what it was like when she told her son he had been given a fake name in captivity: "He kept kicking me in the shins and screaming I was a liar."

Informed that the parent is dead or will harm them, youngsters often faint or run away from him or her, convinced they have seen a ghost or will be hurt. Nabbed at Boston's Logan Airport by customs officials, one father, before his capture, had told his son his mother was dead. The boy's mother remembers the first conversation she had with her son after the arrest: "The police said, 'Andy, your mom is on the phone,' and he said, 'Who?' I got on the line and said, 'Andy, this is your mommy,' and he kept saying, 'Who?' and I kept saying, 'This is Debbie, your mom from West Hartford,' and he just kept saying, 'Who?' "

Kids gone awhile may not even recognize their missing parents—and vice versa. To be settled in one environment and then handed over to a virtual stranger calling herself "Mom" can be mystifying. After four years, a New York educator located his sons in Los Angeles, where they had been stowed. "I walked up to this ranch-style house, and said, 'You must be Joel and you must be Paul.' I didn't recognize my boys. I stared at their hair and hands and ears. When they left they had been chubby babies. Now they were so thin. They were polite young men. If I had seen them on the street, I wouldn't have known them."

Some parents suspect they have spotted their offspring, but are not sure. Their youngsters may be equally skeptical about their parents' identities. Marc went to fetch his children after a five-year disappearance. He thought he could make out his son and daughter playing in a Chicago schoolyard and pulled his car over by the side of some hedges to observe them for awhile. No doubt about it, they were his boy and girl, he decided. Marc hopped out of the car and slowly approached his son. He put his arm on Timmy's shoulder and said, " 'Do you know who I am? I'm your daddy.' Timmy said, 'Yeah,' but I could tell he wasn't sure. To refresh his memory, I sat on the grass with him and my little girl and showed them some pictures of us together. I brought their old toys and coloring books. After about ten minutes I coaxed them over to the car by saying, 'We're going to call Mommy.' Then I said, 'We can't reach Mommy tonight, but we will in the morning.' Then I asked them if they wanted to come back with me to New Jersey, and told them I'd call their mother and ask her if she wanted to come. Of course I didn't invite her, but I told her my plans. Then I took the kids on a ten-day vacation to determine what their reaction would be to their father's showing up after five years. They ended up staying with me."

Reunions are even more strained when the absent parent is not allowed to leave with the child. Even though Rick's mother had custody in New York, her ex-husband had managed to obtain a decree in his favor in Massachusetts. When she finally caught up with him, Martha had to go to court in Massachusetts to fight for her boy, who at age nine and a half weighed only forty-eight pounds. "I knew he was my son. Almost six years of our lives had gone by, and I looked in Rick's eyes. We wanted to grab each other and run, but we both had to keep our distance. What can you do in an hour? We took a walk and I bought him an ice-cream cone and he held me and then I had to let go. It was one of the most painful times in my life. To turn my back and leave was as if someone had taken my heart out of me. I was petrified I'd never see him again. I thought my husband might run some more, but the police had warned me if I left with Rick, *I* would wind up in jail." It took Martha two years to win back Rick, even though the boy had been abused and yearned to live with her.

The homecoming can turn into a confrontation. Take the case of Maggie. Three months after she and her husband were divorced, Bill grabbed their children, ages seven, five, and two, and fled from Oklahoma. In an isolated cabin in New Hampshire, he filled his offspring with false but convincing tales of his ex-wife's promiscuity and mental illness. The youngsters shrank away from their mother when she eventually showed up. Recalls Maggie: "I walked over to my ex-husband's car, where my kids were sitting. He put his body in front of the children to block them from getting out. After witnessing this exchange, they shrieked hysterically and were afraid of me. They refused to get out of my ex-husband's car."

Those kids' reaction—of siding with their thieving parents—is typical of many stolen children. (Some youngsters cling to

53

the snatcher and must be dragged out of his or her arms.) Sticking up for an abductor is a classic response, too, of adults held captive. In fact, the phenomenon is so common, it has been dubbed "the hostage syndrome" or "the Stockholm syndrome" after a 1973 bank robbery in which hostages sought to protect their kidnapers. Prisoners of war and prisoners of parents both empathize with their captors, and believe the other party (other country) has abandoned them.

Social-science observers see more connections between stolen children and POW's. Ask one twelve-year-old youngster, who hardly knew his father (his parents had separated when the boy was a baby), what it was like to be snatched and he will shoot back, "Eight hundred and fifteen days." In many ways, both groups react similarly to the stress of being held captive. Upon the release of the Americans in Iran, hostage experts watched for signs of "entitlement," a personality quirk common to prisoners who are incarcerated for long periods. It is a feeling that their ordeals entitle them to special treatment from their mates, bosses, and friends. Children whisked away may also act self-important. Lavishing attention on them only serves to reinforce this notion. Says one boy from California, who was spirited away to Canada by his father: "When I got back, I got on TV, and that made me different. It's hard to get on TV. Most kids never get a chance to do that."

But the bleak side that POW's and prisoners of parents share is the feeling of betrayal by the home country or the custodial parent. Often they harbor double anger—at one person or group of people for stealing them, at the other for not protecting them, or not finding them sooner. Kids informed a left-behind parent is dead are shocked to find him or her breathing beautifully. They are also mad. "If Dad or Mom did not die," they ask, "then why didn't he or she come get me?" Sometimes the snatcher tells the children the custodial keeper is coming for them. When the absent parent does not show, youngsters assume the searching side does not want to reclaim them. That notion makes them furious, and hurts them as well.

Judy, age five and a half, seethed at her mother when they remet, because she believed the woman had deserted her. "I asked my daddy where my mommy was and he said, 'In Brooklyn, and she's going to visit.' I kept saying, 'When is Mommy going to come?' and he said, 'She'll be here soon,' but she never came." Judy's mother describes their encounter: "I flew to my daughter's school and found Judy's classroom. I picked her up and said, 'That's my baby.' She started to cry. I had brought her toy clown Happy, so I said, 'Don't cry, Happy is here and Mommy is here, and we're going home.' Over and over she screamed, 'Why didn't you come for me before?' "

It takes years for children to completely forgive. Some never do. Thirteen years after he was recovered, one grown boy still sulks. "Time and again," asserts his father, "I ask my son, 'How can it be my fault that I didn't find you for ten months? I was looking night and day, but you kept running.' I explain how hard it was for me to hold onto my job and support his sister at the same time. My son always snaps, 'We don't need to talk about it.' But I know he blames me for not finding him sooner."

Both Mother and Father are under attack. "Aren't parents supposed to defend their offspring?" ask recovered kids indignantly. "Isn't their purpose to provide a refuge from the evils of the outside world?" It is bad enough that the lawful guardian does not rush to their rescue. But when a parent is a kidnaper and a liar—the evil instead of the refuge—a youngster's sense of trust suffers. In fact, the adage "Don't trust strangers" implies that only parents can be counted on. If they cannot be counted on, kids have no one but themselves for support. Forming relationships is out of the question. How can they be sure they won't be double-crossed again? Building back trust is a formidable task for the custodial parent.

According to family counselors and attorneys, most youngsters need three to six months before they are "won over" by the reunited adult. Yet kids rarely make a clean break psychologically from their kidnapers. Although they may find out they were exploited in a power play between the parents, children don't discard the snatcher—even if the snatcher seems to have discarded them. Says Ruth, whose mother sold her favorite stuffed animals in a yard sale and then, with the proceeds, ferreted her to Alabama: "I'm mad at my mom. She took me away from my friends and didn't give me a chance to say goodbye to my dad. Plus all the stuff she said about him wasn't true. She hasn't come to visit me since I've been back with my dad— not once in over a year. But," sighs the seventh-grader, "I still love her."

Sometimes the experience is so excruciating that children can't bear to face facts. Out of an inner need, they defend their kidnapers. Declares clinical psychologist Jeannette Minkoff: "Kids don't want to think their parents don't want them, or are rejecting them. If they say, 'My father wasn't all that bad,' maybe it makes them feel they weren't all that bad, either."

Months after their return, even the most bruised children may play down their ordeals or blame them on someone else. Before Rick's father abandoned him, he told the boy his mother was dead. Uncaring relatives who reared Rick starved and strapped him. Still he protects his dad. Says Rick: "He didn't hit me or anything. My dad was pretty nice." Another child, Larry, also has sublimated his anger. The boy and his three siblings spent six months confined to a broken-down jalopy. Later they were shunted off to an uncle and aunt who battered them repeatedly. "I don't hate my father," claims Larry. "He didn't do anything really bad to us. I hated those people we lived with. My dad was kind to me sometimes. He once bought me a minibike."

Kids may cover up for their abductors. A Tallahassee, Florida, mother has witnessed the welts and heard her three sons discuss their father's cruelty. "Now they are hiding the fact that their father was abusive," says the woman. "They say his new wife was the brutal one. They don't want to believe their dad is bad, and since he hasn't sent them anything for their birthdays or for Christmas, they tell me if he did, I'd only send it back, or he won't give them presents because he knows I'll never deliver them."

Their protests may be hollow and halfhearted, or genuine calls to be rescued. Kids who cannot adjust to a "new" parent may long to return to their kidnapers. While this urge is rare, some children, like Anna, do want out. "When I saw my dad, I didn't know what to do. He was walking up to our house and I started crying a lot because I didn't want him to take me back. I don't want to be with my dad, but when I tell him I want to go back to my mom, he says, 'You're staying.' He doesn't really listen to me. Whenever I ask him if I can talk about returning to Mom, he tells me how bad she is. And that ends the conversation."

Anna may beef about being back, but she is slowly adapting to life with her father. She roller-skates with friends and finds eighth grade enjoyable. Not all kids can cope. Miserable in their new surroundings, youngsters may lapse into serious depressions, or even resort to suicide. Peggy had a couple of near-misses. "When I got back," explains the now eighteen-year-old from Milwaukee, "I was eleven. I had been on the road for four years with my dad. All of a sudden I was living with my mother and I didn't really know her. She was like a stranger. My mother was excited when I got back. I felt weird, but went along with her excitement. I was so used to being with my father, and I missed him. I started to act up in school for attention, like eating crayons, or running around and making the principal nervous. I had missed so many classes, I just couldn't keep up. It was a new school and I had no friends. In fact, I could never make friends. I hated myself, so I decided to kill myself. I felt, Life is no good, I might as well hang it up. Once I locked myself in the bathroom and slit my wrists with a razor blade. Another time I brought a rope into my room and tried to strangle myself."

Children who cannot get used to their custodial parents may crawl back to their captors. This is especially true of those away for years. Kids abducted abroad and returned have an additional burden—culture shock—and sometimes they find their new digs are just too foreign. "They looked as if they had been transplanted into another world," says May, whose two sons were snatched to Argentina when they were toddlers, and sent back to Wisconsin a decade later. "I'd say things to them like 'Get your rear in gear,' or, 'Cool your jets,' and they'd ask what that meant. They were always comparing America to Argentina, claiming the fish were bigger there and South American soccer was better than in this country. They spoke with Spanish accents and pronounced a lot of words wrong and their schoolmates would make fun of them."

May tried to make them feel comfortable, yet after a year, they opted to return to their father. "That year was difficult," reflects the professional horsetrainer, "but I had waited ten years for the opportunity to be their mother, and thought somehow we were going to make it. I understand their decision to go back to their father. They have been with him a lot longer than they have been with me. My boys were two and three years old when they were taken. Their whole life has been spent with him. I have only known them for a year." Incisive though she may be, May was crushed when she had to turn her sons over to their dad. She had spent $35,000 and ten years of her life trying to retrieve them.

It is unusual, though, for kids to part company with their custodial parents. Ordinarily, they weather the rough times— but not without taking out their troubles on their recently reacquired mothers or fathers. Parents may expect paradise, but all too often they find the aftermath of the recovery is hell.

Kids used to mistreatment on the run may push a reunited parent into reprimanding them. Randy was addicted to abuse from her mother and once returned to Dad, tried to provoke him into beating her. Says the bewildered forty-two-year-old stockbroker: "The first two months she was back, no matter where I took her, Randy would have to pick a fight and spoil the day. She'd constantly comment on my cooking. She'd claim the food didn't taste the way she liked it—the way her mother made it—and she would refuse to eat. Randy would goad me until I couldn't stand her whining anymore and would yell. Then she would cry hysterically. Obviously, she was starving for affection, but I gave her as much as I could. How can I make up for what she didn't have? It's impossible."

A paradox prevails: the children want to be close to their custodians, yet they go to pains to alienate themselves. They long to be cuddled and hugged, but when embraced, they push away. Often returned youngsters do not know how to love or be loved, because, as victims of emotional and physical abuse, their sense of self has been assaulted. They take out their rage and their disappointment on the most available persons— their lawful guardians. Acting out may make them feel in control, an appealing change of pace for children stolen back and forth at the whim of their parents. Having to take orders from a "stranger" may also agitate them. For four years, Joan's three sons lived on the lam with their hard-drinking, hard-hitting father. But he was all they had. The boys have been back with their mother for almost a year, and still look for ways to irk her. "They don't like having a new disciplinarian," sighs the weary woman, "so they rebel. If I ask them to do something, they yell, 'No,' or, 'I won't,' or, 'You can't make me.' If I go into their rooms, they tell me to get out. If I sent them to their rooms, they would probably climb out the windows. They refuse to do me any favors. I've tried every approach. We have a swimming pool, so I'll say, 'Bobby, would you go and sweep the pool.' That doesn't work, so then I'll say, 'Won't you please sweep the pool, Bobby?' Next is, 'Bobby, go sweep the pool.' Finally I'll get huffy: 'I told you to go out there and sweep that pool.' It's never done, no matter how I ask. Now they curse at me, something they would never have dared do before they left. I can't even get them to brush their teeth. It's minor to some people, but it's important to me. And these are teenagers! My kids don't act their ages, but the ages they were when they were taken. They stopped growing when they were away."

Eventually kids will usually calm down. Mike, kidnaped three times by each parent in eighteen months, is slowly making progress. Says his father: "I have an eight-year-old boy who will probably need years of counseling before he straightens out. Mike completely resists parental authority. I tell him to do something and he gets mad and cries so hard sometimes I think he's going to have a convulsion. The other day, I asked him to make his bed and he shrieked, 'I'm not going to do that,' and broke down. I went up to him, and for the first time, he put his arms around my neck and hugged me."

The flip side of rebellion is obedience. Recovered children may act like robots, afraid that if they do not comply with their parents' every wish, they will be sent back to the snatcher. States Yale University psychiatrist Albert J. Solnit: "Being abducted puts children in the position where they have to be alert to how to please people so they won't be stolen again. They obey to safeguard themselves." Therapists find some kids overcompensate for having been kidnaped, and take on an array of chores. "They may do things that aren't quite normal for kids," says Jeannette Minkoff. "All children try to get out of doing work around the house. These boys and girls are always looking for Brownie points because they want to be assured of their original place in the family. So they take on extra work, like putting out the rubbish, or doing the dishes, or making the beds. They think, 'If I'm not really good, maybe my mommy won't continue to love me, since I've been away for so long.' "

Kidnaped youngsters act differently, because they feel differently. They aspire to be ordinary, to blend in with the other boys and girls on the block. Yet they can't. Their stolen status sets them apart. For many unable to confide in peers on the run, the cycle of silence continues. Once back, they don't share their experiences because they feel stigmatized. "For three years I couldn't talk about what happened," says John, swiped three times in two years, "but when I reached thirteen, I began to tell my closest friends, just so they wouldn't find out on their own. Then I'd swear them to secrecy."

Youngsters just aren't accepting. How many times has a "Tiffany" or a "Thaddeus" been sorry they were not named "Susan" or "Steven"? Children find anything different is weird, a reason to taunt or tease. Kidnap victims fear that their stories will scare off their friends-to-be. Better to pretend they went on an uneventful trip with a loving parent, they reason, than a terrifying escapade with an odious adult.

Try though they may, abducted children can't hide their histories. How many "regular" kids are escorted to and from school, or watched round-the-clock by a parent turned bodyguard? How many nonabducted youngsters cling, sissylike, to a mother or father? Indeed, this behavior is reserved for jittery parents and their offspring who fear another kidnaping attempt. Other children take notice, too. Says one Philadelphia woman who chaperones her son everywhere: "I drop off David at the school grounds, and he doesn't want to leave me. Sometimes I have to go right up into the classroom. The other kids see this."

Peers also perk up when a former classmate stays back in school. Since kids may have missed years of education while away, they may return to find that they can't possibly keep up. They feel embarrassed and conspicuous; even the dunce of their class has graduated. Infrequent school attendance can permanently scar stolen children. "I'm trying to straighten myself out now," maintains an eighteen-year-old boy, recovered more than a decade ago. "It's so hard, though, because I'm not an educated person, and that depresses me."

Their confidence plummets. Lack of exposure to the three R's makes kids insecure in school and with friends. Due to weakened self-esteem, they blame themselves for their plights. Maintains Santa Ana, California, social worker Peg Edwards: "They think, 'Maybe I was stolen because I wasn't a good enough child, maybe I did something wrong and didn't please Mom' (if their father abducted them). They think their mother let them go. 'What did I do?' they wonder. 'I must not have been loved.' Their self-image is affected. We build up that picture of ourselves as children when both parents tell us they love and accept us. When children feel that one parent hasn't loved or accepted them, only because the grownup is not there, and they don't know any better, then they begin to lower their image of themselves and question, 'Am I really worthy? If Mom didn't want me, who else is going to like me?' "

Like kids of divorce, recovered youngsters think they are responsible for their sorry state. Social worker Judith Nadeau contends it is not necessarily bad for victims to blame themselves. "At least if children blame themselves, it provides them with a certain control. It is easier to say, 'It was my fault because I'm bad,' than to say, 'I'm helpless,' because a child's greatest fear is helplessness. So if they say, 'I'm to blame,' rather than 'I'm helpless,' it feels better. They have more control. They are giving themselves an explanation for what has happened."

Guilt grips children for other reasons, too. Now that they are back, boys and girls realize they might have been able to sneak to a phone or to a nearby bus. Not having taken charge plagues them. "It has changed my life since I was stolen, because I didn't try and contact my dad," maintains Allison, who believed her mother's accusations about her ex-spouse. "That was the big thing. I feel guilty that I didn't call him to let him know where I was. But I didn't think he wanted me."

Therapists who treat abducted children claim kids may feel obligated to make their ordeals sound worse in order to somehow justify their not contacting the searching parent. If their time away was dreadful, they could not be expected to bolt, reason youngsters unconsciously. But they should have, and could have broken loose if the experience were not too terrible. So children say their fingers were taped night and day to prevent their dialing home, or their shoes were stolen so they had no way to flee. What returned children do not know how to explain, often even to themselves, is that it was fear that kept them quiet. Kidnap victims may be so shocked by the knowledge that they could have escaped that they pretend they tried. Telling tales to their custodial parents makes them feel doubly guilty.

Unfortunately, most kids need not fib about their mysterious meanderings. Living conditions on the lam are often so unnatural that children may return with crazy concepts about society. Nathan roamed the country in a car with his father for seven months, dodging authorities. Once recovered, the bellicose boy needed to be deprogrammed by his mother. "Don't tell anyone where you live, or they'll kill you," he instructed his mother. "Does welfare buy guns?" he asked her soon after their reunion. Nathan also requested a pistol to defend himself against policemen. Apparently, the boy's father had also introduced his son to marijuana. Walking by a drug paraphernalia store one day, the five-year-old spotted a pipe in the window. "I know what that's for," he told his mom. "Daddy used to put this sweet stuff in it. It was supposed to make me act funny, but it made me sleepy."

Parents transmit values to their children. In follow-the-leader fashion, youngsters accustomed to hearing lies from an abducting mother or father learn how to fabricate. When they return, they may be such masters of mendacity that they do not even realize they have stopped talking straight. Take Laura, a chronic liar at twelve. For one year she moved around the West Coast with a mother who changed her daughter's name. The healthy woman told neighbors she was dying from leukemia and was leaving town to make a short but new life for herself with the kids. It didn't take long for Laura to catch on to the art of falsehood. Says her frustrated father: "Laura's counselors think it is because she saw so much of it with her mother. Lying was an everyday occurrence when she was away, and it became second nature to Laura. From the day she came home she has lied about her homework, about money that is missing, and about friends. Actually, it is not so much lying as an inability to tell the truth. I can be looking right at her, and she'll be chewing something. I'll ask her what she is eating, not to pry, but because I am interested. She'll swallow it and say, 'Nothing.' Or she'll stick the food in the side of her cheek, and there will be this huge bulge, and she'll say, 'Nothing.' After five minutes she'll end up in tears and say, 'I had a cookie in my mouth.' I'll ask her why she just didn't tell me that, and she'll make up something else, so it turns into a string of lies."

Whether the snatcher is a saint or a swine, most children are affected negatively by the abduction. Child experts debate the extent to which returned youngsters are emotionally damaged, but they agree that the degree depends upon several factors: the length of time the child is away; the child's age and temperament; the child's treatment by the kidnaper; the child's experiences on the run; and, once back, the kind of support the child receives from the community. One child-stealing specialist estimates that out of one hundred kids, perhaps eighty will suffer significantly. The twenty only slightly affected have been stowed away with stable, loving family members, like grandparents, who have allowed them to lead a "normal" day-to-day existence.

A few boys and girls have even blossomed after their ordeals. "Like children of divorce," claims psychologist Dr. Daniel O'Leary, "some snatched kids are able to get back into the mainstream fairly well. I've seen that most markedly where the children tend to achieve in school. They may possibly even overachieve to gain approval from a teacher." Say child-snatching survivors: "The experience has changed my life. It made me grow up a bit more." "Being stolen has made me more sensitive. It has taught me how to understand other people's problems." "I now know I can't let someone else run my life."

A warning, however: the glib talkers usually ache as much as the rest. They just don't let on to their misery. Kids react differently to being abducted. They may gobble their food, or lose their appetites; have trouble sleeping, or stay in bed too long. Some may scream, others may stay silent. They may act up in school, or behave beautifully in class but fall apart at home. Older children verbalize anguish more, while younger ones, less able to articulate their pain through words, may speak through their bodies. For small children, a serious side effect of being abducted is regression—bed-wetting, pants-soiling, thumb-sucking, or masturbating in public. It is their response to stress.

Stephen recalls the deteriorated state of his three children: "They were eleven, seven, and five years old when they came back. The eleven-year-old would suck her thumb, and all were outwardly masturbating and had nightmares. The oldest had bad dreams for a year, and wet the bed on and off for eight or nine months. The middle girl was in such bad shape, I had to buy her a Sears Roebuck machine, which woke her up when she wet. The five-year-old was a mess, too. He still is, even though he's been home for almost two and a half years.

I've had him tested repeatedly, and there is nothing physically wrong. I am told it is emotional. Paul stayed back twice in first grade, and has speech problems. When he was six, he'd say, 'I wuv dis, dis is da thing I want.' Even now he transposes sentences, like, 'The light shut off.' He didn't act his age because his mother never wanted him to grow up. She told him, 'You're my baby. Stay that way.' Paul was in diapers and had a bottle until he was almost four. When I found him at age five and a half, he was making progress. But as soon as he left his mother's side, Paul reverted to being a baby."

Ordinarily, anxiety symptoms last from two months to one year. Dr. Eugene Evans has treated stolen children and contends that kids show similar signs of stress regardless of their age or the length of time they are taken. "The message is usually the same," says the Tucson psychologist, "no matter how long they are gone: 'Your mother was a bad person,' or 'is dead' or 'has moved,' or, 'You can't reach her.' Youngsters go through a tremendous period of trauma when they are away, then when they come back, they find their mother is alive and in the same house. To comprehend all this is a major adjustment."

· 4 ·

Will It Happen Again?

LIKE FUGITIVES FROM JUSTICE, returned children rarely relax. They are nervous and suspicious, convinced their abducting parents are pursuing them. All too often, that is an accurate, not a paranoid, prediction. In about one-third of the cases, sources say, kidnapers strike again. The fear of a re-snatch may be so strong that the child must go into hiding—this time with the custodial parent. Once again the youngster may be forced into living on the lam, saddled with yet another phony name. In some instances, kids find themselves answering to three different names within a short period: their first and given name, another provided by the abducting mother or father, and a third bestowed upon them by the custodial parent for their underground existence. Sometimes there is a fourth, too, if the child adopts the name of a new stepfather.

Everyday events, from telephones to doorbells ringing, ter-rify returned children, who are certain that the caller is the snatcher, come to grab them again. At the sound of the bell, they dive under beds or seek safety behind clothes in an attic closet. A car or license plate resembling the stealing parent's can cause a youngster walking down a street to dart behind bushes and buildings. To an outsider, these movements look like an innocent game of hide-and-seek, but it is not sport to children who feel they are fighting for their lives.

It only takes a second to be stolen, kids tell themselves. Clinging pathetically to their lawful guardians, they refuse to part with a parent for even the most private moments. They won't stay with a baby-sitter, so Mom or Dad must conduct a constant vigil. Watch out if he or she slips away for even an instant. Claims a Massachusetts father who briefly cut the umbilical cord after a bout of cabin fever: "I only went out for dinner. You would have thought I was planning a year-long trip. My son and daughter clung to my legs and neck like toddlers, but they were ten and seven years old. I had to pry them off of me and reassure them I'd be back." Admits one San Francisco boy: "I freaked out when I got home. I couldn't be left alone, and would cry for hours because I was scared. Every time the doorbell or phone rang, I'd hide, sure this was it, that my father was coming for me. I didn't go out the first month I was back because I was afraid I'd see him in the street. My friends would ask me to go places and I'd refuse. When they asked why, I just said I didn't feel like it. I never gave them the real reason. So I stayed inside and watched TV a lot. I remember seeing all these happy little kids on the screen and thinking that I wasn't, and why couldn't I be like them. I had a big sliding glass door in my room, and at night I was positive my father would get me through the window. I'd see a shadow like a cat's, and think, 'That's Dad.' "

Darkness accentuates children's fright. Often abducted kids cannot fall asleep without a parent present, or without the lights on. Separation anxiety may be so severe that youngsters refuse to sleep alone, turning Mommy's or Daddy's only refuge into communal quarters. All kids fantasize about monsters and murderers, but kidnaped boys and girls also must worry about being captured by the ultimate bogeymen—their parents.

Many grownups report that their children's sleep is interrupted by cries of "No, no, no, stop!" from the bedroom down the hall. "I'll be back to get you in ninety days, and this time your mother won't find you," growled a Boston father serving a three-month jail sentence for the theft of his six-year-old son. Every night for several months, the boy would awaken shrieking in his sleep, having dreamed that The Moment had arrived. When first returned, Jenny would have a recurring nightmare. Says the Fort Lauderdale, Florida, child who was spirited away for three years by her dad: "This monster would be chasing me, and there would be this big fiery pit. Right as I was about to fall into the pit, the monster would change into my father."

Youngsters dread bedtime, but also fear school if that was the site of the original steal. Those nabbed during recess may refuse to play outside with their peers, convinced the abductor is lurking behind the jungle gym or basketball hoop. Cliff was class president before his third and final abduction, which occurred while he was playing kickball in the schoolyard. Although he was absent only one month, Cliff could not bring himself to venture outside for recess when he was returned. The principal found him cowering under a staircase. "The other kids asked me why I didn't go play outside," recalls Cliff, "and I'd say I didn't feel like it. Later, I was so scared I dropped out of school."

Children need not be stolen at school to associate the place with the kidnaping. Just being rescued from a classroom is enough to make the biggest bookworms want to play hooky. Take Josh C., for instance, who was hit with a double whammy: not only was he abducted at school, but he was also recovered there. On a muggy Sunday night in 1976, Josh found himself being held against his will by his father. The gruff, heavyset man had failed to return the boy after a routine weekend visit.

At the start of school Monday morning, Mrs. C. showed up to collect her son. She was too late. Realizing his ex-wife might make her move that morning, Josh's father had come for the boy moments before. A concerned teacher sprinted to the parking lot to block the man, and was nearly run over by his pickup truck. Little Josh, trapped inside the locked car, watched the teacher try to save him. Three years and five states later, Mrs. C. traced her newly named, eerily silent son to a Pennsylvania classroom. Her sudden reappearance spooked Josh.

School now symbolizes confrontations to him. To avoid a potential parental skirmish, or a repeat abduction, Josh schemes up ways to stay away—including making himself ill. "He has postnasal drip, which he refuses to take care of," observes his mother. "Sometimes he sucks in the mucus, and that makes him nauseous, but he would rather be sick and skip school than take his medication and get better." Today coaxing him to attend school is an ambitious project for Josh's mother and four teachers. They reassure him daily that he is safe with them. They also point out the private school's elaborate security system: locked doors; entry only after ringing a bell and being okayed on a video-screen monitor; high fences surrounding the playground; and adult supervisors to watch youngsters during recess.

Life is a series of sacrifices for jumpy children and their reunited parents. Private schools are popular, because security is usually more reliable, but tuition is expensive and kids may be separated from old public-school chums. Riding bicycles or playing pick-up-sticks in the backyard—pleasurable enough tasks for the nonabducted child—are viewed as frightening ordeals by children convinced they will be swiped once they step away from their homes. Fear may be intolerable that boys and girls stay inside all the time, or make sure to keep within eyesight and scream-shot of their parents. "Don't go too far," these bodyguards chant constantly, as if the unnerved children could possibly forget.

Hiding is an option for families certain that the kidnaper will attempt another abduction. Innocent victims may be forced to act like criminals, changing their names and canceling their credit cards, leaving no trace to encourage detection. Kids just back from a whirlwind tour of raunchy restaurants and fleabag hotels find themselves on the move once more. Hiding is hiding, whether it is with the "good" parent or the "bad" one. Again, children must cope with being false. The difference, however, is that recovered youngsters and their parents choose their clandestine lifestyle. Kids still in captivity have no say—their lifestyle is chosen for them.

Some children prefer to go underground rather than to live out in the open. They feel more protected, less likely to be exposed by a persistent kidnaper. Muses a boy who "disappeared" for four years with his mother after their reunion: "I thought it would be safer to hide and to change my name. I felt my father couldn't find me if I did. At first it was odd to go by a different name, but then after a while it seemed natural. The precautions we took made our life inconvenient. We weren't listed in the phone book, and gave instructions to my school not to disclose our number." Vanishing was not as simple as it may sound, according to the boy's mother, who devised their getaway:

In the beginning I lived in constant terror, and moved four times the first year. My first step was to pick an alias, so I went to the phone book. I was so angry with the legal system—I had custody and my ex-husband had had my child. I decided our new last name would contain the word "law" in it, because if there weren't justice in the courts, at least I would have it personally. I decided on "Lawton." In California you don't have to go to court to change your name, so I went immediately to the department of motor vehicles and pretended I was getting married, and needed a license with my new name. The clerk told me to come back when I got my marriage license, so I said, "Okay, I'm not getting married, but I want to change my name." Next I put down the new name on my auto insurance and then wrote to credit-card companies and said I was a journalist and "Lucy Lawton" sounded better than my old name for professional purposes. Then I changed my checkbook so it would match my driver's license. I picked yet another fake name for getting a phone, and didn't even list that name. I got the phone by putting down a cash deposit and saying I had just moved into the state and had never had a phone elsewhere. When I needed something, I'd give my parents' number in Ann Arbor. During this period, my ex-husband's mother and father thought their son had committed a terrible act by stealing Michael, and stopped speaking to their son. Even now, I write my ex-mother-in-law by sending letters through my parents, who forward them to her. She does the same, and said she really doesn't want to know where I am. I lived in one place, and went to work in another county, where I kept a post-office box.

Despite my system, my ex-husband traced us twice. We had been at the first place a month, and all of a sudden he called and nonchalantly asked to speak to my son. I slammed down the phone and got hysterical. Some friends packed me up that day and found me a new place. I was there a year, and then my *lawyer* betrayed me. In the past, I had paid his fees promptly, but had run out of money when he sent me another bill for $900. It was for writing a letter to my ex-husband's attorney to collect back payments for child support. For a while, my lawyer also thought I could sue the school for not having an adult on duty at the playground where my son was kidnaped, so I asked my attorney if he would deduct the $900 from the percentage he would get for this other matter. I got a letter back saying I was no longer his client, and saw that a carbon copy had been sent to my ex-husband's lawyer. The letter had my address on it. I was horrified, and moved within two days. It turns out that this lawyer who gave away my address had a stepdaughter enrolled in my son's private school. We figured she would never know who Michael really was, because his last name had been changed, but still every time there was a parents' day or a science fair at school, my son had to stay home. His teachers were very cooperative. A friend of mine worked in the school Michael had come from, and another in the school he attended next, so I literally got handed the records, which were changed so there was no reflection of his new identity. When Michael was seventeen we resurfaced. He's six foot three now, and while he can still get harassed by his father, he can't get stolen anymore.

Fury has replaced fear for Michael. No longer is he the trembling thirteen-year-old who, out of terror, froze when approached by his father at a schoolyard. Nor is he the quaking child who returned from captivity a month later, unable to leave the house or function normally—certain that Father was lurking just beyond the front stoop. Today Michael yearns for a confrontation between his dad and him—and this time, would like to be the one to push and shove. Why the metamorphosis? Getting older has helped, but so has Michael's change of attitude, brought about by the way he views himself and his estranged father. Four years ago: "I felt as if I had no control over my life, that he would steal me again." Now: "I am hoping he will pop up again, so I can kick him in the balls. Anyone who would do to a human being what he did to me— grab me and brainwash me—deserves to be beaten." Michael's confidence took its time returning. "Slowly the fear that my dad would get me went away because Mom taught me what to do if it happened again. She said to scream loudly, and keep her phone number with me at all times. Then she sewed money and telephone numbers into the lining of my jacket, so I could escape by hailing a cab and running to the nearest phone to contact her."

Like other returned children, Michael's ability to control his fear—and to some extent, to conquer it—stems from knowing what to do and how to react. Boning up on these combat tactics ensures kids will be less intimidated by an abductor, and less obsessed with a follow-up snatch. Those most traumatized are youngsters who don't feel they can stand up to a kidnaping parent. Declares clinical psychologist Eugene Evans: "Their fear and anxiety is going to stay with them much longer because they are still dominated by this person, and unable to resist the stealing parent if he or she comes back. These kids don't feel strong enough, either mentally or physically, to resist."

Three adolescent boys, returned recently through the courts, are petrified their indefatigable father will cart them off for the fourth time. Says their equally nervous mother: "Instead of relaxing and letting the love come out, my sons are always tense and on guard, terrified that my ex-husband will strike again. The little one said that if his father does return, he will have to go with him. 'Mama,' he told me, 'if Daddy shows up, my legs won't be able to move.'" One California boy started running track after he returned so he could outdistance his father if there were another abduction attempt. Claims thirteen-year-old Sarah, who turned from cowering to cocky: "For a while, every time I heard someone at the door or walking behind me, I thought it was my father. He had me under his spell. He would call and tell me to pack my bags, because he was coming. When I told him I wouldn't go, he'd say all this stuff that used to get me upset, like I was a bad girl and didn't know any better. But now I hear it better and understand it better and just start laughing because it's almost ridiculous. When he calls and threatens to resteal me, I say, 'I'm old enough now to know what I want, and I don't want to be with you.' One day he warned me he was on his way, so I said, 'Face facts. I'm not going back. I'm not scared of you anymore. You can't keep me under twenty-four-hour guard. I can always take a taxi to a bus station or call up Mom."

Kids have various methods for coping with the fear of a repeat performance. Sarah chose to talk herself out of being scared by talking back to her father. Some children may role-play the inevitable scene between themselves and the snatcher, learning how to act quickly and break loose. One twelve-year-old carried a safety pin for protection, while a four-year-old chose a stick so he could "clunk my mommy if she tries to steal me again."

Even for those feeling well rehearsed or well protected, wielding prepared lines or a "clunking" stick, the fear never completely vanishes. Never mind that the child is too old, too big, or too wise for the kidnaper. States a girl returned to her mother more than five years ago: "I always have the feeling that someday I am going to turn around and my father is going to be there." Perhaps most telling are the larger implications of worrying, articulated by a bruised eleven-year-old girl from San Diego: "I'm afraid of my dad. I'm not really afraid anymore that he's going to come and take me, but that something is going to happen to my mom and I'm going to have to go back to him."

· 5 ·

Lingering Trauma

FEAR FINALLY SUBSIDES. No more nightmares. No more self-imposed house arrest. Life assumes a normalcy for recovered youngsters. Like other kids, they delight in junk food, TV, and water fights.

But then they grow up—or rather, don't grow up. While long-term research on stolen children is unavailable, specialists in the field are beginning to note startling correlations between being snatched and later antisocial behavior, such as delinquency, prostitution, and drug addiction. More "acceptable" problems like mistrust, low self-esteem, and chronic depression are also being linked. Clearly all abducted kids do not turn tricks or pop pills, nor do they all lapse into irreversible spells of sadness. But enough kidnap victims are floundering as adults to make stealing experts take notice. While stress symptoms may have long since vanished, underlying scars from the ordeal may linger indefinitely.

Robbed of regular parent-child relationships, stolen kids may seek substitutions in surrogate "families"—johns acting as father figures, street gangs taking the place of brothers and sisters. Attention is what they want. And love. The real kind. Out of a desperate need to feel wanted, adolescents may lapse into delinquency to prove that they are loved enough, or tough enough. "I think victims of snatching," asserts Dr. Jeannette Minkoff of the Rochester, New York, Probation Department, "are more likely to be candidates for criminality than other kids. There are no hard statistics, but I have noticed that a lot of these kids end up going through the system for shoplifting, petty larceny, burglary, auto theft, and prostitution. You can almost label those who come through the courts on delinquency. Either they've been abandoned or they've been stolen, or have had poor relationships with their parents. Abducted children have been made to feel badly about themselves by their parents' divorce. They have never been able to resolve the blame for that, and have such a need to be part of something that they get into gangs. A lot of these girls are sexually promiscuous and become ladies of the evening. Just to be accepted, they'll do almost anything."

Lack of love pushes these aching mini-adults into acting objectionably. Psychiatrists, sociologists, and school officials have long made connections between divorce, delinquency, and depression. Guilt, misconceptions, and insecurity—which inevitably result from having parents part—may be major causes of adolescent unhappiness and degenerative behavior, report these social scientists.

But not the only causes. Be it divorce or abduction, kids take their cues from their parents. Adults transmit values to their offspring; their obedient charges adopt their systems. If a parent decides to disregard the law and kidnap a child, he or she is telling that child it is okay to disobey established rules. Thus, observant youngsters are transformed into confused junior thugs. For years, they have been taught to be open and honest. Suddenly the snatcher strikes, knocking out these tenets and replacing them with their opposite—lying and cheating. So, like father, like son; kidnaped children learn deception.

The "Simon says" principle applies to solving problems, too. Watching a thieving mother or father "successfully" circumvent a custody dispute unconsciously tells impressionable children that they, too, can avoid unpleasant obstacles with an end run, instead of working through the system. Look out if *their* ex-spouse gives them any trouble with their kids! Dr. Minkoff believes that at least half of all abducted boys and girls will become abductors. Why? They know that it is an option, and they know it causes pain. Those out for revenge are likely to repeat the act. It is well documented that other domestic violence follows this victim/victimizer pattern. Sixty percent of abused kids go on to become abusers, and one study showed that close to 38 percent of battered wives physically abused their youngsters. Divorce expert E. Mavis Hetherington once estimated that three out of four children of divorce will themselves wind up divorced.

Love confuses kids. Daddy hits Mommy because he loves her? She smacks Junior because she loves him? Daddy and Mommy used to love each other before they broke up? Children wonder: "You hit the person you love? You steal the person you love? I was stolen because I was loved?"

One of the most severe long-term effects of being abducted is growing up with a distorted notion of love. Kids conclude that love gives people license to behave any way they want, including illegally and immorally. Says family therapist Dr. Mel Roman: "Love suddenly becomes the justification for almost any kind of act. It means that you can rationalize all kinds of destructive behavior on the basis of saying you love someone, and that you are doing it for their own good. In my view, a child will carry with him a twisted view of what love is all about."

When victims wise up and find out why they were stolen, they

78

are devastated. "When they realize a parent didn't take them because he or she loved them," says Dr. Eugene Evans, "but instead to get even with the other parent, it shatters kids' view of love. Then they think you can't believe someone when he says he loves you, because you're not sure what love means."

Not knowing what it means and not having had healthy role models, they form relationships for the wrong reasons. Often abducted adults end up with unequal partners—people who will "mother" them rather than "lover" them. They seek security and protection more than passion. Frequently snatched sons and daughters wed early to attentive older mates, who unconsciously replace the thieving parent the child never trusted. Child-stealing experts contend that many girls marry men several years their senior, while boys are attracted to older women, if they had an unfulfilled relationship with their mothers (if moms stole their sons, for instance). Like child-abuse victims, kidnaped youngsters also may get married at an early age to escape an oppressive family atmosphere.

The child left behind in an abduction can share a similar mating pattern—early to bed, early to wed. A real catch? Someone who is a perfect parent, more than a perfect partner. Most likely, twenty-one-year-old Jessie will always be scarred by her experience. At the age of nine, she watched her father scoop up her sister Kate from a neighborhood game of jump rope, and hurl her into his car. Locking the doors in Jessie's face, he sped away, ignoring her pleas of "Take me, too!" Even today, eleven years after the incident, Jessie admits her romantic involvements are unhealthy, reflecting the unrequited love from the first important male in her life—Dad. "I felt rejected by my father," says Jessie, "and at the same time, angry at him. Growing up, I was very bitter and could not open up to men. During the dating stage I was vulnerable, and looked for someone who was strong, like a father figure. I found a guy several years older, and our relationship lasted four and a half years. When I met Rick, I had just turned sixteen, and all of a

79

sudden I was this great big woman. He used to buy me clothes that looked like a woman's, and would show me how to put on makeup. I told him what had happened to my father and sister, and he promised we would marry and have kids, that he would never leave me, the way my father had. I just sensed he was going to drop me anyway. I decided I couldn't bear to let him go unless I had something to carry on his memory, so I decided to keep a part of him and got pregnant. He left me with a little boy. I still don't understand why he broke up with me. I want to ask him why, just as if I found my father, I would say, 'Why didn't you want me? What did I do wrong?' I've never been able to go out with men my own age. They act dippy and immature. Rick was five years older. Now I'm more comfortable with a thirty-five-year-old man than one in his early twenties, as I am. But that's really beside the point. From my father and Rick, I feel that I know what men are all about. As far as I'm concerned, they're all screwed up. I don't need them."

Relationships can work both ways: either kidnap victims welcome them, or they avoid them. Grown women taken by fathers as kids may reject all males, while men carried off by mothers may be down on females, not wanting to get hurt again. Some remain single. As grownups, they are often loners or losers at love. They don't know whom to trust or how to maintain lasting liaisons. The refusal to risk relationships or to make the right choices stems from being stolen. Snatched several years ago, one adolescent girl is reluctant to date and mate: "What will happen if I make the mistake of marrying someone like my father?" she wonders nervously. "What if my husband steals my kids? It makes me scared to form long relationships with guys."

Platonic involvements are also scarce and shaky for many plagued by kidnap trauma. The inability to trust—to make friends—is perhaps the most permanent fallout from an abduction. Those snatched back and forth are hit even harder; they can't trust either parent. Just as soon as they have settled down in one spot, they are suddenly uprooted again.

According to experts, returned children may interact normally until adolescence or adulthood, but mistrust will usually surface sometime. Kids are scarred because they have been duped. During infancy, children learn trust from their parents. When the most important people in their lives double-cross them—both through kidnaping and conning—youngsters fall apart. "How could Mom or Dad do that to me?" these anguished children ask. And, "If my parents don't act consistently or honestly, why should anyone else?" Disillusioned and distraught, these lonely, defeated soldiers retreat from humanity.

Social scientists probing the long-range implications of child stealing claim that it can be far more traumatic for kids to be grabbed by parents than by strangers, from the point of view of trust. Society warns children to be wary of strangers. Kids are not expected to trust unknown abductors. But what about a parent who promises a delightful day-long jaunt in the countryside and instead delivers a three-year dash across the continent? It is unfortunate, though more acceptable, for a stranger to steal. It is intolerable and inconceivable to be at the mercy of a blood relative. It can take years to build back trust.

Youngsters must also wrestle with confidence—or the lack thereof. Kids don't trust, so they don't form friendships. They don't form friendships, so they think they can't form them. When they grow up, their self-esteem may be so low that they resort to all sorts of perverted plays to bolster their egos. One Illinois teenager, for example, was grabbed by her father at the age of six in the middle of the night and ushered to a bus they boarded at the local terminal. Today, when upset, she frequents the same depot at night and picks up an older man for a two- or three-day fling.

Depression. It may begin when the child is on the run, and persist long after the welcome home—perhaps when the youngster realizes his almost immaterial part in the parental tug-of-war. He tries to shake his sadness, but can't. Unhappiness becomes a chronic condition. Researchers are discovering the prevalence of low-level depression among children who have been stolen. Broods one young man, kidnaped at the age of seven: "I'm almost eighteen, and I have nothing in my life going for me. I wish I had never been taken, and my parents had divorced regularly. I'm so depressed."

Being abducted makes some children mildly depressed, and in a few cases has been known to cause permanent mental illness. One fourteen-year-old was yanked back and forth thirteen times between her parents. The instability has caused her to become unbalanced. Returned to her father yet another time, the girl tore up her room, smashing the television and windows, claiming it made no difference if she destroyed her room, because her mother would retrieve her anyway, and all those items in the new room would be gone. One Arizona mother wasted no time admitting her daughter to the psychiatric ward of a hospital after she noticed the girl had at least three distinct personalities: one that wrote poetry, another that detested it; a fat side that stuffed herself with food, and a skinny alter ego who practically starved. There was also the prissy "Gosh darn it" girl, and then Miss Gutter Mouth, the formidable curser. Shuttled from state to state, the girl had been sexually molested, left alone a lot, and turned against her mother. Immediately upon her return, she was placed on potent tranquilizers for eight months. That was more than a decade ago. Observes her mother: "Being stolen has carried over into Mary's adult life. She has to be on the move. She can't lead a quiet, normal life, and is happier if things are in turmoil. It makes me nervous just watching her."

Mary's nature is skittish, her prognosis unclear. Although spirited away in third grade, today she is still woefully out of whack. Despite her severe scars, Mary was kidnaped at what child specialists assert is a "good" age. Most experts maintain that kids older than eight years of age recover the quickest with proper help—although how youngsters fare and how they cope are, of course, crucial factors in determining the extent of their injuries and their recuperation. Judith Nadeau believes that babies between the ages of six months and eighteen months may suffer the most: "That is the most drastic time to break a bonding relationship. I'm thinking vis-à-vis adoption and foster-home placement, but it would be identical in terms of kidnaping. There may be fewer problems, though, if the parent who steals is used to caring for the child. From six to eighteen months, infants become symbiotically attached to their primary parents, and breaking that bond is likely to cause severe problems. The child may suffer enormously, but people don't see it as suffering, because he will withdraw and pull into himself and resort to self-stimulation. What he is doing is counting on himself, because he has lost the ability to attach to an object. He can be isolated growing up. Scientists have speculated that even children who appear to have recovered and look normal may have real difficulties as adults. Being stolen may be more tolerable for kids over the ages of seven or eight, because they have a cognitive understanding of what is going on. It may be painful, but they have developed more of a capacity to cope."

Dr. Daniel O'Leary treats snatched kids immediately upon their return. He agrees with Judith Nadeau's theory of recovery: the older the better. "I think it is easier for the ten-, eleven-, and twelve-year-olds, because they think there may be some possibility of getting back with the other parent. The worst time is in the formative preschool and early school years, between the ages of, say, four and eight, when children don't feel they have much control over their lives. Some of the younger kids may be oblivious to what is going on, at least in terms of parental strife. Their problems usually revolve around how much their identity has been masked or changed."

In the end, it barely matters at what age these victims are whisked away. What *is* important is that their ordeals may

83

haunt them for a long time—perhaps forever. Wounded juniors may smart from disappointment and distrust. While they may suddenly seem cured and fancy-free, a relapse attests to a deep-seated problem. Stolen children are scarred children. They don't forget. Says one adult, recovered more than twenty years ago: "You are never all right again. I still have a daily nightmare about my abduction."

II

THE PROBLEM

· 6 ·

The Laws and
Their Loopholes

I had a lot of faith in the legal system when my ex-wife
stole my kids. At first I turned to my attorney. I thought
the New York courts would enforce the custody decree
they had rendered. I was naive. What woke me up was
when the judge said, "I understand your situation, but you
must understand that the courts can only render a custody order, but they cannot enforce it when your ex-wife's
whereabouts are unknown." So I thought, "Here we
have this big judge sitting up there who has made this big
decision about who will get my children, but he can't do
anything to enforce his decision. What kind of a legal
process is that?" I turned to the police, but they didn't
want to do anything. They didn't know where my ex-wife
was, and weren't planning to find out. I got two different
warrants for her arrest. The police couldn't execute them,
though, because they didn't know where she was. I was
told by the chief of police, the state police, and the county

sheriff that if I found her, they would carry out these warrants. Everything was back in my lap. I spent all this money getting the proper legal documents, and after I got them, they didn't do me a bit of good. Then I turned to four private investigators, and all they did was take my money. Finally I found my children myself in Colorado. My lawyer told me I had to pursue the matter in the Colorado courts. I asked him what my chances were of getting custody in this new state. He said they were only fifty-fifty—even though I had already won it in New York. Then I asked my attorney what happens if my ex-wife flees to another state during the proceedings and he told me I'd be out of luck again. He said, "My advice to you off the record is to steal back your boy and girl." That is just what I did.

DAVID NEVER INTENDED, nor did he want, to run off with his children. He kidnaped them as a last resort. Ironically, it is the legal system itself that has spawned child stealing, because it encourages, rather than discourages, this behavior. Abducting parents who break the law are rarely caught or punished, while mothers and fathers who play by the book frequently lose out. Legal guardians may be certain their former mate will abscond with the kids, yet still are compelled to grant him or her visitation—or risk being hauled into court on contempt charges or even jailed.

Those who do steal find they have picked the perfect crime. Child abduction by a parent is illegal only if it occurs after custody has been awarded. Until then, each partner is legally entitled to the child. Thus, a parent has not violated any law if he or she grabs the child when the couple is separated but does not have custody, or is still married. Abduction experts maintain that more than half of all snatches take place during this pre-decree period.

In a few states, parental kidnapings are not illegal anyway.

(While a parent who disregards a custody order may be slapped with civil contempt charges, courts cannot enforce these citations outside state borders. The abductor who moves across state lines may just as well be hiding out in some foreign country.) Often the crime is merely a misdemeanor, the statute casually enforced. Misdemeanors carry little weight. They are not usually extraditable offenses, so once a thieving parent flees outside the state, he or she can't be shipped home and prosecuted. The law becomes unenforceable. Parents catch on quickly: "They can't do anything to me for taking Danny," a man announced to his friends after kidnaping his son. "It's just a misdemeanor, like spitting on the sidewalk."

Even when it is a felony, other states almost always refuse to extradite. Whether or not one state even requests extradition from another depends upon the whim of those in charge. A sympathetic governor may ask for the abductor's return, but a less understanding official may refuse. Parents often decide to steal back their young rather than risk yet another verdict outside their own borders. And just because a father or mother is extradited does not mean the child will be returned; only an alleged kidnaper can be the subject of a request.

Getting a criminal charge filed against an abductor can take months, and may not even lead to an arrest warrant. These warrants are hard to obtain. Unless law officers are willing to look for the fugitive—they often are not—and unless they can find the thief, this document is useless. Since snatchers rarely seek a custody order in a new state, they probably won't come to the attention of authorities, except by accident—if they get picked up for a traffic violation, for instance. They are further able to elude officials by traveling frequently or by changing their names and disappearing into a new community.

Mothers and fathers who abscond abroad are practically never caught. Lawful guardians fortunate enough to catch them are required to go through yet another court proceeding on foreign turf—and often wind up losing custody.

The few offenders who are apprehended in the United States and the even fewer who are extradited and convicted usually receive little more than probation. Fines can be as insignificant as seventy-five dollars, if they are imposed at all. "I'm not expecting anything too severe," confessses an abductor-to-be, "if I get caught. I understand that if I don't create a fuss and come back on my own, I'll probably get yelled at by the judge and not much more."

Parents know they will get off with light sentences. They also realize that if they can hide long enough, a judge may decide to let them keep their children. Jurists dislike disrupting a child's stability, so may "legalize" the abduction for the sake of the kids. In confidence, lawyers endorse the crime by urging their clients to vanish for long lengths of time. They know how judges operate.

Youngsters gone awhile may elect to stay with the snatcher, and then the judge has no choice but to defer to the child. Often the thieving mother or father will brainwash the child against the other parent. It happened to one Wyoming mother of three, whose ex-husband fled with the kids halfway across the country. She finally found them several months later in Ohio. "Their father had told them I didn't want them, didn't feed them," winces the mother, "hit them with sticks, and was crazy. They were so young and gullible when he stole them that now they have turned against me. They testified in court that they didn't want to live with me. The judge gave custody to my ex-husband. I have been in and out of court twenty-eight times. The judge reacts to me like I'm a cancer. Who wants to work with a couple like us? The kids refuse to see me, and visitation is not strictly enforced."

Parents who finally find their youngsters may decide not to fight for custody because they believe their children are so changed or so used to their abductors that they would not adjust well to being home. Washington, D.C., postal worker Arnold Miller, for example, chose to settle for visitation rights when he realized his son's new Orthodox Jewish lifestyle, adopted on the run, would make it impossible for the boy to live a nonreligious life with Dad. "Mason is a completely different person than he was five years ago," claims Miller's second wife. "It's sad. If we had won custody, I don't think Mason would be happy."

Judges are partly to blame for the child-stealing epidemic— not necessarily for their decisions once the kids are back, but for the ones made while they are still away. Often they do not force kidnapers or their conspiring families into revealing where the child is being hidden. Some judges set free snatchers and their relatives who refuse to cooperate, instead of jailing them until the child is returned. "It drives me crazy," says an Indiana mother whose two sons vanished five years ago, "that my ex-mother-in-law tells her attorney while I am sitting in the courtroom what my sons look like, and how tall they are. Yet when my lawyer asks her on the stand where my son and grandson are, she claims she doesn't know. People send Tony letters through his attorney. I was told he was in my hometown last Thanksgiving. It kills me that these things can be done in front of my face and people say they don't know anything, and I can't prove they are lying." While strict jurists may impose contempt-of-court charges on abductors who refuse to disclose a youngster's location, that charge is not terribly intimidating to a parent who has already committed a far more serious act.

There is no uniform approach to parental kidnaping at the state level. Many state statutes exclude parental abductors from their definition of kidnaping, either expressly or by judicial interpretation; others make it a felony. Most state legislatures have now enacted statutes criminalizing this act. Many states differentiate between concealing a youngster within the state (a misdemeanor) and fleeing across the state border (a felony). In a couple of states, snatching is a felony, unless a parent returns a child unharmed prior to arrest. Then the charge is reduced to a misdemeanor. Forty-two states make child abduction and restraint a felony; in thirty-five states, it is a misdemeanor. Three states—New Hampshire, West Virginia, and Idaho—do not have any laws banning this behavior.

Usually the effectiveness of these laws is contingent upon the willingness of states' attorneys and prosecutors to enforce them. Custodial-interference laws may be on the books, but officers may choose to ignore them. Whether or not the police take a case frequently depends upon their attitude toward the crime—not on the crime itself.

At the local level, an abundance of jurisdictional problems invite abductions. One man explains his experience with the system: "I told the Massachusetts court, which had awarded custody to my ex-wife, that she would skip the state of Florida, where she was living with my daughter, and run to Colorado. She went to court and swore under oath that she would not leave Florida. Yet three days later, she moved to Colorado. I went back to court in Massachusetts and said, 'My ex-wife did what I said she would do.' The judge said, 'There is nothing we can do because she is in Colorado.' I went to Florida. I was told they did not have jurisdiction, either. So I traveled to Colorado and found out that my ex-wife was planning to move to San Francisco. I pleaded with the Colorado judge to put a stop to her running. I said, 'I'm begging for relief from this court, because I just can't keep following her all over the country.' The judge ruled that my ex-wife can't move outside of the school district without a court order. If she does, I get custody. But most judges won't do a damn thing. They can dispose of or take a case based on jurisdiction, and they can define *jurisdiction* pretty much any way they want. Once a kidnaper leaves an area, the other side has little chance of regaining the child, unless it is to resteal him."

Another parent had her thieving former husband extradited from Florida to Wisconsin. The father had taken his sons to South America. It took ten years for the mother to track down her boys. When it came time for the trial in Wisconsin, the father's lawyer had the case dismissed on a jurisdictional technicality. Explains the mother, still reeling from the outcome: "His attorney said that when my ex-husband stole the kids, I was visiting a friend who lived outside the county. So the court felt the crime was not committed in that county, and threw out the case. That was a real blow. My ex-husband walked out of the courtroom scot-free."

Police and the FBI—agencies that would ordinarily help a parent if the abductor were a stranger—maintain a "hands-off" policy when a parent is the perpetrator. They consider child stealing a domestic matter; never mind the statutes that make it a criminal, not a civil, affair. "Do you want to treat a loving parent the way you would a robber or a rapist?" asks one assemblyman, explaining why his state legislature has repeatedly voted down childsnatching bills. Perhaps the real reason for steering clear is the fundamental belief that parents steal out of love, not out of spite. Instead of viewing the problem from the standpoint of the child, lawmen and laymen inappropriately probe the motives of the abductor. Implicit in their "hands-off" policy is the attitude that a mother or father should be able to handle a mate—or pay the consequences. Authorities cite the Lindbergh Act, signed by President Hoover in 1932, which specifically excludes parents from the kidnaping statute, as a reason for not getting tough with Mom or Dad.

Since 1973, when Representative Charles Bennett of Florida sponsored legislation removing the parental-exemption clause from the federal kidnaping statute, his bill and numerous others have never obtained the approval of both houses of Congress. Even the recently passed Parental Kidnapping Prevention Act of 1980 (PKPA), the first federal statute designed to stop childsnatching, does not make parental abduction a federal crime.

Many states claim that childsnatching is not a problem, or not *their* problem. The Department of Justice and the FBI are reluctant to get involved, taking the position that family law is a state's, not the federal government's, responsibility, and that no federal law has been broken. Passing the buck has proven convenient for law-enforcement officials—as well as for child stealers.

Parental victims find police are not only indifferent, but often hostile. They resent being called upon to intercede. "What's the big deal?" they have been known to bark at anguished mothers and fathers. Most parents report being treated contemptuously by police. One Midwest woman furnished local law officials with a snapshot of her abducting ex-husband's girlfriend, who neighbors verified had been an accomplice to the steal. When the mother asked the police to question the girlfriend, the officer snapped, "What do you want, lady, revenge?"

Another mother watched aghast as the Phoenix, Arizona, police pulled out a standard complaint form to record the snatching of her two children and then checked off the category labeled "Missing Persons/Bicycles." She has had no word from her son or daughter since they were grabbed seven years ago.

Yet another mom was strolling out of a Chinese restaurant in Brooklyn, New York, with her parents and two-year-old son when two cars suddenly cornered the family. Six burly thugs, accompanied by the boy's father, jumped out and sprayed their victims with Mace. They beat the mother's father so badly he was later admitted to a hospital. In the commotion, the professional hoods yanked the shrieking boy from his mother and sped away. Although the plot was as carefully calculated and brutal as any kidnaping by strangers, law-enforcement officials refused to prosecute the child's father or his hired hands. "Be thankful they didn't have knives or guns," the unsympathetic detective told the mother. She, too, has had little luck locating her child.

The FBI and the police will occasionally enter a case, but usually only if another crime has been committed besides child stealing—or if there is so much blood and violence they can't help but take notice. (The FBI is *supposed* to intercede, however, if there is reason to believe that the child is being abused or neglected, or if the kidnaping takes place in a state that makes child abduction a felony and the case involves interstate or international flight to avoid prosecution.)

Eminent family law attorney Henry Foster, Jr., explains this "lock-the-barn-after-the-horse-is-stolen" principle. One of his clients, a Puerto Rican businesswoman living in New York, was married to a Vietnam veteran. Since his return from the war, he had become increasingly unstable, and the woman filed for divorce. Soon after, the husband absconded with their daughters, ages seven and nine. "The mother went to the Missing Persons Bureau and the FBI and both refused to help," says Foster. "I suggested she get an order from the family court granting her custody. The court would not even let her file a petition for custody unless she could provide the father's address. She was in a Catch-22 situation. She had no idea where her ex-husband was. I made arrangements for her to get the order. About two weeks later, police found the body of the younger girl in a burlap sack tied with barbed wire in the Hudson River. Finally, the FBI decided to look for the father, but it was because of the murder rather than the snatch."

The reluctance of law-enforcement officials to intervene tells abductors that if they don't leave marks on their kids' bodies, and don't kill them, their behavior will be tolerated. In effect, the police are sanctioning child stealing.

Parental kidnaping is a low-priority crime. "On a scale of one to ten," Sergeant Richard Ruffino of the Missing Persons Bureau in Bergen County, New Jersey, confided to a journalist, "police rank missing children minus four."

Officers, overworked and harried, are hesitant to act. Police may be told that a mother or father has abducted the youngster, when the parent may just be late in bringing back the child. Spouses, too, occasionally reconcile, and then the searching parent may withdraw the charges. Why? He or she may drop them out of compassion for the snatcher, out of fear that a criminal proceeding will anger a former spouse and cause him or her to strike again, or because the parent never intended to prosecute after the child was returned. Withdrawing charges enrages law-enforcement agents, who have spent valuable time and may have even risked their lives rounding up the suspect. Police also stay away because they think that district attorneys won't bother to prosecute, but just want the child back. (DA's claim the blame should be placed on extradition officers, who frequently refuse the request, or deny it.)

Police note other prosecution problems. Some states require that "intent" be proved—that is, that the parent plotted the kidnaping, rather than only intended to take the child for a visit. This nuance in the law makes a conviction difficult. So does the fact that sometimes an abductor may not have been told that a custody order was issued before the snatch. Or the offender may have obtained a conflicting custody order from another jurisdiction. In a June 26, 1982, Justice Department report to Congress, the government explained why it prefers not to involve itself with parental kidnaping cases. "We are aware of two recent extradition requests in which the abducting parents obtained temporary custody in asylum states in spite of outstanding felony childsnatching warrants in other states. In two other requests, parents were charged with felonies in spite of the fact that they had obtained custody decrees in other states."

Some authorities are anxious to act, but can't. If the parents are still married, or have no custody papers, no crime has been committed. In some states, there are no laws against parental kidnaping, and newly enacted statutes do not apply to abductions that occurred before the laws were passed. Also, state laws may limit action, especially when the abduction is classified as a misdemeanor, and extradition is almost impossible. While one state may politely ask another to return an offender, the petitioning state may be powerless to proceed further if the request is denied.

There is another obstacle, too: more often than not, police, lawyers, and even district attorneys do not know how to handle child-stealing cases. The laws are so complicated, ambiguous, and ridden with loopholes that even custody experts have trouble advising parents. If the experts aren't sure what to do, how can the average parent know? The Uniform Child Custody Jurisdiction Act (UCCJA) and the Parental Kidnapping Prevention Act (PKPA), statutes aimed at deterring childsnatching, typify the legal complexities and problems.

Until recently, it was easy for a parent dissatisfied with a custody decision in one state to pick up stakes and, with the stolen child in tow, seek a more favorable custody outcome in a second state. "Forum shopping," as it is called, resulted in part because of past Supreme Court rulings declaring that the "full faith and credit" clause of the U.S. Constitution does not generally apply to custody cases. This policy has prevailed since 1962, when the Supreme Court considered its last custody case. Over the past twenty years, it has repeatedly refused to hear appeals on these matters. Because the Court ruled that one state is not required to honor the custody decrees of its fellow states, a snatcher knew he or she could always obtain an award in a different jurisdiction by arguing that the circumstances had changed since the original order was rendered. (Custody decrees are never final and are always subject to modification.) Merely being in possession of the child was evidence enough to change the initial order in a new state. Courts, too, have always favored the local parent and often rule on the side of an abductor who has settled in their area. A second state, fully aware that the petitioning parent had violated the custody order of another state, would still reopen a case. Thus, kids find that they are "owned" by their mother in one state, and by their father in another.

The UCCJA (see Appendix B) is an attempt to put a stop

to "forum shopping" and parental kidnaping by ensuring that only one court has jurisdiction over the child. All custody litigation, including petitions to modify an order, is confined to the court in the child's home state, and when that is not possible, to a state having significant ties to the child. The goal is to put the custody decision in the hands of the court that knows the child best, and can decide where he or she belongs. Under the UCCJA, the "home state" is defined as the place where the child lives for at least six consecutive months prior to an action. If the youngster leaves the state with the person claiming custody, the home state retains jurisdiction for at least six months. The left-behind parent may commence an action in the home state even if the child is not present. Under the UCCJA, merely having the child in a parent's possession in a second state does not confer jurisdiction on the courts of that state if another state, the home state, has initial or continuing jurisdiction.

The act is also designed to foster cooperation and assistance, rather than jurisdictional competition, between the courts of various states, to avoid relitigation in sister states, to make the laws of signatory states uniform, and to bring about the enforcement of custody decrees.

Once a UCCJA state determines custody, all other signatory states must enforce, not modify, the original order, except under rare circumstances. The law also provides that out-of-state custody decrees be recognized and enforced.

The act has international applicability by stating that custody orders from other countries will be recognized and enforced in the United States as long as the parties involved are notified and allowed to object. The law provides a basis for honoring a foreign decree, but most likely will not help an American custodial parent get his or her decree enforced abroad if the child is taken out of the country.

The National Conference of Commissioners on Uniform State Laws drew up the UCCJA in 1968. So far, forty-eight states— excepting Massachusetts, Texas, and the jurisdictions of the

District of Columbia, Puerto Rico, and the Virgin Islands—have adopted the act.

While the statute has been instrumental in clarifying jurisdictional questions, it has fallen short of stopping "forum shopping" altogether. Not all states have signed, and these jurisdictions are not required to join their sister states in carrying out the terms of the agreement. Nonsignatory states have thus become havens for snatchers. The act will not be truly effective until all states sign it into law. Clearly the statute has eliminated some of the incentive to seize and run with the child to signatory states.

Yet crafty abductors can find ways to evade the custody laws—and do. Apparently it is still relatively easy for a kidnaping parent to obtain custody in a new state. He or she can always argue that there has been no prior settlement or that the ex-mate cannot be located. The act does not provide a way to verify whether another state has already rendered a custody decision.

Nor does the UCCJA aid a parent whose former husband or wife decides not to seek custody in a second state. In all likelihood, a thieving mother or father will probably not risk going to court.

Even if a kidnaper elects to reopen a custody case in the home state, he or she still has physical custody of the children. The statute does not require the abductor to turn over the child to the lawful guardian during the proceedings. The snatcher could then argue that it would not be in the best interests of the child to be uprooted from his or her new home. Even if the petitioning parent loses in the home state, he or she still may have the child stowed away in another jurisdiction beyond the reach of the home state's jurisdiction.

The UCCJA says that the home state has jurisdiction. However, if the child has been living in a different state from the one which ruled on custody, the new state may also have jurisdiction, and may award custody to the kidnaping parent, if the youngster's ties to the new state are considered greater than to the original state, and the parent can prove that circumstances have changed enough to merit a new decree. There are discrepancies in states' modification laws, which the UCCJA does not address. The courts of each state have their own interpretation of what constitutes "changed circumstances"—the grounds for modifying an existing custody decree. Some will only grant a modification if the child's life appears to be in danger, while others will reopen the proceedings simply because the court disapproves of the parent's sex life.

The act is flawed in other areas as well. It depends too heavily upon the discretion of the trial judge, who can interpret the same provisions of the UCCJA in different ways. The problem stems, in part, from vague wording. The statute is also weak because it only urges, but does not mandate, interstate cooperation. Thus, a court can refuse to honor the decree of a state that does not cooperate. The UCCJA is only applicable when parents have a custody order; many don't.

A federal child-stealing statute, intended to supplement the UCCJA, has proven as controversial as the reciprocal state act because it, too, contains numerous loopholes. On December 28, 1980, Congress signed into law the PKPA (see Appendix C) which became effective on July 1, 1981. It is the first time the federal government has intervened to help states resolve interstate custody conflicts. Like the UCCJA, the PKPA was designed to prevent kidnaping and "forum shopping," and to encourage states to honor and enforce the custody and visitation orders of one another. The main difference between the two is over the issue of jurisdiction. The UCCJA sets out alternative bases of initial jurisdiction, while the PKPA confines jurisdiction to the home state, as long as the child or one parent remains in that state. Say, for example, that a mother receives custody of her two-year-old daughter in State A. Shortly after the award is rendered, the father flees illegally with the child to State B. Five years later, he goes into court in

State B and requests a modification of jurisdiction, so that State B, not State A, can relitigate custody and decide who should keep the girl. Dad argues that circumstances have changed since the original decree was determined. The child, now seven years of age, is settled in school in State B, and does not even remember life in State A.

Under the terms of the UCCJA, State B could claim jurisdiction because the girl has a significant connection to that state. But under the PKPA, State A—where custody was initially decided—would retain exclusive jurisdiction.

Problems exist with both the UCCJA and the PKPA on this point. One flaw in the UCCJA has always been that an abductor could invariably convince the court in the refuge state to redetermine custody after the child was ensconced in that second state. The PKPA attempts to remove the incentive to "forum shop" by stipulating that regardless of changed circumstances, the second state must defer to the home state in determining custody. Yet this provision is too rigid. How does the home state know what is in this seven-year-old girl's best interests, when the child has not been in that state for five years? The home court will probably favor the mother, but why should the girl be returned to a virtual stranger—to someone she might not even remember? Neither the UCCJA nor the PKPA presents the perfect solution.

Yet the PKPA is effective in eliminating "haven" states, those states that do not honor the decrees of other states, and that have become popular hiding spots for kidnapers seeking custody. Under the UCCJA, nonsignatory states are not required to recognize decrees rendered outside their borders. The federal statute, on the other hand, provides that both the UCCJA and non-UCCJA states enforce, and not modify (except in unusual cases), the custody and visitation decrees of other states when these awards have met the jurisdictional requirements of the law.

Other aspects of the PKPA are impressive, at least on

paper. The statute authorizes the Department of Health and Human Services' Federal Parent Locator Services (FPLS), originally established to trace fathers who default on child support, to help states find absconding parents and their offspring through computer search techniques. The agency hunts parents down in order to enforce state and federal laws pertaining to snatching or restraint. The third provision of the PKPA requests FBI assistance in investigating and snaring snatching suspects who flee interstate or internationally from states where child stealing is a felony.

In practice, however, it is often difficult to secure the assistance of the Department of Health and Human Services or the FBI. According to the statute, each state must enter into an agreement with the Office of Child Support Enforcement in order to have access to the FPLS for parental kidnaping and custody cases. But states may choose whether or not they want to have such an agreement, and if they don't—very few do— parents there can't use the FPLS unless they petition a court (often an arduous and expensive procedure), or obtain the aid of a prosecutor or law-enforcement official who has direct access.

Pretend they do. The FPLS reporting methods may hamper the recovery effort. In order to turn up a kidnaper's home and work address, the computer draws on the records of the Internal Revenue Service (IRS), Social Security Administration (SSA), and other government branches. But these records are not up to date. Both agencies now have annual reporting requirements—the SSA is a year behind in recording changes of address—so that their lists are far from current. IRS records are updated the September following the April tax-filing deadline. A child stealer who moves will not show up for quite a while on the FPLS. By the time he or she does, the abductor may have moved again. If the thieving mom or dad changes names and obtains a new Social Security number, the computer cannot help. Many kidnapers go underground, work off the books, or take up phony identities.

If the computer locates the abductor, it does not have the authority to arrest. A parent must then convince the police to intervene. If the perpetrator is found outside his or her home state, in a state that considers the crime a mere misdemeanor or less, it is unlikely the father or mother will ever be extradited. The statute does not provide the power to ship the offender home.

The third provision of the PKPA is imperfect, too. It declares that the Fugitive Felon Act is applicable in state felony childsnatching cases involving interstate or international flight. The Fugitive Felon Act makes it a felony to travel out of the state or country to avoid prosecution for a felony. It also allows the FBI to locate and apprehend fugitives from justice if the state prosecutor requests. The law is *supposed* to apply to all state offenses, but the Justice Department has been reluctant to intervene in parental kidnaping cases. Thus, the PKPA created this clause to require the FBI to assist the forty-two states with felony child-stealing laws. The Justice Department has balked at this stipulation and imposed special restrictions on FBI involvement in these matters. It claims that it was Congress's intent to ignore child-stealing cases because of the statutory exemption of parents from the federal kidnaping law. Thus, the Justice Department announced that it will not act unless a third party can document that the child is being abused, neglected, or is in physical danger. How can a parent requesting an unlawful flight to avoid prosecution (UFAP) warrant provide evidence that the child is at risk if that parent does not know where the child is? It is tough to obtain a UFAP warrant because of other obstacles: the home state must have a felony statute for child stealing and be willing to extradite; a parent must prove that the abductor crossed state lines; and the parent has to obtain a felony warrant. Most kidnapers do not send change-of-address announcements, nor do they all leave their states.

Senator Malcolm Wallop (R-Wyoming), who helped sponsor the PKPA, is furious that the federal authorities refuse to act. Along with nine other congressmen, he has introduced a bill, S-1759 (presently pending), which clarifies congressional intent concerning FBI assistance to state and local authorities. His bill simply reiterates what has already been written—but not followed—in the PKPA: that the Fugitive Felon Act applies to state felony childsnatching cases, as it does to all other types of state felony cases. S-1759 also orders the Attorney General to remove the additional restrictions the Justice Department has imposed on the FBI in parental kidnaping matters. If the FBI had cooperated from the start, this new bill would not have been necessary. Even if this proposal passes, its impact on the FBI and on a searching mother or father is questionable. The Justice Department is likely to continue its policy of indifference.

The federal government has never shown a keenness for aiding child abduction victims. During House and Senate hearings on the PKPA, the government claimed a variety of reasons for resistance. It objected most vigorously to a section of the statute, which was later eliminated prior to enactment, that would have made child stealing or restraint a federal misdemeanor, punishable by a heavy fine and a possible jail term. The Department of Health and Human Services argued it would cost them at least two hundred thousand dollars a year to locate stolen youngsters and that it constituted an invasion of privacy. The FBI said it would need to hire at least 160 new agents. Both said they couldn't afford these changes. But their greatest objection was articulated by a spokesman for the FBI: "We question whether it is perhaps anomalous for the FBI to withdraw from investigations of bank robberies and escaped federal prisoners and at the same time assume responsibility for a misdemeanor involving essentially a family-relations problem."

Apparently others agree that snatching is a private affair. Outsiders have abetted the crime by refusing to get involved. Usually parents implore an abductor's employer to reveal the kidnaper's forwarding address, only to be told, "Sorry, but no." Credit-card companies and banks routinely refuse to disclose where they mail their clients' statements.

Officials at stolen children's schools are equally hesitant to interfere—even when a mother or father presents a farfetched story about the new pupil. It took a New York custodial mother seven years to find her son. The woman arrived at the boy's elementary school in Massachusetts ready to reclaim him. The principal was stunned to meet the mother, since the boy's father had said she was dead. Even so, the schoolmaster refused to let her visit with her son, because of a court order in his possession protecting the child from his mother. Recalls the woman: "I said to the principal, 'Didn't you ever think about how I could be dangerous and dead at the same time?' His answer was, 'I don't want to get involved. My responsibility is to the child. When he is in school, I won't let him see anyone except his father.' "

Schools often admit students without transcripts, and may not believe a child who reports witnessing an abduction. "There must be some explanation," an instructor informed a girl who swore she saw a screaming classmate being dragged off the kickball field. The teacher turned her attention to the three R's and chose not to investigate. There *was* an explanation—the boy was being kidnaped by his father.

School authorities who discover a child has been stolen may never contact police or the searching parent. Pennsylvania teachers spotted the picture of one of their students in a national magazine article on child stealing. "The principal of the school," fumes the custodial mother, "called my son's teachers into his office and showed the story to them. They agreed that they would decide what was best for John after they got to know the situation better. They had read I had custody and knew a law had been broken. Yet they didn't go to the police. Who are they to play God with my son's life? They are supposed to be professionals, sensitive to children. But they were more concerned with not having trouble and attracting attention than with protecting John." (A school official agreed and, unbeknown to her colleagues, tipped off the mother.)

Unattended, these "domestic disputes" threaten to become the standard alternative for divorcing parents. For some, it appears to be the only way to guarantee they will win the children. Breaking the law is a breeze, so why not? The statutes that supposedly protect victimized parents and penalize offenders are toothless and flawed. Instead of reprimanding snatchers, the legal system *rewards* them, by refusing to enforce laws, or prosecute and punish parents. Turning the other cheek turns off the most decent, law-abiding citizens. They have custody papers, but no children. No one seems to care. Roars a three-time victim: "My anger isn't against my ex-husband. It is against the laws that allowed him to get away with his crime."

Increasingly, frustrated mothers and fathers are questioning the value of playing by the rules when it may mean being robbed of beloved sons or daughters forever. Adults watch as their former partners kidnap their offspring. In many cases, these custodial parents now rekidnap their children. If they had faith in the system, they would never consider stealing back. If abductors feared the system, they would never snatch. "The laws don't mean a thing," huffs a Chicago woman, still hunting for her son after five years, "because people don't respect them. Being in contempt of court or having custody are meaningless. Both are just pieces of paper. The lawyers get their fees, detectives get their fees, judges sit up at the desk and write little notes, and the court reporters wriggle their fingers on the typewriter and want breaks all the time. The whole system is tainted. I'm fed up. It would be terrible for my son if I stole him back—but I just might. I don't think anyone should have to resort to this kind of behavior, but the way the laws are now, it seems as if I have no other alternative."

· 7 ·

Absconding Abroad:
The International Angle

INVOLUNTARILY, America's children emigrate abroad. Faraway continents swell with stolen youngsters and their scheming captors. It is becoming fashionable, and virtually foolproof, for parents to whisk away their kids to foreign countries. If the local police and the FBI seem reluctant to get involved in interstate flights, the State Department and other nations are even less interested in international disappearances. Rather than count on the U.S. government to enforce a parent's rights, that parent must rely on the mercy of foreign judges to honor their custody decrees; only rarely will they recognize them.

Those fortunate enough to locate a loved one must go through the courts of another country to legally win back their babies—even if the parent produces documents proving that he or she is the legal custodian at home. Fighting on foreign turf is difficult, if not impossible. Parents encounter a language barrier in non-English-speaking places, and must pay for yet another attorney in a strange land. They run the risk of having their ex-partners scoot again once they are informed of a court action. Even if a former mate stays to slug out a custody fight, the outcome of a new trial is unpredictable. A judge may favor the kidnaper if the child is ensconced in a community. Or, should a conniving thief obtain custody overseas, the reappearing parent will probably lose in the challenge of that foreign decree. Frequently adults find conflicting decisions in different jurisdictions. In some spots, justice never prevails. Women lose out automatically in patriarchal cultures, despite their proper papers and high-powered counsel. Rarely will a country interfere, too, if a native returns home to stow away his offspring.

The odds are so stacked against winning abroad—and even custodians who do triumph find the process so complicated and costly—that many parents simply steal back their sons and daughters. Although lawful guardians from America can be stopped at a foreign border and arrested, as a practical matter, at worst they will probably be released and sent packing without their kids.

An international treaty that would eliminate custody contests away from home by requiring signatory nations to honor one another's orders is under consideration. It has yet to be ratified, however. In the meantime, American officials are unreceptive to retrieving the children themselves. Even if a parent has managed to procure a felony warrant on a fleeing spouse, the United States would have to ask the "hosting" nation to extradite the abductor, and taxpayers would have to pick up the tab for the procedure. This is unlikely, because America is ungracious when it comes to returning the favor, and refuses to part with childsnatchers from other countries, since kidnaping one's own kids is not a federal crime here. Even laws designed to protect Americans frustrate parental victims. Because of the way the Privacy Act is written, U.S. embassies abroad will not reveal the whereabouts of a citizen—

despite the fact that the child is held illegally. They will only tell a frantic parent if the child is safe.

Kidnapers who research hideouts know they are virtually home free if they can stay away from America. Expatriatism is popular, too, because of the soaring divorce rate, the ease of travel, and the surge of multinational corporations which dispatch employees to foreign offices. Couples from different countries mingle and mate; when their relationships fizzle, one parent may take the offspring and run home.

The nations of the Middle East, the Far East, and South America, as well as Mexico and Canada harbor a substantial number of U.S. child stealers. But Western Europe is an even more renowned retreat. In March 1980, the State Department noted 253 active cases on file of kids stashed outside of America. According to the report, West Germany, Poland, Yugoslavia, and England proved to be the favorite havens, because of the enormous presence of U.S. soldiers stationed on bases there.

The stealing scenario may happen like this: Joe plans to return to the States with his new child, but the mother vows to keep the child with her in Hamburg or Warsaw, so she stows away her son or daughter in a "safe" house with relatives. Or Joe comes back with his bride, but soon realizes that lust, not love, produced their infant child. They separate, then squabble over custody. One day the clever mama boards a plane for her hometown with the boy in tow. So long, Joe. So long, America.

It is "child's play" to successfully slip out of this country with a youngster, claims an architect from Illinois, whose ten-year-old son was spirited away to Amsterdam by the boy's mother: "Short of chaining yourself to your child, you cannot prevent a snatch. I did everything 'right' and still my ex-wife took off. I had my son's only valid passport, and had warned the U.S. Passport Office not to issue another one should my wife pretend she had lost Jimmy's. I assume that she got a friend to lend her another passport for him, and no one bothered to check the photograph."

When the world is the hiding place, there undoubtedly will be some countries that are slipshod in their emigration practices. Parents who suspect their children may be concealed abroad can take precautionary measures to deter a would-be abductor. Once a potential snatcher discovers the other mate has alerted authorities, or legally constrained him, he may bow out. Devising new plans may be too complicated or too much bother. Unless instructed on the ways around the system from colleagues in crime, a snatcher-to-be may be stumped on how to proceed.

Experienced attorneys sometimes advise custodial parents to write a stipulation into their custody orders stating that the children cannot leave the country without their consent. This phrase, rarely included in custody decrees, just might convince other countries to cooperate. It will give parents leverage with the State Department, should the kidnaper defy the order. Once they expire, the government will not renew the passports of Americans living abroad, and this could force expatriates to return home, or at least prevent them from fleeing to yet another foreign country. If that provision is not mentioned in the custody agreement, the Passport Office will renew these passports— even if it knows that the person has illegally absconded with the child and is in hiding.

Noncustodians who fear their former partners will depart with the kids can protect themselves, too. They may incorporate into their custody orders a clause prohibiting the children's departure from the jurisdiction. Then at the request of the parent without custody, Passport Services will deny traveling papers to the parent with custody.

A certified copy of the custody decree (containing the clause forbidding foreign travel) or a restraining order should be sent to the government,* along with the names, dates, and places of birth of the kids and the ex-spouse, and the children's relationship to the letter writer. A parent who neglects to get a special provision limiting travel may still stop a child's passport application from being processed. He or she must send the government his sole custody order and ask that the passport not be issued for the child without his or her consent.

The Passport Office feeds the names of the noncustodial parent and the child into a computer. If parents request the document for themselves or a minor offspring (a youngster under the age of thirteen), it will be denied. The lawful guardian will be notified, and furnished with the address that appears for the child on the application. The same procedure holds for noncustodians and kids still in the United States who ask to renew their passports. Unfortunately, if a noncustodial parent obtains the passports before the custodial parent alerts the State Department, the mother or father may have to wait sometimes as long as four years for the snatcher to renew his or her passport. Passports that have been granted are almost never revoked because of custody conflicts.

It can happen that each side has papers awarding custody in different states, or that no order exists. In these cases, the State Department will give the party who objects to the issuance of the passport time to obtain a decree or resolve the dispute. Should a parent neglect to notify Uncle Sam from the start, the application for the child will be approved. Unless the State Department is informed otherwise, a passport request by one parent is presumed to have the backing of the other parent.

A determined abductor can procure a passport *because of*, rather than despite, government policy. When a snatcher has already fled abroad, the State Department requires that a par-

---

* Office of Citizenship Appeals and Legal Assistance (PPT/C), Department of State, Washington, DC 20520. If the child is abroad, denial requests should be mailed to the nearest American embassy or consulate.

ent who wishes the child to be denied a passport for additional travel obtain a custody order, or an order barring issuance of a passport, from a court in the country in which the permit has been requested. The custodial parent may have a valid custody order from a state court in America, yet must still be granted another one from a court in a foreign nation (where the child has been taken). This policy means that a parent can whisk away a child to any country that does not require a passport for entrance—Mexico, Canada, or the British Virgin Islands, for example—and, once there, apply for a passport. To stop issuance of this document, the searching mother or father back in the United States must fly to that foreign country, hire a local attorney, and obtain a new decree. If the fugitive has already managed to get custody in that country, however, he or she will automatically get a passport. Here is how an adult could skirt the system: a Massachusetts father wants to hide in France with his son. If he were to apply for their passports in Massachusetts, the State Department would turn him down if his ex-wife has informed the government that she has been awarded custody, and does not want her son to have a passport. Notices requesting that passports be denied are effective only within the United States, so the father can still get the proper documents if he first goes to, say, Tortolla in the British Virgin Islands. Tortolla does not require a U.S. passport to enter. Once there, the father applies for the passports. The mother may have a court order in Massachusetts, but unless she can convince a judge in Tortolla to deny the passports to her son and former spouse, they will be granted. However, if the father worked fast and was awarded custody in Tortolla, then his passport would be processed despite his ex-wife's protests.

It is too late. The child is gone. What recourse is there for the adult left behind? Ultimately, the parent must convince a foreign court to hand over the child, since the law of the country where the child is residing, even temporarily, prevails.

In the meantime, the parent encounters a frustrating series of snags when he or she turns to the U.S. government. The message is unmistakable: parents are on their own abroad. The government offers a little help; usually it is little help.

A parent requesting assistance would write to the State Department,* which would ask its Foreign Service posts to conduct a "welfare/whereabouts" search to determine the child's condition and geography. The United States won't help parents if the child's return would violate the laws of a foreign country or a court order. The searching parent must have an idea of the child's location in order for the government to be able to help. Overseas officers may be successful in pinpointing the youngster, but will refuse to reveal where he or she is living, because of the Privacy Act, which forbids their divulging the whereabouts of a U.S. citizen. Through its foreign channels, Washington will report on a child's welfare, but will not intercede even if that child is being abused or neglected. Rather, it alerts local authorities or social service agencies. Never mind that the boy or girl is in danger, or that the abducting parent may have broken the law of the United States.

American consular officers provide lists of attorneys in their districts for parents to engage, yet cannot recommend a particular lawyer, or offer legal advice, or represent that parent in custody proceedings before foreign courts. Mothers and fathers who cannot afford to travel to a distant land, hire help, and sit through complicated court proceedings are out of luck. Having to select an attorney blindly from a list is also risky. Few parents have the money to research the credentials of counselors abroad, and have no way of evaluating them.

* Office of Citizens Consular Services, Department of State, Washington, DC 20520, (202) 632-3444. Parents may also write to the U.S. embassy or consulate nearest the child's foreign residence, if it is known. The letter should include: the child's full name and date and place of birth; passport data; the names and addresses of persons with whom the child is traveling or staying; a current photograph of the youngster; pertinent court papers; and the correspondent's address and telephone number.

Even the most able attorney cannot shield a client from the reality of international politics. A father who had to fight for his daughter in West Germany reports: "It became a nationalistic thing, one country against another. Neither wanted to give in to the laws of the other. There was this attitude on the part of the German court that it knew best, and was not willing to be told what to do by another nation." A private detective who specializes in international retrievals agrees. One of his clients, an American, was a custodial father whose ex-wife had fled with their son to England. The husband obtained a warrant for her arrest in Maryland, and had the child made a ward of the courts of Britain, so that the woman could not leave England with her son. The father hired the detective to bring back the boy to Maryland. Says the investigator: "We got prosecuted for child stealing. The British were insulted that someone had come across the ocean with a foreign court order and had taken it upon himself to presume he had all the rights in England that he had in America."

Some places "welcome" snatchers and virtually ignore their searching ex-mates. But others will not tolerate international abductions. Israel is one of the most accommodating countries, because it defers to American custodians and serves snatchers with papers that are similar to a writ of habeus corpus. A parental kidnaper who refuses to return a child faces criminal charges. The Balkan nations, such as Greece and Turkey, and numerous African nations almost always favor the father, regardless of prior legal claims by the American mother. Off the record, many attorneys urge clients whose kids are hidden in patriarchal societies to steal them back. Besides recommending resnatching, lawyers may also secretly suggest that parents pay for an advantageous custody outcome. In parts of South America, for instance, bribery is common. "There are countries where custody can be bought with wealth and connections," claims a New York family law attorney with expertise in international child stealing.

Even nations that play straight and will recognize American custody decrees still insist upon a hearing in the new country. Usually a parent must hire a lawyer, but some courts make the parents represent themselves, and don't permit them to retain an attorney. How can mothers and fathers who cannot speak the local language and do not know the law convince a court to give them custody?

Some foreign judges make the children themselves decide between Mom and Dad. This was the case for Dennis, his sister, and their five step-siblings, who were kidnaped to Rhodesia by their mother and her new husband. The children were told they were being taken on a two-day trip to a Maryland beach cottage from their home in Richmond, Virginia. But when they arrived in that state, Dennis's stepfather left the car to make a call. Moments later he emerged with the news: their rented beach house had burned down mysteriously. Would the children like to go to New York instead? asked the adults. While the kids played at a Coney Island amusement park, the stepfather sneaked away to buy tickets for part two of the plot: a jaunt to England and Luxembourg, before they reached Rhodesia, their new home. Once he arrived, Dennis begged his mother to let him leave Africa. For two years Dennis felt imprisoned. The break came when he and his stepbrother were sent to South Africa to compete in a baseball game and had to produce passports to cross the border. South African authorities notified Dennis's father that his son had visited their nation and was living in Rhodesia. During the children's absence, Dennis's father had written letters to countries around the world inquiring about them. He flew to Rhodesia expecting to flash his Virginia custody order and then to walk away instantly with the kids. But his official American papers did not impress the Rhodesian judge. After another trial, the court let the children choose whether to stay or go. Six kids hopped the next plane home; only one elected to remain in Rhodesia.

Parents of boys and girls abducted to U.S. territories are not exempt from going to court, either. A Texas mother explains her week-long effort to regain her children from U.S. Samoa. While she had permission to keep the kids back on the ranch, she still needed a Samoan decree.

A U.S. marshal delivered my Texas order to Bill, the children's father, and demanded he hand them over. According to the deputy, Bill told the kids to run, or they would be sent to jail. So they bolted. A female marshal grabbed my daughter and tried to comfort her. Emily shrieked, thinking she was being kidnaped or would be thrown in jail. In the meantime, Doug, who was five, dashed through the dense foliage to the village. He ran to someone's *fallee* [a thatched house with a cement floor and no sides], and the owner hid him. I hadn't seen my kids for six months, and when I finally did, my daughter was angry with me and frightened. I found my son huddled under a bed and a young girl hovering over him. We all were subjected to mental health evaluations. It was bizarre—in this god-forsaken place, they were requiring mental health evaluations. I was assessed by three people, and so were my mother [who had accompanied me], Bill, Doug, and Emily. At the end of mental health day, they decided that the kids should return with me to San Antonio. I still had to undergo a trial, though, to get custody a second time. We stayed with the head of the clinic. Unbeknown to me, she had given Bill permission to keep Doug until court time. At noon Bill drove to her house and demanded Doug. Not knowing the arrangements and thinking Bill would take off with my child, I protested. He proceeded to grab Doug. Then my mother jumped in and grabbed Doug, too. His arms were being ripped apart. My ex-husband won the tug-of-war. By then my son was petrified and clung to his father. He wouldn't come to me. I thought, "Oh boy, I don't even have a son anymore." I didn't see Doug until the trial. There were five judges—one American and four Samoans. The kids were allowed in the courtroom and could hear what was said. I was expected to find witnesses in a place I had spent only three days. Fortunately, two neighbors testified on my behalf. The judges awarded the children to me. I wanted to leave with them immediately, but there was an airline strike and only one plane a week was flying in and out of the island. . . .

Someday soon, parents like this mother from Texas may be spared duplicative court contests on faraway turf. If an international treaty under consideration is ratified, participating countries would ship those children to Texas and let the local courts decide.

In October 1980, thirty nations, including the United States, convened for the Hague Conference on Private International Law. They conducted a convention on the civil aspects of international child abduction, and drafted a treaty to help resolve custody disputes.

The convention proposes the prompt return of the child by the country of refuge. The foreign court does not determine or redetermine which parent keeps the child. Rather, it will decide whether a youngster under the age of sixteen has been wrongfully removed or retained by the alleged abductor. If that is the case, the foreign court will order the child returned to his or her home country. The nation of refuge pays the expenses. The thieving parent can beat this mandate if he or she can prove that the other mate was not actually exercising custody rights, or consented to or yielded to the removal or retention, or that a risk exists if the child returns.

The Hague proposal is a civil, not a criminal, remedy. It covers parental kidnapings that occur both before and after a custody order has been rendered, as well as abductions by joint custodians. The treaty also addresses visitation-rights griev-

118

ances—although children will not be returned because visitation has been violated.

Under the convention, each participating nation sets up a government office called a Central Authority, which will process applications for help by aggrieved parents. Each Central Authority will be linked to those in other countries. Their aim: to try to locate the child; to bring about a voluntary return of the child or to resolve the custody or visitation conflict; and to offer legal representation.

The treaty is designed to provide for extradition and to promote cooperation between nations vis-à-vis custody. Without some kind of international agreement, snatchers can continue to carry off their crimes with the tacit approval of their hosting nations. If enacted, the treaty will make some snatchers reconsider country-hopping. Still, only thirty lands plan to participate. This means that those that do not sign—the rest of the world—will be havens. While the Hague agreement is important, it will not eliminate child stealing. Instead, kidnapers will congregate in "safe" nations.

The rampant trend of fleeing abroad will not end until the U.S. government and other nations take action. All countries in the world need to sign the Hague treaty and refuse to harbor abductors. But America cannot count on others. It has to tighten up existing loopholes within its own borders if kidnapers are never to leave here, and if they do leave, are to be forced back home.

Passport renewals need to be turned down automatically if a noncustodial parent flees illegally, or applies from a country that does not demand a passport upon entering. If possible, the Privacy Act has to be revamped as well, in order that child stealers may be handed over to the embassies and consulates for extradition. Custodial mothers and fathers who locate their kids should not have to be required to undergo new trials on foreign turf. The lawful guardian needs to be allowed to claim the child, provided the youngster consents. If the child is old enough to make up his or her mind, or does not want to leave, there should be another hearing back in the United States, where custody was originally determined.

New York City family law attorney Henry Foster, Jr., proposes a way to abort international abduction attempts. He suggests that the names of the child and the noncustodial parent be entered into the computer now used by U.S. customs officials for screening criminals trying to leave the country. A custodial mother or father who fears a child might be stolen could notify the Passport Office and have these names fed into the computer. Today only parental kidnapers for whom federal felony warrants have been issued—a tiny percentage of child stealers—appear on the customs computer. Foster's recommendation eliminates the need for a federal felony warrant for this purpose, an important revision since child abduction is not considered a felony in many states.

Unless the government overhauls its current policies and invents creative ways to discourage international stealing, snatchers will continue to make their safe and simple exodus.

III

THE ABDUCTORS

· 8 ·

Motives and Madness

S P I T E. Snatchers may swear they steal for their kids' sake, but in most instances, their motives are mean, not altruistic. There is no other way, they claim. Father knows best; the children are better off with him. She is sure they are in danger with Dad. Some have tried the system, some have skirted it. All rationalize, many agonize. However they delude themselves, parents abduct with little understanding of child development. Uprooting a youngster from a secure, stable environment can be devastating. Dr. Daniel O'Leary, who treats stolen children immediately upon their return, attests to the damage: "If parents had the foresight about what was going to happen to these kids, some knowledge of the importance of peers at that age, the impact of lying to a child across time, or deriding the custodial parent, then they wouldn't do it." Judith Nadeau agrees. "If you abruptly take a child away from his primary parent, or move without telling the other parent or preparing the child, then that is abusive." Laments one woman from the

Midwest who has not seen her sons in five years: "My ex-husband took them away from the house they were born in, from their mother, their neighborhood friends, their aunts and cousins. That is called love? Kids are little people who are vulnerable. Their sense of identity is very tenuous."

Thieving parents sometimes cannot, or will not, see the harm. "My child has not suffered at all," insists a father who lived underground with his daughter for ten years. "I apologize to no one." Another father did not believe his son suffered from a snatch, even when the withdrawn twelve-year-old told a television crew that he was "confused" about being physically yanked between his parents. When the father was asked why he thought the boy was confused, the man shrugged, "I guess he wasn't sure what he wanted to say. I don't know what he was confused about."

Kidnapers see themselves as saviors, not scoundrels. They point to the sacrifices they must make, without considering what their children must forsake. Says Barry Sandrew, who speaks regularly with male abductors as a director of one New England fathers' rights group: "I've seen kids taken out of love. Parents have said, 'Bad as it is to steal them, it is better than the alternative.' They may have broken laws, but they have given up what little they had for the sake of the children." Kidnapers rarely examine the trauma that almost always follows for youngsters. That their offspring have not asked to be rescued—to be sacrificed for—is of no consequence.

It is easier for child stealers to delude themselves than most other criminals. A bank robber, for instance, could not argue persuasively that he would enrich anyone but himself by his actions. Parents, however, are supposed to protect their children. When fathers or mothers feel that the children are in danger, whether or not it is true, Mom or Dad may abduct, convinced that she or he is merely acting as any conscientious, duty-bound parent should.

Their belief that the child is in jeopardy is central to the problem. Only rarely is this the case. Even then, most parents refuse to try to rectify the situation legally. They find fault with their former partners, minor though the transgression may be, and decide that the youngster is in trouble. "Parents pull anything out of the air," asserts social worker Peg Edwards, who has handled more than fifty child-stealing cases. "They'll say their ex-mates are sleeping with other people and exposing their children to immoral behavior, or that the kid isn't fed well or isn't clothed properly. But it is something ridiculous in that it is unfounded. It has nothing to do with the dirty clothes, because you don't punish a youngster and take him away from the other parent forever because he has dirty clothes. Snatchers are not concerned with the children. All their attention is on themselves, on hurting the other parent, and on getting control, being powerful." Sometimes a mixture of spite and love spurs them on. Parents may genuinely love and care about their kids, but get caught up in petty skirmishes with warring mates.

.   Regardless of the reasons, therapists and social scientists who treat and study parental kidnapers note their tremendous sense of self-justification. Like law-enforcement officials, abductors often do not consider child stealing a crime. "How can you kidnap your own child?" asked one father incredulously after he had been arrested and a state governor had signed papers to extradite him.

Those who agonize over whether to steal also feel absolved simply because it is a tough decision. Probing the process—how to abduct, where to go, and why—convinces kidnapers that their motives are selfless. "I'm going to an analyst now to really look at everything," confides one snatcher-to-be from the South. "Am I taking my son for myself or am I doing it because I feel it is best for my child? I am examining my reasons very carefully. I'm not doing it lightly."

Quite often a snatcher acts impulsively, however, deciding on the spot not to return the children after a routine visit, or a spat with a former spouse. Family therapist Dr. Jeannette Min-koff says: "My experience is that child stealing is not a well-thought-out plan. It is impulsive. Some people are so angry with each other that they can't handle their anger anymore and have to find some way to get even. The only way they can do that is to take away the child—something that really matters." The head of one support group for steal victims explained to a reporter how snatchers choreograph their grand finale: "What's one last thing I can do that will really clinch it?" a bitter spouse asks. "It's pretty obvious that taking off with the kids will drive anyone crazy."

It is a successful ploy. Searching parents worry and wonder, constantly tormented by this act. "It is a revenge far sweeter and longer-lived than a beating, or even murder, for it never ends," a representative of Child Find said at a congressional hearing on missing children.

A Get-even Mentality

Malice is the most common motive. United Parents Against Child Stealing, an Arizona organization for abduction victims, estimates that eight out of ten parents snatch strictly for re-venge. Thirteen-year-old Judy of Detroit, stolen twice, remem-bers hearing her father threaten her mother: " 'I'll get back at you. I'll get you,' he used to tell her." The most blunt explana-tion for this behavior comes from an angry Florida man: "She told me to go to hell, so I'm telling her the same."

Snatching for spite can occur without warning when a mar-riage is breaking up. One Texas mother informed her husband that she wanted a divorce. She expected a scene, but Jim was reasonable, almost pleasant. A few days after their talk, Amanda dropped off their twenty-month-old baby at a sitter's, and made plans to meet her husband at home for dinner. When she went to fetch her daughter, a hysterical baby-sitter described how Jim had pounded on her door and then dragged away the

screaming child. Where was the girl? Amanda rushed home—
or what was left of home. The place was destroyed, the furniture gone. So was the refrigerator, the food, the baby's gear, even Amanda's clothes. Jim had left nothing. He had boarded up every door and window, except for one on the second floor, from which he had jumped when he fled. He had literally shut out his wife, depriving her of everything. Kidnaping the baby wasn't enough.

One baffled museum curator is convinced that meanness was the motive when his wife, with whom he shared living quarters, but not the bedroom, ran off to France with their two sons: "In our case, it was pure malice. Some parents steal because their children are mistreated and they want to protect them. It was nothing like that for us. Our divorce proceedings were not messy, and neither one of us was fooling around. We were just two different personalities who could not live together anymore."

Rarely do kidnapers admit their true intentions. Says Dr. Mel Roman of the Albert Einstein College of Medicine's Psychiatry Department: "I have never heard abductors say that they steal to punish the other parent. It is always that their former mates are unfit for one reason or another, or have denied them the opportunity to be with the child."

They may not admit their motives, but often they are all too evident anyway. Bloody Band-Aids arrive in the mail or dead fish. One man sent his ex-wife his daughter's toenails and locks of hair. On the child's birthday and on Mother's Day, he gave the tormented woman another present, a phone call with this crisp message: "You will never see your daughter again." Another victimized mother picked up her telephone. "Listen to this," her husband barked into the receiver. Her child was screaming in the background. Then the line went dead. "I'm leaving you the way I found you—alone and childless," a New York father informed his wife in a note. Soon after, the body of one of her daughters was discovered. The father is still at large with the other sibling.

Some parents are so self-centered, plotting the perfect retaliatory move, that they do not consider the potential danger to their children. The "grab game" can result in violence, even death, if a startled baby-sitter, bystander, or former mate offers resistance. Cody Cain is one such casualty. In July 1976, Steven Cain, accompanied by three detectives, stole his small son from his ex-wife's home. Returning from a shopping trip, she found Steven driving off with the boy and pursued them. A high-speed chase on an Oklahoma road ended when Steven's car crashed, killing father and son. Other kids suffer broken bones and beatings when they get trapped in a struggle.

Abductors may put their children in peril purely to hurt the other parent, without intending to keep them. Some youngsters are dumped with relatives or distant friends, living down the block from the snatcher or in another town, state, or even country. To throw police off the track, one father reported his daughter had been kidnaped by a stranger from a fair in Oakland, California. It turned out he had taken the little girl to Mexico, where he left her with relatives. She knew him as "Godfather" the few times he bothered to visit. All the while, the father lived only a few streets away from his grieving ex-wife in America.

Jay was shunted off to his father's brother when the child was four years old. "My father took me to my uncle's in Maine, and then he took me to my other uncle's in Florida, and then that uncle took me to live in Texas and then back to Maine. In Maine, my father lived ten miles away from me with his new family. I guess he didn't want me around."

According to Children's Rights of Washington, D.C., parents who steal for revenge frequently abandon their offspring after their anger has cooled. Even those who think they want their youngsters can find child rearing too big a burden. Either way, many snatchers cannot cope with the responsibility and part company with their sons and daughters. After an eight-month hunt, for example, an Arizona mother discovered that her kids had been abandoned by their father, then bounced between foster homes before being adopted by a couple of another race.

RESENTMENT

Revenge is not the only reason parents have for kidnaping. Years after a marriage has ended, a snatcher may strike, jealous that his former lover has found a new partner. When the youngsters take to the stepparent, the old parent can feel replaced, and may abduct the children to reaffirm his or her role. "I think my ex-wife snatched my boys because she felt threatened," muses one California father whose sons were hidden for seven years. "I was very close to them, and so was my new wife. Before they were stolen, they had spent the summer with us. When my former wife came to take them home, they didn't want to go. That was too much for her."

Even still-marrieds are vulnerable. Men, especially, may resent it when a wife or soon-to-be-ex gets too independent, and this attitude can precipitate a snatch. Before the days of women's liberation, men were "supposed to" have better, higher-paying jobs than their mates. Females could seek a divorce, but usually only did so if the husband had committed adultery or abandoned them. The Archie Bunker days are over. Today some women net thicker paychecks than their husbands, or even support the family. Women now are flying the coop, directing their husbands to "buzz off" when they are bored. These males may feel emasculated, angry that their "uppity" wives have initiated the divorce or are coping on their own. They steal the kids to make a statement: "Now we'll see just how independent you can be."

Some say it to themselves, others are more open. Out of fear of being spurned, an insecure husband warned his wife: "If you ever leave me, or if you ever divorce me, I'll see you live in hell." He kept his promise. Because the mother walked out, he kidnaped the children—twice. One abducted youngster remembers her father telling her, "You know, you're never going to see your mom again because she divorced me."

"You Can Have the Kids if . . ."

Jilted husbands and wives are not always gracious losers. Many cannot accept that the other spouse wants to separate. Desperate for a reconciliation, they steal the kids and then open the negotiations. "Come back, withdraw the divorce action, and the children will be yours." Bargaining usually backfires, but not always. Miserable without their sons and daughters and convinced there is no other way they will ever see them, a few parents elect to return to their scheming mates. "It was a repulsive thought to go back to this man," says Leanne, a thirty-three-year-old computer programmer, "but I wanted my kids. I was tired of fighting in the courts for three years, of spending thousands of dollars, and of hearing my husband tell my children that I was to blame for their being taken. He'd say, 'If Mummy would only pack her bags and come home like a lady, but she's not with us because she doesn't love you.' He told me he stole them to bring me to my senses and 'give them what they really want, a mother and father together.' Finally I said, 'Okay, I'll move back, but I'm only doing it because of the children.' Our reunion lasted one week."

Some parental victims stay longer, but most eventually move out alone, no closer to keeping the kids. For three months, Lori Eslani of Casper, Wyoming, played "wife." In March 1980, she and her infant daughter flew to Shiraz, a city in southern Iran, where her husband had stowed away their two-year-old son, Seth. Her mission: to patch up her marriage or to pack up and take her little boy. She had been nine months pregnant with their second child when Eslani had disappeared with Seth. The father had never seen his little girl. When Lori realized her relationship would not work and decided to leave Iran, she

130

found herself trapped. Not long before, the American Embassy and hostages had been seized. The government had confiscated Lori's passport when she entered the country, and would not let her go without her husband's permission. Women have no rights in the Islamic republic. Absconding with Seth was impossible, and had she not been nursing her newborn daughter, she would have had to flee without her, too. Finally Lori escaped, pretending to be going on a brief vacation. Unless she returns to Iran, she will never see her son again.

Abductors often have no interest in the children or in salvaging the marriage, but care only for what the kids are worth in a property settlement. "Some snatchers negotiate," notes Dr. Minkoff. "They telephone and say, 'You'd better do this, this, and this, or you'll never see your children again.' Requests range from 'Stop seeing another man' to 'Tell the courts I don't have to pay child support anymore' to 'Sell the house and give me my half.' "

Joel, a Texas CPA, coveted his car more than his little girl, says his wife Darlene. "Our vintage Thunderbird was my husband's baby. He'd spend weekends washing and buffing it, and told me he would burn it first rather than ever let me keep it. But when we split, I needed the car to drive our daughter to day care, so I hid it at a friend's. A week after Joel took off with the baby, his father called me at my office. He said, 'My son wanted me to tell you you can have your daughter if you give him the car.' " Another man found money more appealing than automobiles. After fleeing to Argentina with his sons, the father got caught embezzling funds from the Mormon church. Rather than risk being jailed, he decided to pay the church back, but didn't have the cash. He devised a swap: his ex-wife would get the boys if she paid him for them—just enough to make restitution to the church.

Many parents prefer power to negotiation. They steal to show who is boss rather than to request any ransom. Flexing muscles has always been easier than discussing differences. According to findings at the National Conference for Family Violence Researchers at the University of New Hampshire in July 1981, the chief cause of family violence of all types is the abuse of power, or the wish of the stronger member to control the weaker one. While the conference focused on wife and child beating, its conclusions apply to child stealing as well.

FED-UP FATHERS

They kidnap for power, but also out of defeat. In nine out of ten cases, the courts favor the mother over the father. Given these odds, and the fact that a messy fight can run into thousands of dollars in attorneys' fees, other court costs, and payments to private investigators, many males opt to steal instead of go into debt or gamble on an unpredictable verdict.

The experiences of many men who have tried to play it straight lend credence to the theory that the legal system forces fathers to run off with their kids. At a Senate hearing on a federal child-stealing bill, a snatcher spoke out: "I foolishly went through a court battle. Unbelievably I listened to a judge tell me before and during the trial that the children would be given to me only if I could prove my ex-wife legally insane or a nymphomaniac. Nothing else would do. It mattered not that I was a professional with a doctorate, and had a perfectly clean record both in the army and as a civilian. On the other hand, my ex-wife freely admitted to adultery, a previous felony conviction, an education that went little past high school, and contempt of court. She had taken the children across country, living openly with her boyfriend for three months before returning for the trial. It was later found out that she was three months' pregnant at the time of our divorce and custody trial. After hearing all this and more, the judge still had the opinion that there was no way she would give me custody of our children. In fact, she threatened, 'You had better settle this case now because nothing you have shown me will alter my decision to give these children to their natural mother. If, in fact, this trial continues to waste my time, I have known of cases where the father has been restrained from seeing his children for a year because the court deemed him a disruptive force.' " States a three-time abductor who slugged it out four times in front of the bench: "Stealing my kids was the only way. I tried to go through the courts and it didn't work."

Burned by the paternal prejudice in other aspects of their divorce proceedings, some fathers abscond with their kids before the judge can sock it to them on the custody decision. They have already witnessed the judge's "justice" in preliminary skirmishes. They have been ordered from their homes and kept from their kids. Their property has been generously handed over to their wives. They wonder how they can possibly expect a more enlightened verdict on their remaining and most important mutual "possession," the children.

Picture this scenario from a male's perspective. At first the divorce may be an amicable parting, but the father's attorney coaxes him into an all-out war with his wife. "Fight for your rights," he is told, but a bitter contest seems likely to boost his lawyer's fee rather than to settle their differences. He and his wife agree to separate, but not about who will walk out. Neither one wants to leave, so she has a plan: Her lawyer slaps him with an Order to Show Cause, requiring him to appear before a judge on short notice—sometimes only twenty-four or forty-eight hours—to demonstrate why he shouldn't get the boot. Why should Dad be out on the street? She claims the kids are in danger if he is allowed to remain under the same roof. This charge can be made in an unsupported affidavit, so his wife may not even have to appear in court at this stage. Since the judge has nothing on which to base a decision, other than her word against his, His Honor is likely to protect the kids until there is a full trial. That means Dad lands in a motel room or an apartment. Once he gets his day in court, the mother will, in most cases, be awarded the house, the kids, child support, and alimony. And him? He is stuck with that apartment on the other side of town, meager time with the little ones, lots of debts, and gnawing loneliness. There is also rage at a system that has permitted him to be displaced. A new man on the scene playing "Dad" can sometimes be too much for the natural father to bear.

Let's say he abides by the judge's order and leaves the house, kisses the kids goodbye, promptly pays child support and alimony. Still, there is no guarantee that his ex-wife will follow the court's order and let him see his children, or that she will not move far away, which will mean he can't be an active father. In many states, lawful guardians are legally entitled to move anywhere they want, as long as it does not jeopardize the child's welfare. Forget the feelings and rights of the noncustodial parent who may lose contact with his kids. Maintains one fed-up father: "This system requires that one parent, or both, cut up the other to win. I'm not sure what the prize is. The men get their homes, children, and their pride taken away. Suddenly a man has little or no say-so in his children's lives. I am one who, out of desperation, resorted to stealing my child. I know how emotionally devastating a divorce can be. Attorneys are a large part of the trauma, as are the courts, which still live in the nineteenth century. I cannot sympathize with a totally defeating, helpless situation that can bring about any emotion, including violence." Barry Sandrew, of Fathers United for Equal Justice, echoes this attitude: "Fathers lose everything through the courts—their money, their homes, and their children. They are financially and emotionally wasted. Snatchers say, 'This can't be happening to me, and if this is happening to me and this is justice, then there is nothing I can respect as justice. Why not just run off with the kids?' All socialization leaves them. They have little respect left for society and the judicial system. The only way to survive in that situation is to take what they believe is theirs and to leave. They feel they have been violated and are doing nothing wrong by taking back what is theirs."

DENIAL OF VISITATION

When a parent is not allowed to parent, he or she may feel compelled to kidnap. Abductors claim that the main reason they steal is that visitation has been thwarted. Every time they get ready to see their children, many mothers and fathers wonder, "Will my ex-spouse pretend, again, that the child is sick or is going out of town? Will I be allowed to take my son sailing or to the circus, or will I be ordered out of what was once my home?"

Sporadic or brief visits can be even more unsatisfying to noncustodial parents than not seeing the kids at all. They provide a tantalizing glimpse of what a close, loving relationship might have been like, or a reminder of what once was. Those tormented by what "could be" or "used to be" may decide to steal. Steve Brown, co-founder of Children of Divorce, a fathers' rights group, condones kidnaping when mothers refuse to cooperate. "The reason for childsnatching is that husbands are put under incredible stress, and when you back any animal or human into a corner and begin to abuse them, they've got to retaliate. I'm in favor of snatching if the father isn't given the opportunity to be an equal parent. When alienated from their families, fathers feel they can't relate to their kids, and don't know what to say to them. It's pathetic. A lot of men say, 'This is too painful, I'm going to leave,' so the children are brought up by their mother. If the father steals them, they're still brought up by one parent."

Thirty-two-year-old Walt agrees. He plans to run off with his newborn daughter. "My girlfriend and I were supposed to get married, but we broke up before the baby was born. Since her birth, her mother won't let me visit. She says I can't see the baby because I don't talk to her correctly. I went to my attorney to try to force the courts to let me see my child, but the lawyer said even if I were to get legal visitation rights, she still can decide when I can be with the baby, and the courts won't do anything to her if she doesn't cooperate. So I told the mother, 'You have two choices: let me see my daughter, or I'm going to kidnap her.' She says, 'I'm not going to worry about it, I'm not going to let you see the child, goodbye.' I don't want to steal my daughter, because I believe every child needs a mother. But doesn't she need a father, too? The way things are now, the baby is cut off from either me or her mother anyway."

CHILD SUPPORT

When a father is prevented from visiting his children or is reduced to a "zoo daddy," and is still required to support both mother and child, the resentment and frustration may lead him to steal his offspring. Many kidnapers believe that since they pay child support, they are entitled to "own" their youngsters. In fact, some thieving fathers tell their children that Mom only wants them "so Daddy can pay child support." Their reasoning may be flawed, but so is a system that tracks down and prosecutes fathers who default on payments but refuses to get involved when mothers—the recipients of these checks—deny visitation. A custodial parent, according to law, need not reveal her whereabouts to the other mate, so fathers across the country send support money to post-office boxes, not knowing where their kids are, or even how they are. The Uniform Reciprocal Enforcement of Support Act and the Federal Enforcement of Support Act police payments only; kids are not their concern. Pained by the indifference of the child-support system, fathers are refusing to pay for children they are not allowed to see.

Alan is one "post office" dad who has stopped sending money. He feels so brutalized by the bureaucracy that he may drop out. Alan's story: "I cut off child support because my ex-wife has refused to let me see my daughter for the last fifteen months. When I call her at my ex-in-laws', they say, 'I don't know where she lives.' I paid seventy-two dollars a week—a third of my salary—in child support, which the courts took directly out of my paycheck, even though my ex-wife's parents bought her a house and both she and her boyfriend work. I was subpoenaed by the family court in New York seven times in the last few months for nonpayment of child support. I explained why I stopped paying, but was told, 'It is not our concern why. If you want to discuss visitation problems, go to Florida, where custody was decided, and settle it down there.' I spoke with an attorney in Florida, who thought I had less than a 50 percent chance of getting the agreement enforced, because I have joint custody. This lawyer estimates it would cost me at least five thousand dollars to fight in court—eighteen hundred for legal fees, plus air fare and accommodations. I earn only two hundred and ten dollars a week as a locksmith.

"The courts are making it impossible for me to pursue the matter in Florida, because I can't afford an expensive proceeding. If I can't solve my problem legally, I'll solve it illegally. If the courts continue to harass me about support money, I might skip town and disappear. New York wouldn't look too far because I have joint custody. I might also concede defeat, give my ex-wife what she wants, and pay blackmail, hoping to God she lets me speak to my child. So far that hasn't worked, though. I'm considering stealing my daughter and bringing her back to New York, but I have nothing to offer her now, so I might wait three or four years until I'm in a better position and have established myself in another state under a different name and then snatch her. I don't want to hide, though. Living on the lam would be terrible for my daughter."

An unsympathetic support system that gobbles huge chunks of a father's salary can sometimes cause a kidnaping. One state policeman with five children was ordered to give his entire paycheck to his ex-wife. When he asked the female judge how he was going to live, she replied, "I know you policemen, you can work overtime or moonlight. You figure it out." "Let's face it," says the head of one men's rights organization, "what is a parent going to do? He's either going to leave without the kids, not make his support payments and get thrown in jail, or pay them and not be allowed to see the children. Or he can steal them and go and lead a decent life."

Not all fathers tired of the support structure are bent on stiffing their ex-wives. One desperate father tried to pay support, thinking the money might force his wife to let him see his daughter. He phoned Legal Aid, the district attorney, the police, and the sheriff, asking to pay support. "I was told support doesn't work that way. The DA's office said they don't handle custody or support, so I called the support office and was told they don't have anything to do with a man who *wants* to pay, but rather track down those who are supposed to and don't. I feel like a man on the moon—no one else is in my position. Lots of fathers don't want to pay support and don't care about their children. But I do. I'm thinking of stealing my daughter because I've tried everything else and nothing works."

FEMALE SNATCHERS

Women kidnap, too. They steal out of anger, embarrassment, and a sense of entitlement, since only one out of ten mothers loses custody. "Surely everyone knows women make better custodians than men," they rail at the judge. At the same time that they feel superior, they also experience self-doubt. Psychologist Daniel O'Leary equates noncustodial mothers with rape victims: "For a long time, women have been told that if they are raped, they probably did something unintentionally or unconsciously, which prompted someone to act sexually toward them. Similarly, if they lost their children, they must have done something to make the judge think they were incapable of taking care of the kids. In some states there is a tendency to award the child to the mother unless she is deemed unfit or an alcoholic, so that a mother might reasonably believe she must not have been a very good parent."

Women wonder how the judge views them, but equally important, what their neighbors, relatives, and friends think. They feel humiliated and exposed. Some mothers seek custody because they feel it will look bad if they don't—not because they want their kids. Society still stigmatizes an absentee mother. Many women, then, feel justified in stealing their children, regarding mothering as an innate talent and their natural right. Housewives, especially, rationalize their crime by pointing to a husband's busy work schedule, which they say leaves little time for child rearing.

"Rescuing" the Children

Peer pressure motivates women to snatch, but so does the belief that their kids are in danger with their ex-mates. Husbands and wives share this "SOS" notion, which is usually false. Grandparents steal grandchildren, too, if they think their own kids, or their former sons- or daughters-in-law, can't raise them as well as they.

Ordinarily, parental kidnapers have an exaggerated fear for their youngsters' welfare and need not intercede. The issue, however, is not whether the children are in jeopardy, but that the parents *believe* they are. Judith Nadeau recalls how a confused father misinterpreted the normal fantasies of a three-year-old. "She was visiting her father for the weekend, and when he put her to bed, she began talking about monsters. He thought that the monster was his ex-wife, and that was what the child was complaining about. So all night he slept with her almost under him, 'protecting' her. The next morning he decided he should take her away with him permanently." Another father, eventually prosecuted for child abduction, was convinced his former wife was insane, and if he let his kids stay with her, he would be allowing them to become "two more headstones in an emotional graveyard." One man objected to the neighborhood in which his sons lived, and to their new stepfather, because he had multiple sclerosis and was confined to a wheelchair. The natural father failed to see that the house was really lovely and that the stepdad, though ill, was a university professor with a Ph.D.

Kidnaping mothers and fathers usually cite their ex-spouses' shabby living quarters, lack of employment or income, or live-in lovers as evidence that they are unfit to parent. The kids don't always agree. Twice one father stole his children from their mother's backyard, and even though they pleaded to be returned to Mom, they were forced to stay. "It's terrible," explains the father. "I spent fifteen thousand dollars to find them, and was fired from my job because of the time it took. Now they're here and they don't like it. But I think someday they will come to realize that what I did was right, and why I have gone to such lengths. My ex-wife doesn't even have a shower. Her house is very primitive." His daughter's opinion: "I loved being with my mother. I had my own pony and would go horseback riding and swimming, and play with my stepsister. We lived on five hundred acres in northern California and played outside until it got real dark. Then we'd go inside and watch TV and eat popcorn. We didn't have a shower, but we could go swimming or take a bath in the creek. It was fun."

One newspaper in Iowa ran an article on childsnatching and asked abductors to present their positions. Wrote one angry male: "The fact is there are large numbers of divorced mothers who are not able to cope without turning to alcohol, drugs, prostitution, or worse. Are fathers simply to stand by and, because of ill-informed judicial decisions prejudiced with the 'matriarch' doctrine, allow their children to grow up in such an atmosphere?"

Curiously, the death of another child in the family can also trigger a steal. Thieving parents frequently blame their ex-spouses for the death and hope to "save" the remaining siblings from similar doom. That is what happened to a mother whose older son died of a brain tumor and whose younger son was taken. Out on a picnic after his two-year ordeal with his dad, the boy nervously queried a nurse: "My father said my mother killed my brother, but I thought he died of cancer. A person can't make another person get cancer, can they?" The father had asked the court to protect the boy from his mother, claiming she was already responsible for one child's death. "My son died at Sloan-Kettering, a cancer hospital," says the mother, "after being treated there for five months. The doctors told my husband they don't know what causes malignancies."

If a spouse kills one child, a parent may reason, what assurance is there he or she won't destroy the rest? So on mercy missions they steal, saving their remaining kids from a similar fate. Some snatchers simply go berserk when their loved ones die. Take Paul, for instance, an all-American corporate executive turned leftist expatriate on the run. Until his first son was born retarded, Paul bragged a business degree from Columbia University and had distinguished himself as an army pilot. He had a good job as a management consultant and a solid twenty-three-year marriage. Convinced chemicals in the environment were killing his son, Paul began feeding the failing boy health foods. When Jerry died at the age of eight, Paul flipped. The grieving father first shunned meat and then bought goats for the backyard so he could drink organic milk. His neighbors were appalled. Paul lived in a white, ranch-style house in a wealthy suburb of Phoenix, and when it rained he would insist on milking the goats in the living room. He decided the children had to be protected, and wouldn't allow them to have birthday parties, because of the cake, soda, and candy, or to watch TV, because of all the advertisements for sweets.

Eventually, he sold their television set, accusing his wife of getting the idea to divorce him from watching *Masterpiece Theatre*. Paul began making anti-American remarks and when his wife filed for divorce, he flew to Central America to scout a commune on which to live. He said if his wife was going to leave him, he wasn't going to leave his son and daughter, the way his father had left him. His ex-wife told the judge he would run, but Paul was granted visitation rights anyway. He took the kids for the weekend and disappeared. That was six years ago. Paul later wrote the judge saying he was obeying a law higher than a human law, and he would teach the children to love their mother, but they would never return.

Occasionally a noncustodial mother or father is justified in worrying about the child's welfare. Occasionally courts do goof and award custody to an unfit parent. One hysterical mother, for example, was convinced her ex-husband was a pornographer who was forcing their fourteen-year-old daughter into sexual games. She sought the help of a hired hand who flew to Florida and verified the sordid tale. He stole back the girl. The paid muscle told reporters, "You can call that childsnatching if you want. I call it a rescue."

A prominent Boston attorney with a thriving practice and an elegant home in the suburbs suddenly disappeared one day, leaving clients in his office and plants in his living room. Even though his ex-wife had been hospitalized twice for nervous breakdowns and the neighbors testified she repeatedly abused the children, the courts gave her custody. Several weeks before the abduction, the father had written an article on the detrimental effects of parental kidnaping on youngsters. Apparently, he felt he had no other choice.

A little boy's letter to President Jimmy Carter reveals a distraught mother's inducement to steal:

Mr. President Sir:

My name is John. I am ten and my brother Jeff is eight. We are big for our ages, but we are not big enough to be heard, so we write to you and hope you can help us. When we were in Tennessee with our father and his wife, she was very mean to us and our father didn't do anything to stop it. She has a very bad temper. When we went with our mommy at Eastertime, she saw all the bruises and marks and how skinny we were. She took us to the doctor's. We went to court and the judge said he wouldn't do anything to help us. He did not even hear any of the doctors or other people or us who were there to tell what had happened to us. We love our mommy and stepdad. They have never treated us bad [sic] and the judge man said we had to go back with our father and his wife. We are and always will be afraid of our father. We cried and begged our mommy not to let us go there again. So our mommy took us away. If we try to go back, Mommy will be in trouble and we'd have to go back to our dad. Sooner or later our father's wife will kill us. We know. We can't let our daddy know where we are. No one seems to care what happens to us, only our mommy listens. Why can't the judge listen? We had to live that stuff, not him. We know where we are loved and treated better and are happy. Why can't we be allowed to stay where we are safe and happy?

Still, those who abduct for the "right" reasons are rare indeed.

MANY MOTIVES COMBINED

Stealing is complicated. Snatchers may grab out of love *and* out of spite, to help their children *and* to hurt their spouses. Usually many motives work simultaneously, goading abductors into action. Jim's case illustrates how these conflicting emotions overlap and can culminate in a kidnaping. The Los Angeles insurance executive was frustrated with the courts, and furious with his ex-wife; jealous of her new husband, and unhappy with the way his daughter was being reared; unsure he would be allowed to see her, and sure she was asking him to steal her. Here is Jim's account:

My lawyer and I thought the judge was going to ask my ex-wife and me to go to conciliation court to discuss custody, but instead he made the decision on the spot to give her permanent custody, along with permission for her to move halfway across the country with my daughter. I was awarded "reasonable" visitation, but when one person is unreasonable, there is no such thing.

For the past two years I have had a terrible problem seeing my child. My ex-wife is always making excuses about why my daughter can't visit me, and I had them checked out and they aren't true. She also had me thrown out of my home when we first separated, and it took me three repeated court sessions to even get anything out of the house. She ruined my business, which had fifty thousand dollars' worth of stock, and I had collected antiques and jewelry, which all disappeared. She never had to account for them. A guy has no rights whatsoever. I'm fed up with the system. I know it's against the judge's order, but I plan to steal my daughter because I feel it is my right to have her at least half the time. I'll steal her just to tell off the judge, to show him what poor judgment he used, because my little girl would be in a much better position with me than with her mother.

Since my divorce I have gotten remarried to a woman who is a schoolteacher, and she is better qualified to take care of a small child than my ex-wife. Between the two of us, we speak several languages. My ex-wife speaks only English. I don't want my daughter to be brought up by dumb people. Her stepfather is a Southerner, an army man, and you know they aren't very smart. I have been knocked off, so to speak, by this man. He tells her I'm a "Chink" because I'm part Chinese. He says I'm just a little nobody, and she repeats it.

I feel my daughter isn't being brought up the way a child should be. She's only three and a half years old and already she's too much like her mother—a shrew, not a princess, a cheat, a liar, and I don't want that. I want her to have the best of everything. That doesn't mean I'm going to hand her everything, but give her the opportunity to be a young lady who will be looked upon, as she gets older, as a well-bred, well-educated person. She is picking up a lot of bad habits from her mother. She's very moody one minute and screams, and the next minute she's nice. She has poor manners, too, and never says "please" or "thank-you," just "I want this, give it to me." I have this beautiful little girl who looks like a child model. She has platinum blond hair and blue eyes mixed with Oriental features. She's one of those kids whom people stop on the street and say, "Oh, what a beautiful child!" Just imagine a beautiful child who is going to act like a pig! And it hurts me to think I can't do anything about it. I have no power. I've become what is called a Disneyland father, around for a superficial good time only.

My first daughter from a different marriage died, so my second daughter became more important to me. My first wife also stole my sons and I had no idea where they were for three years. She brainwashed them against me by the time I found them, and that's terrible for any parent to do. Because my kids were taken, I became aware of what a child needs. Not long ago, my daughter and I were at the playground and I said, "Everyone loves you," meaning Mom and Dad. But she repeated three times, "Mom loves me only a little bit," and I said, "Why do you say that? You know Mom loves you." But she said, "Yes, but only a little bit." There are reasons why children say these things. They must know the difference.

Jim's statements are all too typical of most snatchers: reasoning that is both sensible and selfish, logic that is ultimately twisted and flawed. Dissecting his argument will show the inconsistencies in his thinking:

145

Reasonable	*Unreasonable*
Concern that his daughter is not being brought up properly.	It is unrealistic to expect a three-year-old to have impeccable manners. He also wants to steal his daughter to get back at the judge for denying him custody, and at his wife's new husband for calling him a "Chink."
A victim of snatching himself, he knows how excruciating it can be and how it can affect the children, especially since the other parent is almost always bad-mouthed.	Rather than realize how destructive it is for a searching parent and child, he claims having his kids stolen has made him more sensitive to a youngster's needs.
Since his first daughter had died, his second one became even more important to him.	Instead of doing what was best for her, he planned to do what was best for himself.

· 9 ·

Who They Are and
How They Live

"'SAVE ME, SAVE ME!'" snatchers swear their children
shout. No matter that no one else hears their pleading. The
abductors' belief that their offspring are in danger, or their
former mates are unfit, is ironic, for it is they, not their ex-
spouses, who are the menace. Child-stealing experts agree that
youngsters are almost always at greater risk with parental kidnapers than with legal guardians. As a group, abductors are
unstable and disturbed. One confused father wrote a Cincinnati
court explaining why he had spirited away his daughter, who
first lived with her mother and then with her grandparents in
Nassau. "I'd be a poor parent if I allowed my child to grow
up where kids learn about Lord Nelson instead of Abe Lincoln.
I'm taking her to Brazil."

Of course, a person need not be sick to steal. When relationships fall apart and couples spar, it is easy to decide the other
spouse is an incompetent parent, or simply to want to wound
an ex-lover. Yet one California organization, the Stolen Infor-

mation Exchange, examined five hundred cases of child stealing and discovered that 90 percent of these abductors had a prior history of physical or emotional abuse. Add to that another support group's statistic that 60 percent have criminal records, and the extent of their potential harm is evident.

A person with a history of emotional disturbance makes an immature and often violent partner and parent. The stresses of a broken or failing marriage can push that bitter grownup over the edge. Confused to begin with, he uses his muscle instead of his marbles. A day after her second birthday, a Wyoming father kidnaped his daughter from her grandmother. Even though the woman handed over the girl peacefully, he tied his mother-in-law to a chair and beat her mercilessly. Another father, cornered by police, pulled a knife on his six-year-old girl and threatened to cut her up and then kill himself. In a macabre childsnatching chase, an estranged husband grabbed the couple's seven-month-old daughter and heaved his wife out of their moving car onto a highway. The father watched as a passerby scooped up the shaken woman, and then he pounced again, dragging her from the stranger.

Whether abductors act this way because they are sick or just really mean is impossible to say. Most likely they are mean because they are sick. Declares clinical psychologist Minkoff: "Ordinary people have control over their impulses and are able to tame their anger before they do something for which they will be sorry. Otherwise, every wife in America would be battered. If you look at people who commit delinquent acts— and to me, child stealing is a delinquent act—you can pretty much predict that person's future and find out he is probably not going to have any better control in another situation. It has been my experience that there is something not quite within normal limits about this kind of behavior." Confirms Daniel O'Leary: "My impression is that most parents who steal their children have committed legal infractions in the past, and are desensitized to doing something illegal again."

Because they are often warped, snatchers are likely to act inappropriately with their abducted children. An East Coast support group knows of a kidnaped boy and girl whose mother belongs to a religious cult. When they misbehave, she forces them, bare-kneed, to pray for hours kneeling on kernels of rice. Her other punishment: two boards with which to beat them, called "Mr. Ouch" and "Mr. Persuasion."

One of the sickest stories of emotional abuse involves a father who snatched his son at the age of three, when he could barely remember his mother. The ex-wife's *sister*—the sister-in-law of the abductor—made a visit to an upstate New York farm where the boy was being hidden, and posed as the child's mother. She left after only a week, explaining to her "son" that she was taking off because she didn't want him anymore. "My mother's sister came to see me," says the child, recently reunited with his natural mother. "I called my aunt 'Mom' because I thought she was my mother. My father took pictures of us together so I would think she was my mom."

Also bizzare was Karen Boyd Mellon's behavior when she and Pittsburgh banking tycoon Seward Mellon took turns kidnaping their daughters in what has become the most celebrated case of child stealing. For two months, Karen and her girls, Catherine, then five, and Constance, three, moved fourteen times and lived under nine aliases to elude her ex-husband. She spent a thousand dollars a day on round-the-clock bodyguards, and according to newspaper accounts, once had six thousand dollars in her pocketbook but refused to buy her daughter asthma medicine because, she allegedly told the girl, "your father doesn't love you enough to spend the ten dollars to pay for it."

While abductors may be unstable in their relationships, they must be lucid enough to plot their getaways. A steady source of income is essential for relocating, and for the *ifs*—if the kidnaper can't snare a job immediately, or hates his hideout and wants to take off again. Therefore, snatchers are usually employed until their departure, but also count on relatives for cash and creativity in lying low. Kinsmen act as go-betweens, feigning ignorance when frantic mates phone, and ferreting the mail through clandestine channels.

On occasion, relatives turn into co-conspirators, taking to the road with the thieving parent. Because of the maternal-custody bias, mother-and-son snatching teams are more common than any other family combination. One such couple in cahoots eluded authorities for more than a year. With the son's fourteen-month-old child, the Long Island duo fled underground, living under an assortment of aliases in Nevada, California, and Washington. They had accomplices in New Jersey, New York, Massachusetts, Vermont, Arizona, Nevada, California, Washington, and England, who fed the searching mother false information.

Phyllis's ordeal began on April 30, 1978, when her ex-husband failed to return their daughter Martha after a weekend visit. A telegram told all: "Martha and I have decided to emigrate. Don't worry. Michael." The mother suspected they were in England because Michael's mother had a cousin who lived near Manchester. Phyllis frantically phoned the airlines asking if an elderly woman, middle-aged man, and baby were booked on any flights to England. Indeed, the grandmother had bought tickets to make their scheme seem authentic and to confuse Phyllis. They had never left the country, but were in New York the night of the abduction. Michael's mother, Louise, had her real estate partner call Phyllis that night to say her ex-mother-in-law was in London having back surgery. The partner claimed a local orthopedic surgeon had set up the operation. The implication was that Michael and Martha had joined her abroad. If there were any doubts, the telegram would confirm it.

Phyllis called the orthopedist in town to get the name of the British surgeon. Louise's back was perfect, he assured Phyllis. Surgery in England? Impossible! Louise had had an appointment with him ten days before and had asked if she was physically able to care for a baby. When the physician learned

Martha had been stolen, he offered to help. The next time Louise called for an appointment, he had his receptionist request her phone number, claiming he needed to call her back. Louise did phone. She was reluctant to divulge her number, saying she was at a friend's, but a persistent receptionist coaxed it out of her. Phyllis traced the line to a woman who had hid them, but by the time the police arrived at her house, Louise, Michael, and Martha had fled.

Phyllis would have realized her mistake soon enough had she continued to believe Louise was in England. Phyllis's father had seen a postcard from Louise bearing a British postmark. She wrote that she and her friend Mary Higgins were enjoying a leisurely tour of the British countryside. When Michael had walked out on Phyllis, however, he had abandoned an extensive collection of files from his legal practice. One of the documents was Mary Higgins's last will. The old lady could not possibly be traveling in Europe or elsewhere—she had died several years before. Louise had mailed the postcards to her English cousin, who had mailed them back to the States. One hundred twenty-five thousand dollars and fourteen detectives later, Phyllis found Martha, answering to a different name, in Seattle.

Sometimes "brothers" will aid abductors when relatives refuse. A small, strident faction of the men's rights movement provides parental kidnapers with false identities and refuge in "safe" houses. They steal children for other men and, word has it, will even keep the kids until the father obtains a favorable custody order, on the rare occasion when he bothers with the courts. These "helpers" advise fathers on how to abduct, as well as how to avoid detection and where to disappear. It is a loose but well-established network, introducing kidnapers to one another, and sometimes to a sympathetic employer or realtor, who will fix forms in the event the police come around. Working for "the cause" rather than for money, this underground is scorned by most of the fathers' groups, who prefer to stay within the law and lobby for change.

The majority of parents, male and female, are on their own when it comes to concocting escape plans. They may sniff around for suggestions, but ultimately act alone. "The United States is one of the easiest countries in which to go underground, because of a person's ability to move about freely," claims one father who is making plans to disappear with his daughter. "In Europe, on the other hand, the police constantly ask for identification and do periodic spot checks. How many times are you stopped for doing something wrong in this country?"

Those in the know agree that establishing a new identity is a cinch. The first step is a new birth certificate, and with that, a person can get a driver's license, Social Security card, and credit cards. Only a birth certificate is required to obtain a passport, too. But how to get that entree into the world of the illegal, the birth certificate? Two men, one the head of a men's rights groups, the other an "underground" father, explain their different approaches to assuming a fake identity. "You hunt someone up, a friend, or a person you meet in a bar," says the founder of the fathers' organization. "You ask him his age, or his astrological sign, and say, 'You're thirty-five years old?' or 'You're a Sagittarius? I don't believe it. Let me see your driver's license.' Act casual, and from that, get the guy's birth date and ask him where he was born. Then go to that town and tell the city clerk you want 'your' birth certificate. If you don't work on the books, you'll never get caught." An on-the-run dad explains his technique: "If you don't feel like waiting for a phony birth certificate, you can buy a fake Social Security number for as little as one hundred dollars."

Wily women can get away with even more. One mother had eight aliases in twenty-two months. One name was on her birth certificate and another on her driver's license. Even though she had documents with different names, she convinced a welfare clerk to put her on their payroll, explaining that she lived with a man whose last name appeared on her driver's license. She also had her son baptized several times in various states in order to stay on welfare.

Parents who kidnap their children and those who consider it scheme perpetually, searching for ways to successfully pull off their crimes. One father, still in the planning stages, provides insight into the plotting process: "I object to forcefully removing a child from a parent, so I would snatch my daughter during my visitation period. I would tell her we were going on a vacation—most children would accept that—and after a while, tell her her mother loves her and that she will see her later, because I don't intend to disappear forever. I would let her talk on the telephone with my ex-wife, so it wouldn't be so traumatic. If I stay in the United States, I would have to change my name and my daughter's. She's very small—only three— so it's not too hard. Even though she knows her name well, you can give a child a new name and say it's a nickname. I probably wouldn't change it if we leave America. I'm a dual citizen of the United States and Denmark, so I might choose either country. I also have twenty-six cousins scattered around the world, and could settle near them so my daughter would have some family, and there would be other kids her age. The problem is I've been in this country for twenty-three years and it is hard to suddenly start all over someplace else. The switch might be too drastic for my daughter, too.

"I'll definitely have to change professions. People in this country think once they do something, it's the only thing they can do. I don't feel that way. If you have been observant all your life, you have learned a lot of different things without realizing it. I am in the fashion accessory business, but I could be a maitre d' in a restaurant or a waiter because I know the fine art of cooking and serving by going to good places, or I could be a business manager or consultant in any country. Whatever I do and wherever I go, I'll probably be forced to lose touch with my relatives in this country and my two sons from a previous marriage. Even though I risk being arrested (although I've talked to other people who say I'd probably only be sentenced to probation), cutting off contact with family and friends is a punishment in itself."

The strain on snatchers can be intolerable. The constant fear of being found out makes them skittish. Kidnapers must be skilled con men, persuasive in deceiving school officials, neighbors, employers—even their own children. Those who disappear underground and change their names must find fake ID's. Their lives are phony and lonely. They leave jobs and lose roots.

Sarah's story captures the continual conniving and terror many abductors experience. With her four-year-old daughter in tow, Sarah hopped a plane to Dallas with twelve thousand dollars in cash stuffed in her boots. She made reservations under a fictitious name, and chose Dallas because she knew no one there. Sarah took an apartment with no lease and had an unlisted phone number under yet another alias. Searching city death records for an infant girl born on her birthday, she procured a birth certificate under the dead child's name. She also altered her Social Security number, and worked at minimum-wage jobs because she couldn't risk having a prospective employer check her resume. "I never did relax," Sarah told a journalist when she came out of hiding. "I lived on the verge of hysteria all the time. I was afraid I would get a traffic ticket, afraid to be too friendly with anybody. I always felt temporary. I'd go to the grocery store and buy a pound of sugar and a quart of milk, because I knew for that entire three years we would be going home at any minute."

Another woman on the run with her three children in Mexico was equally spooked. "You've really no idea what it's like to live this way. I see a police car coming down the street and think it's coming for me. I'm always nervous." Her ten-year-old daughter, who adopted a new name, also was jittery about being discovered, especially when the principal called her into his office on a routine matter. Says the frightened girl: "I thought somebody was coming to get me."

Marriages also suffer. Parents who consider kidnaping or are already underground may find themselves suddenly single again when their present partners refuse to join them in their furtive lives as fugitives. One California woman said goodbye to her new husband when he decided to snatch his child from a previous marriage. She had a stimulating teaching job and family and friends she would not give up. "My desire to steal has ruined my life," says the driven father. "My wife doesn't realize what it is like to lose a child. I spent years trying to be a father and I don't get the chance. I have to resort to taking my daughter just because I want to be a father."

Abductors often have an idealized vision of what life with their kids will be like without the other parent. Many naively assume that their youngsters won't mind leaving home, and that jobs will be plentiful. But the practicalities of toilet training and kitchen duties may make thieving moms and dads return the children. So can the knowledge that the kids can't stand their company. After his third successful grab, Warren has decided he will never again steal his son. "I wouldn't kidnap Billy again, because I'm afraid it would be too much for him. He'd only be bitter with me since he told the court he wanted to live with his mother. He also might run away. It hurts that he's not with me."

Kidnapers may be angry that their children want out and abandon them altogether. Some snatchers never even wanted the responsibility, only the revenge, while others thought they could hack the obstacles, but realize they can't. Still fuming at former spouses, abductors vow never to return their children, even if the parents can no longer keep them. One father spent $51,000 to find his two daughters the first time and $57,000 the next. When his ex-wife stole his kids yet a third time, he discovered that one of his girls may have been sold. Though broke, he wrote to a detective pleading for help in confirming his story and locating his daughters. The letter read: "It is rumored that my ex-wife sold my younger daughter Jennifer to a couple in California, but I have not been able to verify this. I did hear from a woman who baby-sat for Mary, the older child, and was told she is now called Molly. This woman also claims that Mary told her on several occasions, 'Mommy used to have another baby, but we don't have her anymore.' The baby-sitter said she never saw Jennifer, only Mary."

Who are these parents who discard their offspring, or hide them from the other spouse? While research on the subject is still scanty, a profile of a snatcher emerges from two sources: a study of Los Angeles County offenders, and a survey conducted by the New York support group Child Find. Criminologist Michael Agopian examined ninety-one cases of Mom/Dad kidnapings and found that 35 percent of the abductors and victim parents are between the ages of twenty-seven and thirty-one, and that more than 70 percent are thirty-six years old or younger. Culled from registrants, telephone callers, children's rights advocacy groups, law-enforcement officials, attorneys, and mental health experts, Child Find's profile concurred, contending that most abductors are in their late twenties to early thirties. Seventy percent are men, claims the Los Angeles study, while Child Find estimated the figure is closer to 65 percent.

The chief disagreement is over their past histories. Agopian maintains that most are stable, steadily employed, and law-abiding, with clean records prior to the kidnaping. On the other hand, Child Find found that more than half have criminal records.

The organization also discovered that the majority of snatchers have abused their children before they hit the road. Spouses are targets of violence, too. Thus, those prone to stealing usually have little respect for the legal system, little respect for their youngsters—both during and after the abduction—and least respect of all for their mates. If kidnapers do not beat their wives, they frequently degrade them in other ways.

Gloria's partner illustrates how this second-rate treatment can trigger a snatch. "In 1967, in front of his mother, my boyfriend asked me to marry him," says Gloria. "I said it was a big decision and had to think about it. A few weeks later I said yes. After his proposal, I was bedridden with a back injury. I lived twenty minutes from him, and every day he would visit. Finally he convinced me to move in with him so he and his housekeeper could take care of me. It took a lot of convincing because he was the only man with whom I ever had a physical relationship. I totally trusted him and decided it was ridiculous for me to be by myself because I was helpless and we were getting married shortly. After I got pregnant his attitude was, 'I have you where I want you. Any man in his right mind wouldn't stick out his neck to get married, if he had a woman in this position.' I kept forgiving him and waiting, and I was going crazy but tried not to let it show because I didn't want to push him or upset him. I thought he would come around once the baby was born, but after I had my daughter, he said he had no intention of marrying me, that I had no money, no family who cared about me, and I had no choice. I wasn't ever going to leave him anyway. He'd say, 'If you don't behave yourself, or if you give me any trouble, I'm going to take away our daughter, or give her up for adoption.' " Gloria's five-year-old girl, who screamed and wept as she was violently ripped out of her mother's arms, has been gone since December 20, 1974.

IV

THE CUSTODIAL PARENTS

· 10 ·

Hide-and-Seek

''I WAITED AND WAITED for my sons to come home from their weekend away. Finally a woman refusing to identify herself phoned and said, 'Your children are with their father.' Then she hung up. It was like out of a grade B movie." A heartless tactic perhaps, but Mary's despair, anger, and loneliness would have been the same, regardless of how the message had been delivered, or who delivered it. For five years now, she has been deprived of early-morning cuddles, reading bedtime stories, and witnessing milestones: first steps; first shoes; first day of school.

Abductors may never even bother to call, but may make their statements through silence. In this case, no news is bad news. Not hearing, not knowing, not getting cooperation from authorities haunts helpless parents. They do what they can. To finance the search, they sell their furniture and family heirlooms, and frequently wind up sacrificing their present marriages for The Cause.

Worry and terror consume them. Over and over, they wonder: "Are my children safe? Are they being well treated? What has my baby been told? Will he recognize me when I find him? Is she even with my ex-spouse, or has she been abandoned?" Grownups may have to trick themselves to carry on. "I need to rationalize that my kids are fine and happy and really don't miss me that much," confesses a worn-out mother plagued with uncertainty. "That is the only way I can cope."

Mothers and fathers may be spurred on by speculation that their children are being fed falsehoods. "I want my sons to know that I'm not dead, that I didn't voluntarily give me them up, or abandon them," says Terry, who has been hunting for eight years, "that there was another choice they didn't know about." Devastated adults hire detectives or hop planes and trains, searching for the ultimate clue. They grill the kidnaper's cronies and cousins, business partners and banks. When they don't get answers, they panic. When they do get answers, they think they are being misled by a co-conspirator.

Waiting is excruciating; it may never end. Parents ponder that idea, too. More insightful sufferers may even understand their ex-partner's motives, but ache from their children's absence. "I know that my former wife was desperate not to lose the children, and that's why she did this," muses a New Orleans neurologist. "But I'm desperate, too, because I want to touch them, and hold them, and have a say in their lives."

Frantic parents stalk the country night and day, day and night, hoping to crack the case and corner their elusive little ones. Sometimes they get lucky, especially if a thieving former mate exits with a wanted accomplice, or has committed other crimes. Police may perk up when they hear the kidnaper has a checkered past, hauling the person in for auto theft or armed robbery, rather than for child abduction. The charge is unimportant to parents wanting only one thing: their offspring. Snatchers with clean records are tougher to snare.

Success is usually tied to finances. No money may mean no

kids. Rarely do childsnatchers relocate down the block. More likely, they move out of state, or across the country. Traveling can be prohibitive to an impoverished parent who also may have to hire a lawyer or detective, or snoop extensively on his or her own. Housewives with no independent resources are left with the least recourse. "Have-nots" often remain childless. Conversely, wealthy abductors can usually remain hidden indefinitely.

Irrational though it may be, parents frequently blame themselves. "I should have prevented the kidnaping," they moan. "I could have prevented it. Why didn't I foresee it? The signs were all there." Guilt envelops them. "They think they must have done something wrong in caring for the child," explains Dr. Daniel O'Leary, "or else the other parent wouldn't have gone so far as to steal the kids." Searching parents are bad parents, as they view it. Their self-esteem suffers, especially if they have drilled their kids before the abduction on how to escape and then are never contacted. They agonize over why the child does not call, convinced that he or she does not want to live with them. Other parents fault themselves for not teaching their offspring how to break loose from a snatcher.

Tactless outsiders reinforce grownups' feelings of guilt. "Neighbors tell me my son must be happy now," states Martha, a three-time parental victim, "or else he would have tried to get in contact. Or I must have done something wrong, or my husband would never have kidnaped John. I have even been told, 'It is better that the boy was stolen by his father, because boys belong with their fathers.'" Complains Alice of Colorado Springs: "People don't believe it when you say you can't get help from authorities. They won't accept that." When police did not help her find her children, Alice set up her own detective operation. Friends disapproved of her snooping style. A year after her two daughters were stolen, she took a job as a cook at a fishing camp in order to make money to continue her quest. In a detailed diary she kept during her seven-year search,

Alice wrote: "Because I chose a lifestyle of individual development with excitement and adventure, rather than the conven-
tional and traditional way, I am ridiculed. 'You're just having
fun, you're not looking for the kids!' they say. But I am used
to narrow-minded people."

Judgmental neighbors cannot comprehend the pain of being
left behind. Nor do they understand the peculiar plight of searching parents, who are in limbo, not knowing if their children will
come back, or be gone forever. Dating is difficult, because missing moms and dads are reluctant to resume their lives, believing
they must grieve full-time. What will the kids say when they meet
a new stepmother or father, or step-siblings? Will they think
they have been replaced? Waiting parents are afraid to remarry
and mate, or to even discuss their dilemma: "I have to live as if
Gary were here and not here at the same time," says an Indiana
mother, who has yet to hear from her son after four years.
Reveals one embarrassed victim: "I hem and haw when people
ask me if I have children, after they find out I'm divorced. I
don't want to sound self-pitying, but I don't know what to say."

Parents don't know how to act in part because of confusion
over their children's status. Might the child *really* be dead?
Youngsters are almost always alive, but not knowing can be
agonizing. According to people who have suffered both a kidnaping and a fatality in the family, an abduction can be harder.
At least there is closure with death; with a snatch there is no
finality. "Having Nick gone," says Jill, a marketing analyst, "was
worse than going through the death of my first husband, who
developed a malignant brain tumor. It was a horrifying experience, but I knew I'd never see my husband again. With Nick,
everything was unknown." Pamela suffered the loss of two sons:
one taken by leukemia, the other by an unstable ex-husband.
The two years her son Ted was gone were, in some ways,
tougher for Pamela than the premature death of little Bill. "Not
knowing where Ted was felt far worse than my other son's death
—if that is possible. Someone told me, and it's true, it's as if

God took one of my children and the devil is after the other one."

Child stealing is hell enough for parents without prior tragedies. For both, the questions are the same: not only, "Is my child alive?" but "How will I know if my child dies?" A justifiable concern, indeed. Custodial parents may not be notified because their kids' names are often changed—unless, of course, the abductor informs them. (Since when are kidnapers considerate?)

In December 1974, Gloria Yerkovich's daughter, Joanna, was grabbed. She has had no word about the youngster since. "Until two years ago," says Gloria, "whenever I would hear of a disaster anywhere in the world, like a plane crash, I'd wonder if Joanna were involved. I would have no way of knowing if she was killed."

Parents whose children vanish claim the feeling of being powerless, of having no control, is the most difficult emotion to bear. "You feel totally helpless," says one woman from Atlanta. "You want to kill. My ex-husband acted without any concern for me at all, as if I were a total nothing." A San Diego father feels emasculated: "I had just come home from work. I was on my bed and heard a scream. I thought maybe one of my boys fell down and got hurt. I kept hearing this scream, so I jumped up and ran to the door. Kirk had already been thrown off his bike and was being pushed into a car, and Jeff was hanging onto a post on the front porch with one arm, while my ex-wife took ahold of the other. He was yelling, 'Daddy, get me.' All of a sudden, I saw these guys run up to Jeff. I said, 'Oh God, I have to do something.' But it was too late. They already had my sons in their car and were taking off. I jumped into my car, but I couldn't catch them. I blew the engine up on the freeway."

Where do they look? How do they look? Even the most competent amateur detective feels overwhelmed. Admits a father whose daughter was stolen by her grandmother: "Once I packed

165

my suitcases, withdrew all the money from my checking and savings accounts, and started planning the search. Then I sat down on the bed and realized that I didn't even know in what direction to go. That is when frustration set in." Parents can't possibly comb the globe. Even if they are able to do so, their exes and kids may be living under assumed names. "With a math background," laments a mother, looking for the last six years, "my ex-husband could be anything from a clerk in a five-and-ten-cent-store to an executive in a bank. He could also be self-employed. Who knows if he has changed his name, or if he is even filing for income tax?"

Sorrow, bitterness, and fear eventually give way to depression. The blues can be so bad that parents never recover. They become recluses. Alcoholics. Anorexics. Bulimiacs. One San Francisco mother is so shaken by her child's abduction that she can no longer eat normally. Periodically she is hospitalized and fed intravenously. Sufferers may not take care of themselves because they may not care about themselves. Nervous breakdowns are common; some consider suicide. One two-time parental victim almost did both, but was rescued by the reappearance of her three sons. Right before their reunion, Mary told reporters: "I don't know how much more pressure I can handle. I don't know where I am heading. I don't know if I'll ever see my kids again, I don't know what is to happen to me, and I don't know how much more grieving I can take." In a letter to the *Arizona Daily Star*, a thirty-eight-year-old waitress shared her anguish after her daughter was swiped by her father. "This is enough to make people do their self [sic] in. I have come close so many times, but I realize when I find her, she'll need me. So I suffer on and on every day."

Women especially smart from the experience. Society expects them to be mothers, and most women expect to be as well. Without their young, they feel stripped of their role and robbed of their identity. Weeps one New York City woman: "I'm a mother yet not a mother. I'm a childless mother. I had my family, my son, a purpose in life. Now I have nothing." For her, Mother's Day and Keith's birthday are terribly difficult. On these occasions Ronda sends packages of books, puzzles, and gift certificates to her ex-husband's brother's house outside Chicago. "I always get them back marked 'Return to Sender,' " whispers the twenty-nine-year-old mother, "and when I'm unusually depressed, I open the packages and then reseal them." She pauses. "I've been doing this for seven years."

Experts claim dejection has more to do with their being women than mothers. On a radio call-in program in Boston, only male victims telephoned the station. Kristin Brown of Child Find speculated about the absence of female callers on the show: "My feeling is that women whose kids are stolen are treated with such contempt by authorities that they feel helpless. A woman who pounds on their door and says, 'My children have been taken, what are you going to do?' is viewed as hysterical. When she stops pounding on the door, she is seen as neglectful. They are damned if they do, and damned if they don't. It seems that men get treated better by police."

Better treatment does not mean better results, however. Fathers do not seem to be much more successful at retrieving their kids than mothers. Both sexes feel helpless and vulnerable. Explains California social worker Peg Edwards: "Parents experience severe depression because the core of a parent is the belief that he or she can protect the child. When that youngster is taken away, it's as if the parent's life were being taken away. A lot of their strength goes, too. It is totally inconceivable to them that they can't protect their children."

When Mother or Father suspects abuse, the wait is even more agonizing. Parents harmed in a snatching scuffle often wonder if their offspring are faring any better. If the abductor could do this to me, what might he or she do to my child? Cat-and-mouse child-stealing games between parents can confirm a grownup's fears. Take Patsy, for example. Three times she tracked down her former husband and sons; three times he took off, his boys in tow. Her brief moments alone with Scott and Mike haunted her in their absence. Once she traced them to a school in Oregon: "We spent five minutes together in an empty classroom. My younger boy told me they were being mistreated by their father, and whipped for little things, like putting too much milk on their cereal. My sons were so skinny. One boy was wearing a shirt I had given him three and a half years before. All of a sudden, their father barged into the classroom and grabbed them. He fled the state in the middle of the night. It took six months before I found them again, all the while wondering how much skinnier they were getting and how little milk they were putting on their cereal to avoid another beating."

Equally draining and depressing are false leads. One Westchester, New York, searcher was sure she had found her daughter Joanna after a national magazine ran the child's picture. An anonymous caller from California claimed her daughter was the missing girl's best friend. The source divulged the alleged victim's fake name, "Wendy," and her unlisted telephone number. The photograph in the magazine was taken when Joanna was five; now she was twelve. Still, a Xeroxed copy from Wendy's school yearbook seemed remarkably similar to the way Joanna's mother thought her child would look seven years later. The mother was delighted, until a West Coast detective traced Wendy's birth certificate. Says the New York woman: "It turned out that 'Wendy' was really someone else's Wendy, not my daughter, and that she was born to the parents with whom she lived. I don't know why that woman phoned, but the emotional strain on me was enormous. I had to wait four and a half months to verify her report. When I discovered the truth, it took every ounce of energy I had to keep myself together."

False hopes, false leads, no leads. Usually parents give in to depression for a while, and then vow to shake it, growing angry instead of complacent. They *must* stop guessing about their

168

loved ones' welfare and find out, firsthand, how they are faring. They *must* endure because the children *will* return. Lisa articulates this despair-to-action swing: "When Ned was kidnaped, I lapsed into a deep depression. I quit work, and wouldn't leave the house. I kept faulting myself, thinking, 'How could I not have known?' I was sure that I would never see Ned again. One day I called my ex-husband's father to ask if he had any new information. He said, 'I'd never tell you where Ned was even if I knew.' Then I realized he was in on the kidnaping. I went from being depressed to being angry. Until then, I had treated the abduction like a death, but then I thought, 'My son is alive, why shouldn't I see him? All I have to do is find him.' "

Lisa got out of bed and took to the road, traveling to Massachusetts, New York, Virginia, and Florida. She plastered "wanted" posters with a photograph of her child wherever she suspected he might be, briefed her hometown police on a newly enacted child-stealing statute they had never seen, and then got the FBI to intervene. Within seven months, the boy was back.

Not all parents are as successful as Lisa. Nor do they have the funds for such elaborate odysseys. Frequently moms and dads go through hunting spurts and then, when frustrated or financially depleted, suspend their searches. Yet parents rarely call it quits for good. "When somebody steals your child," claims sociologist Michael Agopian, "it's like a shadow that follows you everywhere. You're always looking, always searching. There's a cold silence, and things are never the way they used to be." A microbiologist from Atlanta agrees: "For me it was indescribable anguish. I was totally lost when my ex-wife absconded with my daughter. I did everything I could to get her back. I know another colleague to whom this happened, and he said, 'Fine, my wife is gone, my children are gone. I no longer have a wife and children.' Some people can do that. I can't."

Few can. Those who stop looking don't stop thinking or

hoping. They told onto the Tinkertoys and the train sets, the doll carriages and the coloring books. Parents may take a break from their unnatural eat/sleep/search routine, and perhaps even leave town or start a new career. But giving up, as Mr. H. chose, is unusual for victim parents. The same day a Queens, New York, judge awarded him temporary custody of his two sons, Mrs. H. ran off with them. Over the next six months, the father spent several thousand dollars on detectives. He became disenchanted with their methods, and realized that even if he did find Jim and David, the grab game would continue indefinitely. According to Mr. H., "I gave up looking because I realized the detectives I hired didn't really care about my children; they were only a source of income for them. An investigator would say, 'I'm going to find your sons, give me three hundred dollars.' Then he'd call back a little later and ask for another two hundred dollars, or say that he had found my boys and I had to give him five hundred more. Then I thought, 'Suppose I find them, what are the detectives going to do, throw my boys into a car?' I couldn't bring them home, because my ex-wife would only steal them again, and this would go on and on. I couldn't disappear with my sons, either. I had a job. I was active in politics and known in the community."

Fed-up mothers and fathers may decide that the only way to beat the custody battle is to play dirty—the way the abductor did. Desperate, they are willing to break the law to locate their kids. Some parents obtain telephone bills illegally, and pilfer mail. Sometimes they burglarize homes to get information. According to one New York support group, parental victims are usually model citizens—until their children are stolen. They have trusted the legal system, and gained custody the "right" way. Yet their decree sits uselessly in a drawer while their children sit somewhere unknown.

Pushed too far, they forsake the law and practice a justice of their own. Alice was one such "clean" citizen contemplating turning criminal. After a year, she had exhausted the traditional channels: police; lawyers; district attorneys; attorneys general; detectives; newspaper reporters. In a journal she kept on her progress, Alice explains her considerations for abandoning her by-the-book approach. In a March 1977 entry she wrote: "Since Christmas of '76, I have tried to work within the guidelines of the law. There have been demands made upon my body, mind, heart, and soul. I am innocent of any crime, and facing the possibility of never holding, playing with, talking to, or seeing my children again. One attempts to respect the legal process, but it doesn't deserve mine."

Parents sacrifice substantially for their kids. Besides risking arrest, they lose their jobs and their nest eggs, forsake their social lives, and say goodbye to present spouses. The hunt gobbles up all their time and money. Long-distance telephone calls, lawyers, and detectives are expensive. Following up on a tip may mean paying for a plane trip, hotel room, and meals away from home. So searching parents mortgage their houses and move to rented rooms, exchanging credit cards for food stamps. Or they try to hold onto their homes and their married names, just in case the kids come looking. Victims borrow from friends and family, and when they run out of funds, borrow still more. A North Carolina mother spent forty thousand dollars on four detectives. Finally she gave up. "I had nothing else to sell," explains the former librarian. "I got rid of everything of value—my house, my car, my jewelry. Now I rent a one-room apartment in a low-income neighborhood."

Even a bare-bones sleuthing operation can cost thousands of dollars. One young woman did most of the legwork herself. After digging through public records, she discovered her ex-husband had gotten two traffic tickets in Las Vegas. She bet he had fled there, and scoured nursery schools in Gambling Town, U.S.A. On a busy playground the mother spotted her two-year-old son. She hired a detective to distract a school official while she made off with the boy. The tab for the recovery: between twelve and fifteen thousand dollars. Had she not played Columbo most of the time, the woman would have spent thousands more.

Searching is costly in nonmonetary ways, too. Romance and relationships get short shrift. Parents on the prowl are married to their work—the work of bringing back their offspring—and may be unattentive to remaining mates and children. Second spouses are under strain. They must act supportive, but may find it difficult to *really* ache for someone else's kids. Though they can intellectualize that parent's pain, resentment follows nonetheless—at their husband or wife for neglecting their needs, and at the victim child for causing the pain. Even the most selfless helpmate has a hard time watching a paycheck shrink to finance yet another hunting expedition. Marriages frequently dissolve during the searching stage. Confides a man whose stepdaughter was stolen eight years ago: "I go through a range of emotions, from wanting things to turn out positively to wanting to back away from my marriage, and even from finding the girl."

For Andrea, being a newlywed almost meant being newly divorced. One month before she tied the knot, her husband-to-be's ex-wife absconded with his three children. "The kidnaping put the worst damper on our marriage," says the advertising executive from Hartford, Connecticut. "I spent the first six months trying to cheer up my husband. He would have these tremendous mood swings, which were unpredictable. We would be out to dinner, laughing, and a little blond boy would walk by and that would remind him of his own kids, who are all blonds. Suddenly David would plunge into a deep depression, wondering where his children were. I'd beg him to talk, but he would sulk silently. I felt cheated out of a normal, fun marriage. Every so often I'd go into a tirade, and start screaming. I'd denounce his ex-wife, and yell at him for getting involved with her. There was never a relaxed feeling in the house. But as soon as David found the kids, he was his old self again. I almost walked out on him before they came home, though."

Say he's alive. Say she's safe and sound. The kids have been located, but they are still with the snatcher. Now what? How to get them back: rekidnap them alone or with a detective and risk a messy confrontation? Take the nonviolent legal route— slap the abductor with a subpoena, and pray he or she doesn't scoot before the hearing, or try the informal approach of coaxing an ex-spouse to turn over the child?

Jerry, a Las Vegas construction worker, chose the first method. He hired a child stealer to fetch his two sons. "It takes so long through the courts," the father told a television crew filming the retrieval in California, "and I could run into difficulty. The judge might just turn my boys over to their mother anyway. Then I'd have to come back to California and it could take months and months. Using a detective is a lot faster."

Faster, yes; less traumatic, no. In fact, being restolen by a stranger can be more terrifying for a child than sitting through a vitriolic court proceeding. Sarah opted to get back her boy and girl through legal channels even though her *lawyers* suggested she use the services of a kidnaper-for-hire. When the child's father sent Emily and Doug two round-trip tickets from Boston to Samoa for the summer, Sarah never expected him to cash in the return portion and keep the kids. When she consulted her attorneys at a prestigious Boston firm, they said: "We really shouldn't suggest this, because it's unethical, but it may be expedient to hire someone to go and kidnap the children." "They acted as if this was the most fascinating case they had ever had," says Sarah. "It fulfilled their *own* sense of adventure. They pretended I had unlimited funds and came up with schemes that were impossible and prohibitively expensive. They advised me to hire a couple of detectives and then charter a private plane to Samoa and fly the kids to Australia, and then back to America. They said it would cost ten thousand dollars to have the detectives go to Samoa just to check out the best way to get my children back, but while they were there they'd *consider* stealing the kids.

"I vetoed the idea of detectives because my lawyers didn't want me to go to Samoa. They thought I might get hurt, but I didn't want my kids to be grabbed by people they didn't know. I decided to hire an attorney in Samoa to concoct a plan, figuring he would know the culture and how to proceed. Even the Bostonians' approach to finding a Samoan attorney was ridiculous. They said to one another, 'Is there a Harvard man in Samoa? Whom do we know from Harvard there?' Then they got out their book of Harvard Law School alumni and the closest they could find was a Harvard person in Hawaii. They called him up, and he recommended a local lawyer in Samoa." The local lawyer suggested that Sarah accompany U.S. marshals to her husband's hideout, and then go through the courts. Less than a week after Sarah arrived, the kids were back with her in Boston. No professional child stealer. No chartered plane. No Harvard counsel.

Neither courts nor private detectives appealed to forty-two-year-old Harold, a secondary-school administrator from Long Island, New York. Instead, he chose a more informal, straightforward method. "I got a tip on where my ex-wife and boys were living. For three days, I didn't know what to do. Should I call her at work? Should I call her at home? Should I fly to California and surprise her? My kids had been gone for four years, and I knew nothing about my ex-wife, or her situation, or if she would run again. About three years ago, I decided that if I found my boys, I would not see them before okaying it with their mother. I didn't want to do anything that would threaten her, because she would be angry and upset, and then the kids would get it.

"Finally I decided to call her at work. Her secretary answered and I told her my name. There was a long delay before my ex-wife picked up the phone—I think she was trying to decide what to do. When she got on the line she said, 'Harold, what do you want?' I said, 'I want peace, I want to be your friend, I want to be the children's father.' She said, 'I'll call you back.' Later, we made arrangements for a visit."

Not all abductors are so civil to mates who catch up with them. Mothers and fathers may be warned to stay away or else the kids will be gone, next time for good. Other kidnapers adopt a you-can-look-but-not-touch attitude: searching parents are allowed to see their children on the snatcher's turf, but may not leave the house alone with their youngsters. Ironically, a similar supervised visitation setup exists for convicted child stealers!

To visit or not to visit? Parents who have located their little ones may choose not to resteal them. Grownups may be physically afraid of an encounter, especially if there was a scuffle in the initial steal, or if they fear their former partners. "I wanted to get back my daughter," explains a Colorado mother, "but not at the risk of jeopardizing my life. My ex-husband had promised to have some of his hoodlum friends do me in if I ever came to Indiana to retrieve her. I had six other children to think about."

Some parents do not recover their kids because they have run out of money for lawyers, court fees, or detectives. Others decide their youngsters have been gone too long, and would not recognize them, or want them. Those who opt for a reunion claim the wondering and the waiting may be the worst part. Louis, a Toledo dentist, was ready to *kiss* his snatching ex-wife when, after a four-year absence, he learned that his two sons were alive. "Part of me died when they disappeared. There was so much pain, constant pain, until I heard from my boys. I felt so relieved, it almost didn't matter if I saw them or not."

Successful searchers ponder their reception: Will their sons and daughters run to them, or run away from them? As one jittery mother described the feeling: "I didn't know what my sons had been told about me, if they'd say, 'I don't want to see you,' or, 'I want my father.' Maybe they should have stayed with my ex-husband, maybe they would have been happier with him than they'd be with me. I always thought that when I found the kids I'd only be elated, but I was so frightened they'd reject me."

Striking out is also a fear of mothers and fathers who have yet to uncover their children. Adults perpetually rehearse their reunions. "This is how the scenario goes," says a woman who has been looking for her daughter for eight years. "I would tell her what happened, but I'm prepared for rejection. I would understand that she would not be rejecting me, but it would be a combination of very complex emotions. Perhaps she was brainwashed against me, or we didn't have enough time together. We've lost so much. I believe that the basic relationship is there. She and I had an incredibly close bond, and I don't think that could ever be destroyed. But outside forces pull people apart. It's going to take a long healing period to put it all back together, and I'm worried that because of the initial rejection, we won't have an opportunity to work it out, to get close again."

Adjusting is difficult for both parents and children. In fact, it may be so difficult that the parent has second thoughts about the successful recovery. Parents have a double burden: their kids' problems plus their own. They must cater to their children, yet rarely receive sympathy in return. Adults are victims, too. After the reunion, the parent needs nursing, not negativism; reassurance, not rejection; lots of love, not the cold shoulder. Yet youngsters have a hard time coping, and punish their parents for their problems.

Often children go home and find a new "daddy" at the dinner table, or an unfamiliar baby brother sporting their favorite clothes. They feel replaced and resentful, and blame their reunited parents for abandoning them. These angry, uncooperative refugees rebel and cause hell. Parents are weary. They are mad, too. Whatever happened to gratitude? They have sacrificed and searched, in order to rescue their young. "Didn't they want to be rescued?" grownups wonder. They may momentarily question whether it was worth the bother, and even regret having found their thankless offspring. While the kids were away, the parents idealized them and contemplated their idyllic reunion, with the children leaping into their arms. When confronted by reality—sometimes not so much as a handshake for a greeting—parents may break down. The aftermath is equally grisly: the clinging and crying, the regression and the fear. The more scarred victims may refuse to call their custodial parents Mom or Dad. Adults are upset when they realize how much, and how long, it will take to gain back that title.

Other surprises ensue, too. If the marriage was on the rocks before the kids were retrieved, it is guaranteed to be shaky once the kids return to the nest. A new mate may decide to fly the coop. Adults accustomed to the intimacy of just husband and wife may find a screaming or sullen youngster a third wheel. Even the most sympathetic stepmom or dad can resent the rift the child has brought between them. The parent who binds them is caught in the middle, feeling responsible for the child, yet unable to control him or her; responsible for the marriage, yet committed to the child.

Spouse number two may look longingly at the door, and sometimes exits stormily. When Michael returned on the scene after five years, his stepfather, a stranger, untied the marital knot. Julia's explanation: "Jim was very jealous of my child. He made me make a choice between him and Michael." Although Harriet and her second husband stayed together after her child came home, she still smarts from the husband-versus-daughter tug-of-war. "I kept thinking," says the Minnesota mother, " 'To whom do I owe my loyalty, my husband or my child?' Kathy almost destroyed my marriage because her demands were so great. She was used to being beaten and abused by her father. It was all she knew. That's how she would get attention. She'd yell at my new husband until he'd get so upset he'd berate her. It was a terrible time. Kathy was jealous of my husband, and wanted me all to herself. Sean wanted me all to *himself*. He wanted her out of the house and in a foster home. He was tired of the expense—twenty-four thousand dollars—it cost to find her, and tired of her trying to break up our marriage. But she was a sick girl. He just couldn't deal with her. I still resent him for not understanding."

A stepmother who speaks for the other side explains the strain three returned stepchildren put on her relationship. "Paul and I have suffered as a couple. Since his kids have been back, it has been hell. The children have hurt my marriage. Not that they have come between my husband and me, since he is very supportive and always backs me. But after three years of putting all my energy into helping his kids, I don't feel I have any energy left over for my husband. Or myself. All three kids have severe emotional problems. When they came home, I went in as Supermom, all gung-ho, thinking I've got to help these youngsters get over a rough time and readjust. I went from being Supermom to being drained. I as the mother have had to take all the abuse when they are angry at their natural mother. I represent Mother. There's no other female figure on whom they can take out their anger. If Patty, the oldest, is watching a show on TV she once saw with her mother, it may set her off and she will be impossible with me. I have considered giving up. I feel that I don't want their problems anymore, that I don't want the responsibility."

Sibling struggles also plague parents. The prodigal son or daughter, welcomed with fanfare, may irritate a well-ensconced child left behind, or a stepbrother or stepsister. Like a new parent, nonabducted siblings may seethe at the newcomer for having to share their turf. If grabbed at an early age, a child may not even remember a sibling.

Father or Mother is expected to play peacemaker, but what about his or her own peace? Besides wrestling with warring children and a discontented mate, they may also have to deal with their own feelings of disappointment and depression. "It's hard to get back those maternal feelings after six years," confesses a woman struggling to keep her household intact. "My son was taken away as a toddler and brought home as a grown boy." Her child echoes the difficulty: "My mother was a stranger. I was told, 'Here is your mother,' and this lady was sitting on a courtroom bench crying." "Parents may have to learn about their children all over again," declares social worker Judith Nadeau. "That adult is also angry with the child, because anyone who causes you severe distress will anger you. It's like mourning. Part of your grieving for a loved one is also getting over the anger at them for leaving you."

First, parents are mad because their young are away; then, that they won't leave the adults alone. Frightened of a resnatch, the child may follow Mom and Dad from room to room and place to place, mimicking their every move. Without privacy, life changes for parents. They take precautions, too, by staying and playing with the kids to head off a repeat steal. No provision for grownup time, for free time. They can't risk a bus-stop abduction, so they must walk or drive their offspring to school, and fetch them at the end of the day. Parents turn into guards. Lenny lives in a run-down cabin on an empty country road outside of Worcester, Massachusetts. He has no telephone to alert police if his ex-wife strikes again, but has an SOS system of his own—"self-help." Late at night he stays awake, waiting for his former mate to pounce. Reasons Lenny: "It only takes a second to steal Philip. I'm a machinist collecting worker's compensation, so I can watch my son all the time. I have a shotgun, and just filed for a pistol permit. No one is every going to take Philip again."

Some eminent child specialists question whether parents whose kids are gone awhile even have the right to recover them. Child-development experts claim that disturbing a youngster's stability can have devastating effects. Children become more settled in the new environment each day they are away. If years have elapsed, they may not want to leave the snatcher's side. Yet should an abductor be "rewarded" for his or her crime by being allowed to keep the child? Believes Yale University child psychiatrist Albert J. Solnit: "The question is, whose needs come first? I think children are more vulnerable, and must have their rights protected more than adults. The best interests of the child would be with the parent with whom that child has the strongest relationship, regardless of how it came about. The searching parent might like to know what happened to the child, but I would hope that society would protect the child from having that relationship broken. If the abductor is not neglecting or abusing the youngster, you might say to the psychological parent, 'By the way, the other parent has now shown up, would you have any objection to their seeing the child? They would like to know how he is.' You might say, 'Do you even have the right to ask to intrude?' "

Judges seem to agree that in cases where youngsters are entrenched in their new communities, it is disruptive to uproot them, and only under unusual circumstances should they be returned to their legal guardians. A dilemma, indeed: Is it better for a child to stay put with one parent—the kidnaper—or to be returned, and then know both mother and father? "If a child is doing well," maintains Dr. Mel Roman, "it would be detrimental to the child to be sent back a few years later to the rightful custodian. It would be a significant problem for that child to readjust. On the other hand, I feel very strongly that it is critical for a child's development to have as much access to both parents as possible."

Mothers and fathers still looking for missing sons or daughters have ample time to consider their options. Until they spot their children, however, there are ways to ease the ache. Instead of wallowing in self-pity, adults who have recovered their offspring suggest keeping active. Lobbying to change child-stealing laws may seem futile, but can make a parent feel useful, and is a way to meet other victims. Support groups are cathartic, as well as superb sources of information on the latest legislation and shortcuts for locating stolen children. Therapy also lets a grieving parent vent anger, learn to cope, and resume her or his life. "There is a lot of self-searching that goes on for a parent," explains one Chicago father, "and even if you may know you are doing everything you can to locate the child, and it's not your fault, you still blame yourself and lose your confidence." Family and friends can be supportive too; often victim parents move in with their own parents. Being alone, being inactive, is hurtful, not helpful.

Adults must not give up. They must be patient. Kids *are* returned. But while grownups hope and hunt, they grieve for what can never be. Searching parents know that even if the children come marching home, it is often too late. "I expect to see my sons when they are young men, when they come looking," muses a woman from Pennsylvania with premature streaks of grey hair. "Maybe I'll see them sometime, but not in time to be a mother. There is a difference between mothering a seventeen-year-old and a seven-year-old. What I've lost is not replaceable."

· 11 ·

Detectives and Custody Vigilantes

H O W   M U C H   I S your child "worth?" Five thousand dollars? Ten thousand dollars? Fifty thousand? It is a crass but realistic question for the victims of child stealing. Parents may have to put a price tag on their youngsters in order to see them again. Increasingly, mothers and fathers are engaging professional kidnapers to retrieve their girls and boys. Due to the abundance of abductions, the sluggish, often unsatisfactory results received through the courts, and the indifference of law-enforcement officials, the snatching-back business has turned into a lucrative racket.

These hired hands are usually private investigators, but they may also be "custody vigilantes"—unlicensed, overzealous muscle men who use unsavory tactics to snare children. Detectives can have a rough touch as well. Many were once bounty hunters who tracked, or hounded, fugitives from state to state. Today they may specialize in spy-game weapons and strategy that can backfire and injure the child.

Adults whose kids are stolen are desperate and vulnerable. Investigators know this, and some of the more unethical members of this new breed of child catchers prey on parents. Victims report unscrupulous operatives who demand five thousand dollars from a searching parent, locate the snatcher, and then tell the abductor: "Give me ten thousand dollars and I'll say I couldn't find you." At a legislative hearing, one congressman testified that some private eyes abduct a boy or girl from one parent and then rekidnap that child from the other, collecting a fee from both parents.

Not all such investigators are fee-building opportunists, of course. Many are effective and sincere. Rather than gouge clients, a few charge poor parents on a sliding scale, depending upon their ability to pay.

Still, recovering kids is a business—a profitable business—and those inexperienced in child retrievals may be tempted to take on a distraught mother or father willing to pay top dollar. One Boston investigator, a criminal surveillance specialist, exemplifies the mentality of many greedy but well-intentioned detectives. He had snatched a youngster only once, and cringed when the same client suggested he do it again—until big bucks were flashed in front of him. "I wouldn't touch another child-stealing case," he told a journalist. "It depends upon what you can live with. The effect on the boy I recovered was so devastating that I swore I'd never snatch kids again." Five minutes later he modified this principled stance: "I wouldn't participate in one for less than ten thousand dollars."

When do parents feel hiring an investigator is necessary for restealing a child? It should *never* be necessary for this purpose. Snatching back a child will only further traumatize a youngster, and using professional kidnapers can only compound the problem. Still, it is a fact of life: some detectives do abduct children. Consequently, it is important for anyone involved or potentially involved in a parental kidnaping case to know how these investigators operate. In addition, detectives *can* be useful for the limited task of locating children only—after which the custodial parent can follow the proper legal channels to retrieve the child.

There is no consensus among child-stealing authorities about when—and if—an investigator should be called. Detectives themselves are uncertain of what their role should be. One California private eye recommends that parents hire him immediately after a snatch, when a kidnaper's trail is hot and the child remembers the parental victim. On the other hand, a Boston agency advises parents to wait six months to a year after an abduction in order to give the fugitive time to settle down. Children's Rights, Inc., of Washington, D.C., a now-defunct support group for parental victims, eschewed the use of professionals. It once estimated that mothers and fathers spend five thousand dollars annually on investigators for several years, but claimed that most of its members had eventually found their offspring through jilted boyfriends or girlfriends of the abductor, not through hired help. Yet most custody experts contend that investigators can be effective, especially when police refuse to intervene, the kidnaper has gone underground and has changed his or her name, or there are no leads on the kidnaper's location.

A skilled private eye has the manpower to search several areas simultaneously, and access to resources unavailable to most parents. Through an underground network of contacts, the detective may be able to extract ordinarily unavailable information on credit cards and car records, forwarding addresses and bank statements. Working through an unknown third party may catch a childsnatcher off guard. An unsubtle parent who quizzes the same sources may have no luck and may risk having a tattletale tip off the thieving parent. In addition, investigators often possess a wide range of effective, if unethical, tactics. For instance, "Fake correspondence is one of the oldest ways of tracking down a person," reveals one successful detective. "Say the abductor is an executive in an advertising agency. You would print up a phony letterhead, and make it look as though you were a potential client, and would deal only with that individual. Often people on the run contact their offices, so when a kidnaper calls and hears a prospective client wants him to phone, you can sometimes get his telephone number by asking him to call back, or by tracing it."

It may be advantageous to hire agents in international cases, say experts, since these professionals should know how to operate in different milieux. A California detective explains how he ingratiated himself with the Ecuadorian authorities. It cost his client, an American heiress, eighty thousand dollars to retrieve her four-year-old boy from her Ecuadorian ex-husband. Explains the private eye: "You can do anything you want in South America as long as you have money. I paid off certain officials, and they did pretty much what I told them to do. Never once did I let them know that I was a private investigator. I said I was a friend of the grandfather's, who was an important man in America. I said I was on my way to Switzerland and thought I would come to Ecuador to see what the status of the case was. The boy was hard to find, since he had been moved from house to house. I informed the chief of police in this small town that I would offer a reward of fifty thousand *sucres* (around two thousand dollars) if he found my client's child. I also promised to pay for the use of police cars and personnel. I said I would like him to disperse the money. (I upped the fee to six thousand.) Well, he dispersed the money right into his left pocket! He assigned me four uniformed cops and two plainclothes detectives, and they stayed with me the whole time.

"They issued a warrant for the father's arrest. All I had to do was tell them whom to arrest, and they did. They crashed down the doors of the father's friends, relatives, and neighbors, and hauled them into jail on trumped-up conspiracy charges. Then I'd interrogate them in prison, demanding to know where the boy was being hidden. I also went to a printer and had ten 'wanted' posters made up, announcing a reward for the return of the child and showing a picture of the father. I brought a couple of these posters along to the father's attorney, and told him that I had had *ten thousand* of these signs printed. I also reminded him that the money was there for him, too, if he led me to the boy. The father was so intimidated by the pressure that he had his brother hand over the child in front of the courthouse."

One cloak-and-dagger detective located a four-year-old girl from Cedar Rapids, Iowa, on an isolated island called Nexas, south of the mainland of Greece. Her father had whisked her away to his homeland while on a routine visit with her in America. According to the investigator:

The island was so small that we couldn't go in posing as tourists, let alone hide the mother there, since she was known to the family. So we persuaded her to fly to Nexas on a one-way ticket, throw herself on her husband's doorstep, and say she couldn't live without the child and wanted a reconciliation. As a good-faith measure, she gave her husband her passport, so he would think she intended to stay. (She had gotten a duplicate before leaving America.) The mother rented an apartment on the island, and spent time with the child, whom she hadn't seen for nine months and who now spoke Greek and had forgotten English. After the girl had gotten readjusted to her mother, two colleagues and I, by prearrangement, chartered a yacht and sailed to Nexas. We arrived at the harbor pretending to be yachtsmen sailing around the Mediterranean. We made contact with the mother, and instructed her to show up one night with her daughter so we could take off. But she chose a night when a terrible storm was brewing, and we could not leave the harbor. They couldn't leave the boat, either, because the daughter was at the age where she would have told her father about the yacht.

We decided to lock the mother and child on board and

go to a hotel, where we could watch the boat from our room. When the daughter failed to return to her father that night, police began swarming around the yacht. It was the only one in the harbor that didn't belong there. Every two hours officers patrolled our boat with binoculars and police dogs, but the storm had killed any scent. On the fourth day, we took some barometric readings and decided the storm would subside and that we should set sail. One at a time we "yachtsmen" snuck back on deck. The police returned just after we had untied the lines, so we had to hide flat on the side of the boat and hand-hold the lines. The cops took their time inspecting our boat from the outside, and stayed awhile to smoke cigarettes. We cut the lines as soon as they left. The thirty-eight-foot ketch made a lot of noise, but the storm muffled the sound. We had a rough passage that was forty hours long, and sailed into a Turkish harbor. Suddenly a mass of police surrounded us—not, it turns out, because we had fled with the child, but because we were flying the Greek flag in a Turkish port. That was a definite "no-no" so we quickly removed it. Then we took a sixteen-hour bus trip along windy little roads to Istanbul. We got eaten alive by fleas, and arrived at the airport in time for a huge riot. We had to physically fight our way through the terminal. There was an airplane strike, and the first plane out went to Rome. We grabbed it, then hopped another to London, and then on to America. The father back on Nexas was sure his wife had reached the United States long before. To confuse him, I had arranged for my client's parents in Iowa to send their son-in-law a telegram saying the mother and child had landed safely in America. At the time, they were holed up on the boat less than a mile away from him!

Not every adult has the resources to buy an Ecuadorian police department's cooperation or fly to the Greek islands. For many

victims, detectives' rates are excessive for more mundane retrievals closer to home. Generally speaking, private eyes almost
always charge a flat fee for child recoveries rather than work
on an hourly basis. (Those who do make fifteen to thirty dollars
an hour, although some get as much as fifty dollars an hour.
This translates into a hundred and sixty to four hundred dollars
a day, or eight hundred to two thousand dollars a week, plus
expenses.) Detectives differ on their payment plans. Some demand one rate for both locating and rekidnaping, but most
break down the bill and command one fee for finding the child
and another for the actual grab. A few investigators refuse to
abduct, but will track down the child for one thousand to three
thousand dollars. The parent must then retrieve the youngster
through the courts.

Usually detectives want a certain portion of the fee up front—
say a thousand dollars or so, or sometimes half of the total
tab, including estimated expenses. Or they may ask for part
of the locating costs, and then once they find the child, collect
the difference. They may request part or all of the retrieval
money before actually abducting the child.

An average snatch costs between three and six thousand dollars, plus expenses—fifteen hundred to three thousand to locate
the child and a few extra thousand for the kidnaping. Of course
the sum can be far more—in the tens of thousands—for
lengthier, more complicated operations requiring several helpers
and extensive travel. Ordinarily, parents must hire at least two
agents, who often tail the child until the rescue mission begins.
With three agents, costs can climb to seven hundred dollars a
day—before expenses are added. It is not unusual to find figures
of ten to twenty thousand dollars for services rendered within
this country. Steeper fees are often cited for maneuvers abroad.
(Although it is rare in the United States, some overseas agencies
request a bonus for a successful job.)

Why the hefty charges? Detectives know that desperate parents are willing to pay these sums, and may cash in on their pain. But bills are big for other reasons as well. Doing the dirty work can be dangerous. Investigators sometimes break the law to get results—opening mail, tapping telephones, even burglarizing houses. In addition, kids are not always delighted to be reunited with their lawful guardians, and may run away. Often, investigators have to play psychiatrist and coax a hysterical youngster into the absent mom's or dad's arms. Grabbing a child may mean warding off an irate, sometimes violent, gun-toting parent. Then there is the possibility of being slapped by that parent with assault and battery charges. Huffs a Baltimore private eye who makes frequent court appearances: "It is so easy for a parent to claim assault and battery. Just brushing up against someone is battery."

If detectives are not careful kidnapers, they risk losing their licenses, and clients pay for that risk. Some states outlaw retrievals by parents or their agents, so investigators have to decide whether to abide by the rules and turn down a case, or take the chance of getting caught and charged with child abduction or a similar crime. Even states that do not specifically forbid "self-help" can find ways to arrest an investigator. The general rule, though, is that a detective is on safe ground if he or she works for the lawful guardian, and is accompanied on the recovery by the client. A hired hand who steals for the noncustodial parent could be rounded up for kidnaping, along with the client.

When custody has not been decided, a detective is free to serve either side. What is considered legal or illegal action by an investigator depends not only on the parent's rights, but also on the reasonableness of the retrieval method. Tommy-gun tactics, for example, could endanger a child, and may merit the arrest of an agent. The detective would probably not be treated harshly for merely holding hands with the child and leading him or her to the getaway car. What is right and wrong in childsnatching is a fine line, frequently defined at the discretion of a judge.

Whether or not a detective can touch a child without incurring legal liability is also debatable. Because their colleagues have been imprisoned for this behavior, many private eyes refuse to grab boys or girls, instead making their clients do it. Other investigators prefer to yank the children themselves, maintaining that having the custodial parents' permission and presence will provide the necessary legal immunity.

Sky-high fees result from taking this gamble and from exposing the detective to danger. One professional wound up in an Argentine prison surrounded by police officers pointing machine guns, even though his client had custody and had joined him for the abduction. She, too, had landed in jail. The agent and the Wisconsin mother had flown to South America to reclaim the woman's two sons, stowed away abroad for ten years. The detective traced them to an English-speaking school. They were stunned to meet their mother, a virtual stranger, whom the now-teenagers had last seen when they were three and four years old. Although they agreed to accompany her back to the States, they set one condition for their trip: that they be allowed to say goodbye to their father. "I knew we would run into problems," recalls the detective, "if we granted their wish, but we felt they would not return otherwise. As soon as the boys saw their father, he grabbed his older son and took off, leaving us with the younger boy. The police arrived immediately and set up roadblocks around the house. I told my client that we should consider leaving with the one child and return another time for the older boy. She said, 'No way I'd split them, they are brothers.' We had to drive through back alleys to skirt the roadblocks. Then we spotted the father and the boy in their car and tailed them until they pulled over. The father was very wired. We didn't want to take the other boy, we said, we just wanted him to see his mother. I invited the father to have coffee with us and discuss the matter. He said, 'Okay, but first we had better go to the police station and tell them it's a false alarm, because I've reported you.'

"It was a trap. When we got to the station, I was thrown into a cell, and my client was locked in an office for two days. The father had filed a complaint, and in Argentina a complaint cannot be withdrawn without an order from the judge. Luckily the investigating officer was married to a girl who taught English. We became friendly with her, and it turned out that her father was the judge on our case. So he said that if we made a statement saying we had come to Argentina to negotiate custody, then he would write a special order to release us. We left the country—but without the boys."

For another detective, stealing was equally harrowing, although more successful. He was well paid for the risk. Terry was hired to steal back a boy being guarded around the clock by police officers. His client, the child's father, had custody, yet the thieving mother had something even better: a father who was mayor of the Texas town to which she had fled. As mayor, the father had ordered twenty-four-hour police protection for his little girl's son. Terry tracked the child to a secluded nursery school. He noticed that once a day for five minutes, from 2:05 P.M. to 2:10 P.M., the child ventured outside to romp with classmates, and the officers guarding him used the time to relax. (The rest of the day the preschooler was confined indoors, because his mother feared a resnatch.)

The playground backed up to a wooded area. A high fence separated the two. The plan was to have the father hide in the woods and during the boy's five-minute airing, Dad would call his son to the fence. The detective would heave his client over the fence, so he could grab the boy, and then they would climb over again and flee through the woods—all without the police on duty noticing. For the first three days, the father was unable to position himself properly, but on the fourth day, father and son sprinted through the woods to a waiting car. The detective drove them ten blocks. There they abandoned that car and switched to another, which the agent used to get them to a nearby airport. A private plane whisked the duo across the state line to safety.

That desperate stage has been reached: a searching parent decides he or she needs investigative help. How does the father or mother find a retrieval expert and not a con man? Support groups, detectives, lawyers, custody experts, and victim parents have offered some guidelines on how to choose an investigator and what to expect once he is hired.

They claim that a family-law attorney can recommend a reputable detective. Many specialists in divorce work use one routinely in their practices. A family-law professor at a nearby law school may also give a referral. The teachers are up to date on domestic problems, and may be aware of an expert on child stealing in the area.

The local police department can also suggest an investigator, who will more than likely be a former police officer. Child-snatching support groups (see Appendix A) or men's rights groups can usually recommend a private eye, who will probably have a sound track record for returning children.

All experts queried agree that it is preferable to get more than one name, and then to interview detectives in person before settling on one. They say it is wise to ask the investigator for a reference from a former client with a similar case, although they will probably be told, "Sorry," since it is privileged information. Because of this confidentiality code, detectives have little accountability. Even so, there are ways to ensure they are aboveboard. For example, support groups urge prospective clients to ask an agent for the name of a lawyer for whom he has worked.

They also insist that a parent choose an investigator who is licensed by the state. If a licensed detective takes advantage of a mother or father, she or he can complain to the licensing board, a division of the state police. If there is cause to investigate, the state will probe the matter. (There is no recourse if an adult is unhappy with an unlicensed operative.) Not all states have a regulatory body, although most do. A few require that a person merely pay money (usually one thousand dollars) for a license, and waive the experience requirement demanded by stricter states. Experts advise parents to check with the state police to see if any complaints have been filed against the licensed hand. A dishonest detective may receive no formal complaints—parents may not know how to protest or simply not bother—while a successful sleuth may have several complaints on file because he has an abrasive manner. The ratings from local boards should not be the only reference check.

Those in the know tell mothers and fathers to find out how many similar cases the agent has handled. They say that someone who has not had any child-stealing experience should be passed over. But they also warn against private eyes who claim their expertise is child recoveries. These people should be scrutinized, since not too many operatives are snatching experts, but quite a few are cashing in on the abduction epidemic, bragging about as many as a thousand retrievals. Obviously, this is an inflated figure. While experts maintain that it is better to hire an investigator with experience in the field rather than someone with no track record, they stress that big talkers may be just that—big talkers.

Plush quarters may also impress a parent. Again, mothers and fathers must not be misled. The investigator may have bought his overstuffed sofa and Levolor blinds with cash earned from divorce surveillance or fender-bender assignments, not from child stealings. At the same time, a one-man, hole-in-the-wall office with fraying furniture may also indicate that the person behind the empty desk has had little luck in any kind of investigative matter. As a rule, say seasoned parents, it is wiser to choose an agent who has several associates, instead of someone who works alone.

Authorities urge parents to judge detectives partly on their toughness. Do they demand to see a client's custody papers to make sure he or she is the lawful guardian? (Unless neither side has custody—the client is still married or was never married or never bothered to file papers—the private eye is supposed to work only for the parent with custody.) Will the detective agree to confer with the parent's attorney about getaway plans? A by-the-book detective will be eager to comply, not wanting to risk arrest. Is the private eye planning to research the laws on child abduction in the state where the child is hidden to make sure the detective and the client can't be slapped with kidnaping charges? To find out if the noncustodial parent has obtained a court order in his new state? If the case is international, is the private eye going to look up the laws in the country of refuge?

One responsible detective turned down a lucrative offer to steal back a child after doing some homework. His client-to-be was German. Her absconding ex-husband was Mexican. Both the mother and father lived in Italy, but the father had grabbed their son and packed him off to live with relatives in Mexico. "When we looked at the law," says the British detective, "we realized we couldn't take the case because our client and her child would be at risk. The mother had been living with another man in Italy, and under Mexican law, an adulterous wife cannot be granted custody. Written into their law is also the rule that any man who finds his wife having an extramarital affair is entitled to kill her and her lover, and never be charged with murder. So if this woman went to Mexico, her husband could kill her."

How detectives handle money indicates whether they are on the up-and-up, report the experts. If they seem vague when a parent brings up finances, authorities warn parents to beware.

Detectives may not be able to compute the costs without doing more research, though. It is reasonable for them to request more money to investigate so they can come up with an estimated tab.

To keep a ceiling on the bill and control other conditions of the agreement, parents should only use an agent who works with a written contract. This document sets down the specifics: how long the assignment will take; when fees are to be paid; what happens if the client wants to bow out, or the detective and the client have a disagreement. An investigator who is legally compelled to carry out the terms of a contract is less likely to take advantage of a parent, claim detectives themselves.

They also suggest that these agreements include a time factor. This means that the detective must recover the child within a designated period (usually thirty days to one year). After that, the contract is renewable. If the detective does not deliver the child and the client does not choose to extend the contract, the client may dissolve the agreement without having to pay the full fee. For example, the document might state that a mother must spend two thousand dollars to have her child located within six months. She would be obligated to furnish one thousand dollars in advance. Should the detective fail to find the child within six months, and the mother wanted to stop searching, she would be required to pay the investigator the extra thousand. In an ideal contract, clients pay expenses and part of the fee in advance, and owe the balance upon completion of the case.

Richard Stenzel, president of Allied Systems Investigators of Santa Ana, California, offers the only money-back guarantee contract of its kind in the country. He promises to retrieve a child, and if he can't, he will return a client's money in full— expenses included. Stenzel never even sees the money until he recovers the child because it is put in escrow by the client's attorney or bank. Allied works on a time clause, which can be extended by mutual agreement. If a client opts not to renew, he has not lost a cent. Still, it is expensive; Stenzel charges $17,500 for the average child-stealing case.

Experts believe it is important to incorporate a reporting clause into an agreement. This would require that an agent submit full reports of his progress to the client at frequent intervals (at least once a month). Otherwise, the operative could stop searching for several months at a stretch, while the meter ticked on.

Another point to be covered in the contract, say authorities, is what happens if the client and detective have a falling-out. As a precaution, they suggest that parents add that a mutually acceptable arbitrator (whose decision is binding) can settle disputes. A client should always keep the detective's fees in escrow through an attorney. In the contract, mothers and fathers should include a clause stating that they have the option of calling off the recovery up to the time the kidnaping is carried out—without being penalized and having to pay full price. Once a detective attempts an abduction, regardless of the outcome, parents must dole out the total tab.

Victim parents report that the most crucial question adults must ask an investigator is about his snatching style. Does he grab the kids himself, or make the parent do the actual abducting? Adults should stay away from investigators who kidnap without the parent's being present, contend experts, since these agents are proposing a flagrantly illegal move, and may bend the rules in other areas as well. Without the client around to watch, a detective may not be too concerned about the tactics he uses—or the feelings of the children being recovered.

Drilling operatives about their plans is essential. Parents must find out if they will be face-to-face with their ex-mates during the retrieval, or if the agent insists on restealing when the abductor is out of sight. Skirmishes can be avoided if parents don't have a chance to confront each other, say mothers and fathers who have taken part in a snatch-back.

Here are opposing viewpoints by two equally accomplished professionals:

Mr. R: I never have a situation where a child is faced with both parents at the same time. That way you are putting the child on the spot and he or she will feel torn between the two.

Mr. L: I am not looking for the best time for the child. I am looking out for the interests of my client. I frequently grab a child when both the custodial and the noncustodial parent are together.

Not all adults would be thrilled with the all-business approach of Mr. L., and would prefer to hire Mr. R. But mothers and fathers must ask still more questions before choosing the right representative, such as how many days it will take the detective to recover the child *after* the boy or girl has been located. Some investigators steal on the spot; others stake out a site for one day to one week. A detective who claims he can do the job in two hours should probably be passed over, advise experts, as should one who says he needs at least one month. The longer the planning period, the more the retrieval will cost. But counselors say that it may make sense to wait to learn the snatcher's pattern rather than be precipitous and risk bungling the abduction because of poor preparation.

Usually investigators who handle these cases spend about four days or so setting up the recovery and another two to three days to execute it. Stage one entails sending one to two detectives to the hideout to figure out the child's schedule (and, of course, the abductor's), to learn the best time to resteal. Often agents arrive on a weekend and then take two or three weekdays casing the youngster's home and school.

They prepare for the getaway phase, too, plotting tricks to foil a parent who tries to pursue the child after the kidnaping.

Investigators might make phony airplane reservations in the client's name, for instance. A pursuing parent who calls the airlines and finds a reservation in the ex-husband's or wife's and child's name will assume they have been found, and charge to the airport to reclaim the child. Of course, the agent would have arranged for the client and child to have escaped earlier by train, or have put them on a different flight to a different city. Sometimes detectives will reserve tickets for their clients on several flights to several places simultaneously. Should the noncustodial father or mother phone the airlines, he or she will be confused, not knowing which time or which town is the real one.

Before a recovery, investigators also frequently put down a deposit on a room at a motel (under a fake name this time) in case the lawful guardian and child need to lie low for a while. Planners often rent a couple of cars for the kidnaping. One is for speeding away from the site. A few blocks away is another automobile, the "switch car," into which the detective, client, and child transfer to continue their trip. Some private eyes plant yet another vehicle, called a crash car, at the scene of the abduction. Usually placed in the middle of the street, it blocks a parent or bystander who tries to recapture the child.

Occasionally parents forsake safety for results. They want their children back, no matter what—or how. Detectives and attorneys may have been a dead-end route. Out of desperation, some parents desert the traditional avenues of help and turn to custody vigilantes, unlicensed kidnapers for hire. "Antichildsnatching specialists," "vigilante recovery teams," "civil rights workers," they call themselves. These self-appointed sellers of justice often charge less than private investigators. For two hundred to two thousand dollars they will work for either the custodial or the noncustodial parent, although most of their clients are noncustodial fathers. Some steal kids for the money, but most do it because they believe that custody arrangements are unjust and want to rectify them.

Vigilantes seem more committed to violence than to straightening out the system. It is not their problem if the client's former spouse or even the child gets roughed up during the abduction. Frequently inexperienced thugs, sometimes losers at custody themselves, conduct these kidnapings. Parents who hire these hit men have little recourse if they are displeased with their services. Vigilantes can be found through a few of the more strident men's rights groups or through word-of-mouth.

One of the most notorious vigilantes is a man let's call "Bad Bill." In his eighteen-year child-stealing career, he claims to have carried off five hundred successful recoveries. Outraged by the custody system, he has made kids his cause. Full-time he roves the country, recapturing children with the help of helicopters, boats, and cars. His wife remains in the Midwest, while "Bad Bill" beds down at his clients' homes. While he claims to work only for the custodial parent, he cannot claim a clean record. The publicity hound spent several months in jail for assault when a district attorney charged him with child torture and aggravated assault and battery. "Bad Bill" was arrested after he had telephoned the news stations to brag about his latest scuffle. He was convicted on one count of battery.

He can't go home, since he is wanted for questioning back in his state on an abduction case. "Bad Bill" enjoys being so indispensable that his family does not even have a telephone. When he speaks with his wife every Thursday at seven P.M., she must run over to a neighbor's to take the call. Why no phone? "I have too many enemies," he pronounces with pride, not fear. "I have been head to head with the Mafia four times, and the CIA rightists twice."

"Bad Bill" considers himself the meanest and the best super-sleuth around. He takes the "dirty" cases everyone else gives up on, he likes to tell anyone who will listen. A juicy newsletter he writes regularly smears his competition and lauds his own tactics. In one edition, "Bad Bill" revealed one of his escape plans: he attaches tacks to a piece of string and places them under the back bumper of a car wheel. If an irate parent tries to follow him after he has stolen a child, the abductor simply pulls the string and blows out Mom's or Dad's tires. The vigilante kingpin's style is best stated in "Child Snatching, Search and Recovery Techniques," a mimeographed volume he wrote. His advice to others who want to kidnap children? "Use violence if necessary, because you are going to be accused of it anyway."

And to hell with the children—a cautionary tale, indeed.

· 12 ·

How to Prevent a Snatch

U N L E S S A C H I L D is placed under twenty-four hour guard, he or she is game for any snatcher. Yet even this impractical approach won't necessarily deter a determined thief. With round-the-clock security, a crafty kidnaper can still strike. Nevertheless, a watchful mother or father may be able to head off a snatch if savvy to the ways of child abductors—their pouncing patterns (the most common times, locations, and ruses) and warning signs (suspicious behavior that will tip off a custodial parent). Ways exist to prevent an abduction, which have been gleaned from attorneys, criminologists, sociologists, psychologists, and parental victims.

"It will never happen to me," most grownups swear. Yet every year between twenty-five and one hundred thousand parents are robbed of their young. Many of these men and women are two-time losers. In fact, the chances of a second kidnaping are high, say experts.

All children are potential targets: products of separated or divorcing parents; of amicable or bitter partings; of couples still married but contemplating a breakup; even of unmarried mates. Offspring born of international unions are especially easy prey; a disgruntled partner can successfully hide out in her or his home country.

Parents must not be tricked. A father may *seem* disinterested in his children—he may skip visitations and not contest custody—but that does not mean he won't abduct. Numerous child stealers have appeared on the scene after several years' absence. Conscientious visitors are equally suspect. A noncustodial parent may comply with court schedules for a while, picking up and returning the child punctually. It may be a setup, though. After gaining the lawful guardian's trust, the parent may slip away with the child during a routine weekend visit.

Anytime is prime time for an abduction. But parents must be particularly vigilant if there is no custody decree—at the beginning of a separation or divorce before papers are served, or between the serving of papers and the securing of temporary custody. This is a period when adults frequently spar and look for ways to punish a partner for a failed relationship. Should a kidnaper flee, adults are out of luck; without a custody order, they have no legal recourse.

Common belief holds that snatchers attack immediately after they lose in court. Often they do. But according to a study conducted by criminologist Michael Agopian of ninety-one child stealers screened for prosecution by the Los Angeles County District Attorney's Office, the most popular time for thefts is two years or more after a custody determination or divorce.

To stave off an attempt, parents should study the preferred operating patterns of "successful" snatchers. What are abductors' favorite stalking grounds and seasons? Do they nab more at dusk or at dawn? Do they work alone? Like all generalities, these observations apply only to the majority of perpetrators.

Most kidnapings do not involve fist fights or force, high-speed chases or stakeouts. While shopping centers, schools, and backyards are fashionable locations for grabs, more typically children disappear during court-sanctioned visitation periods. Weekends are extremely attractive to childsnatchers, because they give them an extra couple of days to escape without arousing the suspicion of school officials or former mates. Youngsters, too, may be easily deceived, assuming they are only off for a minivacation and will be back in their beds Sunday night. Holidays are tempting for the same reasons, particularly summer vacations.

. Michael Agopian's California study confirms these findings on peak places and periods for stealing. His work also reveals other fascinating insights into offenders. It is essential to note, however, that Agopian surveyed only a small sample of abductors, and that his conclusions do not necessarily reflect the behavior of most kidnapers, although in some cases they may. This is what Agopian, Director of the Child-Stealing Research Center in Los Angeles, discovered: stolen boys and girls were mostly eleven years of age or younger, while the three- to five-year-olds were taken most often. The mean age of offenders was thirty-four, and of victim parents, thirty-three. Fathers stole twice as frequently as mothers. Most thefts took place at the victim's home. The second most common setting was the child's school, while the fewest kidnapings occurred outdoors. These statistics substantiate the theory that snatchers duck out with their kids under the guise of court-appointed visitations. It follows, then, that Fridays were especially dangerous, and that Saturdays and Sundays also proved popular. Midweek days, like Tuesdays and Thursdays, registered only a few abductions. Each season received a relatively equal amount of violations, although fall and summer were somewhat more busy for child stealers. The increase may be attributed to summer visitations, which the kidnapers decided, on their own, to prolong. Most perilous hours were late afternoon and early evening, with 2:00 P.M. to 7:59 P.M. fetching the most victims, and 2:00 A.M. to 7:59 A.M. accounting for the least. Most crimes were accomplished by a lone abductor, but in the few instances where kidnapers had company, often the extras were relatives or siblings of the child.

Of course, not all snatchers will make their move precisely at 7:59 P.M. on a Friday in the fall. But being attuned to potentially vulnerable times can help an alert parent thwart a would-be abductor. So, too, will recognizing warning signs and precarious situations. Kidnapers rarely announce their plans to steal—although some do, and must be taken seriously. Still, certain types are more prone to being candidates, and certain circumstances may make an abduction more likely. Obviously parents who fit these profiles and conditions won't necessarily flee; but then again, these signs may be significant.

What to look for: several child-stealing support groups have noted that men who beat their wives are often abductors. So, too, are adults with criminal records. In fact, the organization Child Find discovered that more than 60 percent of their registered parents' kidnaping spouses had been arrested for prior crimes. Also, parents should take heed if a youngster in the family dies or is seriously ill. The remaining or healthy sibling has a chance of being stolen, since the kidnaper may blame the custodial parent for the child's death or disease, and think the surviving brother or sister must be rescued.

Parents who suddenly make more requests to see the children should be watched. Often abductors ask for more visitation time before they steal their offspring. They may be blatantly uninterested in getting together with the little ones, either while they are living under the same roof or after the divorce. Perhaps they stand up their kids, are late when they do come around, or are leisurely about returning them. Parents may ask themselves, "What makes the child so attractive to visit now? Is it really him or her my former husband or wife wants, or is it revenge?"

Grownups must be particularly vigilant if the noncustodial parent's pattern changes or if she loses touch, only to resurface and make more demands for the child. Her absence may mean she was away scouting hideouts for the two of them. New circumstances for her could indicate trouble, too—a new job, a new mate, a new home, or a new hometown. Lawful guardians must be extra wary when their own situations change—when they remarry, or have more kids by a different partner, or make plans to move away. Either jealousy (of a new man or woman on the scene) or fear (of not having access to their young) may spur an angry, frustrated mother or father into action. If a former spouse begs for a reconciliation and is met with unrequited love, he may use the kids as bargaining pawns to try and force a reunion. "I didn't see the signs," groans a Baltimore woman whose ex-husband stowed away their daughter for five years. "John was furious with me because he thought I had left him. He pleaded with me to remarry him, but I told him to forget it."

Usually parents steal when they feel slighted, replaced, or rebuffed. The trick is not to antagonize or alienate a former spouse. "Don't give anyone a reason to abduct," suggests Dr. Jeannette Minkoff. "Let the noncustodial parent have access to the kids. If the child is sick, I would encourage the custodial parent to invite the visiting adult into the house to see the child, rather than have that person think that maybe the youngster is not sick at all. If Daddy comes to visit and he doesn't have the fifty dollars for child support, don't say, 'You can't see the kids if you don't have the money.' Don't drag the children into it. Go to court the next day to get that money, but don't withhold the kids."

Still, being conciliatory and sensitive does not always work. The parent should take precautions to discourage kidnaping. In the event it does occur, he or she will be prepared with detailed information for authorities, and enough leverage with in-laws to make them squirm, and perhaps squeal. Proper documents and "dope" will guarantee cooperation; cooperation may speed the retrieval.

Even if adults have just separated, they should get custody immediately. A temporary or permanent order will give police the authority to track a spouse. No decree may mean no investigation. To further protect a parent, an attorney should be asked to include in the temporary custody order a provision prohibiting either party from taking the child out of state until custody is formally resolved. Permanent papers, too, can restrict travel with the youngster. The document may require that a parent wishing to leave the area obtain written consent from the other parent, or make a prior agreement with the court of jurisdiction. In this way, a parent could also prevent issuance of a passport for a child. (Adults who fear their kids may be hidden abroad should consult Chapter 7 for tips on how to limit foreign travel.)

The custody agreement should also include a clause restricting the exes from having access to their youngsters' school records. The Family Educational Rights and Privacy Act (FERPA) allows both noncustodial and custodial parents to obtain copies of their children's written records and have them sent to other schools—unless there is a provision in the custody order forbidding an ex-mate from having access to these transcripts without the other parent's consent. That parent must give the original school a copy of the custody order with this clause. If the former spouse tries unilaterally to obtain the child's transcripts, or asks to have them forwarded to a new school, the request will be denied. This policy can help in narrowing the hunt if an ex-spouse steals the kids and asks for the records from a hideout. The searching side will be able to learn where the request originated.

Some mothers and fathers find the "hit-'em-where-it-hurts"

monetary approach effective, and try to incorporate these clauses into custody agreements with the consent of the other party, or by judicial decree. Making an ex-spouse post bond every time he or she takes the children for a visit is one way to discourage stealing. Should the ex fail to return them, he or she must forfeit cash or valuable property (such as a home or his business). Bonds must be big enough both to deter a would-be abductor and to pay the expenses of the parent victim—for attorneys, detectives, and travel. If a parent is too poor to post bond, perhaps relatives could. Having their money tied up and conceivably lost would further ensure that they would not aid the abductor. Rather, they probably would do everything they could to dissuade him or her from skipping town.

Other forms of protection resembling bonds are security accounts kept in escrow and liquidated damages. In the first case, an independent escrow officer can hold a specified sum of money, provided by the potential snatcher, in a special account. If that parent returns the child, those funds will not be spent. However, once the ex-spouse violates the visitation agreement and kidnaps the kids, that money is paid over by the escrow agent to the mate who is left behind. Liquidated damages work on a similar principle. One parent is liable to the other for certain sums of cash if she or he neglects to bring back the offspring. Assessing damages on a cumulative basis— money due for every day of the violation—makes this method even more powerful. Combining the escrow procedure with the provision for liquidated damages in the settlement agreement saves investigating parents the time, expense, and trouble of having to find the abducting mates and sue them for damages.

Convinced an ex-partner will flee with their child, some frightened parents request a writ of habeas corpus—an order of the court requiring the party to appear before the judge—and explain his plans for the child. The judge may revoke visitation privileges. If a noncustodial parent takes the lawful guardian to court, the judge can set rigid restrictions to help prevent the custodial parent from kidnaping, too. Since the judge will demand proof of plans, a parent should jot down the times and places an ex-husband or wife forgot to visit, or returned the kids late, or refused to turn them over for the weekend or holiday.

Fair and precise custody and visitation agreements may just be the best insurance against child theft. It is essential that the noncustodial parent not feel deprived. Also, being vague can be costly. "Reasonable visitation" clauses may frustrate both sides: the custodial parent might deny visitation, or the noncustodian might refuse to return the children when the weekend is over. These actions could be legal, simply because parents neglected to spell out the specifics in the custody agreement. To avoid acrimony and a possible abduction by a miffed party, parents must incorporate into their papers the days, weeks, months, and holidays owed the visiting parent. Not only will it clarify each side's rights, but should the noncustodial parent spirit away the child, this document will prove that the kidnaper violated, and was unreasonable about, "reasonable visitation."

Adults pleased with custody arrangements rarely steal. That is why joint custody—where both parents have an equal say in their youngster's welfare and upbringing—should be considered. It might be uncomfortable to keep in close contact with a just lost lover, and the logistics of switching from one parent to the other may be inconvenient, but it is worth staying on the good side of an unpredictable mate.

As important as a mutually satisfactory piece of paper is peace of mind. After a separation or divorce, it is ideal to get the family into therapy to work through anger, sadness, aggression, resentment, and guilt. This route is often impossible, though. A family member may balk at exposing his or her feelings, or fees may be prohibitive for a household suddenly faced with two dwellings and two sets of dishes.

Even a parent who assumes a former spouse is coping and will not bolt would be wise to prepare for the worst. One childsnatching group suggests school-age kids have a clear photograph taken of them annually, while shots of preschoolers should be snapped four times a year. Occasionally, newspapers, magazines, and television programs offer to run a picture of the child; they cannot help much, however, if the photograph is hazy or out of date.

While it may be opportunistic, lawful guardians should stay chummy with ex-in-laws. If there was no feeling for them before, or bad feeling, it might seem hypocritical to call or write. But if parents ingratiate themselves, former in-laws are less likely to dismiss them if they ask for help after an abduction. Letters and telephone calls also provide a way of keeping tabs on an ex-mother- or father-in-law. The kidnaper's parents may just be the key to the case, too, since thieves frequently dash home to their own parents for funds and support.

In-laws aren't the only ones who need to be trailed. The kids themselves must check in continually with a worried grownup. If more than one child is at risk, and a kidnaping appears imminent, a parent should try to separate the siblings outside the house. This tactic will discourage an abductor bent on running off with the brood. When visiting parents come to claim their offspring for a weekend or a holiday, the other adult must insist upon a detailed itinerary, if not of events, then of telephone numbers and addresses where the youngsters will be staying.

Parents should make older kids memorize their area codes, telephone numbers, and addresses. They must also be drilled on escape plans should they be abducted. Telling children they may be stolen can traumatize them needlessly if they end up not being taken. Yet staying quiet to protect them may be disastrous. Maintains Dr. Daniel O'Leary: "You have to weigh the advantages and disadvantages of alerting a youngster, but the disadvantage—being kidnaped—is far worse. I have seen instances in which an abduction has been avoided by children's being wary of situations—kids being told that under no circumstances should they walk more than one house away or leave the eyeshot of an aide on a school playground. These warnings are realistic, because you hear that, in fact, that parent has been lurking around the house or the classroom trying to snatch the child."

Admonishing adults to be on the lookout is sensible, too. School authorities can watch for unexpected visits from the non-custodial parent, and so can baby-sitters, ballet teachers, camp counselors, and day-care instructors. Keeping a copy of the custody order with these grownups can refute a smooth-talking ex-spouse's claims that he or she is entitled to the child. It is prudent, as well, to leave another copy with the local police, along with the visitation schedule. If a former husband or wife absconds with the child, law-enforcement officials will, with documents in hand, be able to respond quickly (should they choose). They will also want extensive information on a former mate. Even before the spouse departs, a parent should play amateur FBI agent, compiling data on an ex-partner. Being thorough will impress police. According to one Baton Rouge, Louisiana, mother, her detailed presentation won support from initially indifferent officers. "They say, 'Just the facts, ma'am,' " states Janice, a dental hygienist, "and are turned off by hysterical parents who fall apart when they file a report." A list will also help mothers and fathers who decide to sleuth themselves. Instead of wasting time learning where a former mate banks and works, they are able to start scouting immediately.

This list should include: a spouse's date of birth and Social Security number; driver's license, bank account, and credit-card numbers; information on passport and insurance policies; addresses and telephone numbers of past employers, bill collectors (if there are any debts), relatives, friends, lovers, and families; military status; magazine and newspaper subscriptions; property interests; and shops frequented.

Parents should also include the kids' birth dates, current photographs, school records, teachers' and playmates' names and numbers, and medical information. A child with a medical condition may be easier to track than a healthy adult.

Precautions may be sophisticated or simple, straightforward or surreptitious. Still, a resolute mother or father will grab anyway. The mate of one such willful woman imparts this poignant advice to divorcing parents: "Oftentimes when kids are stolen, they are told that Daddy or Mommy does not love them anymore. So tell the child that you love him or her and always will. No matter what happens."

· 13 ·

What to Do If . . .

S T O P   W E E P I N G and start working. Bringing back the children is the absent parent's responsibility. It may be unfair that the victim has to organize the search party and oversee their return, but chances are, the kids won't call home and a thieving ex-spouse won't hand them over voluntarily. Without your efforts, they may stay hidden forever.

There are two strategies for snaring a snatcher and child. One plan is designed to find the fugitive and youngster, the other to haul them home. For either situation, hiring an attorney and contacting police is the first task. A parent must have a custody decree before law-enforcement officials will consider the case. While a permanent order is preferable, a temporary one should provide enough proof that the abductor has no legal right to the child. Parents who have not yet filed for custody should sprint to a lawyer's to obtain a decree. Police will not help if the feuding couple are still married, though, because until there is a custody award, no crime has been committed. Both parents have an equal right to their children, until a court orders otherwise.

It is also doubtful whether law-enforcement officials will intervene when an unmarried mother or father absconds with the child, unless one party has previously received an order from the court appointing that person the legal guardian. If a parent suspects the youngster may have been whisked out of the country, consult Chapter 7—but not before reporting the incident to the local police. They have access to resources unavailable to the average parent—from telephone taps to mail covers to bank records—and don't cost a dime, either. Detectives may snoop secretly, too, but their thousand-dollar-plus tabs are more than most people can afford.

Local police are notorious for refusing assistance when they hear the words "parental kidnaping," but a sympathetic cop may agree to investigate. Since it is often a matter of luck and the attitude of the officer on duty whether or not one agency takes the case, it would be wise to contact all law-enforcement groups. Sheriffs and state troopers, for example, may have broader jurisdiction than a local policeman. Missing persons bureaus, which eagerly get cracking on stranger kidnapings, have a reputation for steering clear of parental abductions. Yet the clerk behind the desk has been known to make an exception and use the bureau's network of contacts to locate the child. Still, the bureau usually will insist that the youngster be missing for a certain length of time—at least twenty-four hours —before it will act.

Under the Missing Children Act, however, signed into law October 12, 1982, local police are required to enter the names of all missing children into the FBI's central computer, to which police agencies across the country have access. What is more, the bill eliminates the twenty-four-hour waiting period most agencies require before getting involved. The federal legislation also establishes a nationwide computer clearing-house to help identify the bodies of missing children. If the local police refuse to contact the FBI, the searching parent may call his or her local FBI office directly and ask them to enter the material into the data bank.

Still, how a parent presents the case—and herself or himself —may determine police response. A mother or father who wails uncontrollably and forgets the specifics may be branded a scatterbrained hysteric and ushered out the door. On the other hand, a calm, informed adult might just impress a skeptical and busy officer. To this crucial meeting, adults should bring in-depth information on the former spouse and missing children, as detailed in Chapter 12. This information should also include the date of the divorce or separation; the date and place custody was granted; a copy of the custody agreement; and the time and place from which the children were taken. Current photographs of the ex-spouse and the child should also be a part of the dossier.

Mothers and fathers must bone up on the laws. A lawyer will tell his or her client how the state regards parental kidnaping. Is it a misdemeanor or a felony, or isn't it considered a crime? In some states, it is a misdemeanor if the snatcher stays within the state and a felony once the abductor crosses the state line. Can a parent prove the ex-spouse has fled the state? Sometimes an officer will upgrade a misdemeanor to a felony if the child's life is at risk. Does the thief have a prior history of emotional disturbance or child abuse? Police may think these accusations are exaggerated, the tall tales of an overwrought parent. But if the parent brings along a neighbor or a landlord to attest to a former mate's violent tendencies, the men in blue are more likely to listen.

Grownups should shoot for a criminal arrest warrant for their ex-partners. Although police may still make a parent find the abductor, at least they will arrest kidnaper and put him or her behind bars until bail is posted. The prisoner may consider taking off before the trial or extradition hearing, but may decide against it if it means forfeiting the bond money. Preventing the snatcher from fleeing again while the other parent pursues legal remedies is essential. Abductors who do run before their day in court may be sought by police on a new charge of jumping bail, an offense that many cops take more seriously than domestic kidnaping. If a private bondsman has supplied the bail money, he may join in the search for the fugitive to protect his investment. Bondsmen are notoriously relentless in tracking down clients who have skipped town, and may be an invaluable ally in the hunt for the children.

The best warrant to obtain is a state felony warrant in the kidnaper's name with a guarantee of extradition. Only states that regard this act as a felony offer a felony warrant. When child stealing is listed as a misdemeanor, parents should request a misdemeanor warrant, and hope the snatcher has stowed the child away *within* the state. A misdemeanor warrant is only binding intrastate.

Felony arrest warrants, on the other hand, are valid in other states. Once they are issued, local authorities can place information on the kidnaper in the FBI's National Crime Information Center (NCIC). If police in another state stop the fugitive (say, for a minor traffic violation) and run an NCIC computer check, that parent can be arrested and held for extradition.

The new Parental Kidnapping Prevention Act of 1980, discussed in Chapter 6, authorizes FBI assistance in certain cases. Parents should scrutinize—even memorize—this law, and mention it to the police. They may not know that it exists, or that they may have the right to request government help. Getting the FBI to search is important, since its nationwide resources are much more extensive and sophisticated than those of any state or local agency.

The PKPA states that the Fugitive Felon Act, designed to permit federal authorities to locate and apprehend fugitives from state justice, applies to parental abductions when the kidnaper has fled the state or country to avoid prosecution, provided the state from which he or she has run makes the crime a felony. The state or local prosecutor must apply to the nearest U.S. Attorney for an "unlawful flight to avoid prosecution" (UFAP) warrant. After the U.S. Attorney issues the warrant, the FBI may step in.

Even if a parent convinces a state or local policeman to ask a U.S. Attorney for a UFAP warrant, this valuable piece of paper is difficult to obtain. The parent must prove the former mate has fled the state for the purpose of avoiding prosecution. If the snatcher's whereabouts are unknown, as is usually the case, this hurdle may be insuperable. The Justice Department has a policy that it will not authorize the UFAP warrant unless there is independent information—such as prior domestic complaints—proving that the child's life is in danger, or that the child is being neglected or abused. Without the warrant, the FBI may not get involved. The Justice Department will not grant a warrant when an abductor's whereabouts are known. Instead, the home state must ask the harboring state to extradite the criminal, and to hold him or her until the extradition proceeding is completed. Even if a federal warrant is issued, the FBI may still refuse to act, or may give the case the "back burner" treatment. This is because of the prevailing attitude of lawmen that child stealing is a family, rather than a police, matter.

Should the FBI intervene and find the fugitive, the person is handed over to local officers in the refuge state to await extradition. The federal warrant is then dropped, and if the asylum state agrees to extradite, the snatcher is sent home to face court action.

The PKPA offers another way to locate the kids—in theory at least. It allows states access to the Department of Health and Human Services' Federal Parent Locator Service (FPLS). Previously, the FPLS could only be used to track fathers who defaulted on child-support payments. Now, however, it is also available when a state or federal criminal law violation, such as parental kidnaping or custodial interference, is being investigated or prosecuted. This nationwide computer service stores data on abductors, from their military files to their IRS forms. The data bank is of limited usefulness, however, because its records are six to eighteen months behind. If the subject skips around a lot, the computer won't have the up-to-date information on the snatcher. It also can't help if the kidnaper is working off the books or assumes a phony name, since the FPLS is a system that relies primarily on tax returns and Social Security numbers.

In order to use the central computer, each state must have entered into an agreement with the Secretary of Health and Human Services. The state child-support enforcement office can tell a parent if it has such an agreement. If it does, moms and dads must find an authorized person to plug the information into the computer, since neither a petitioning parent nor his or her attorney has direct access. The chosen few who do are agents or attorneys of states that have agreements to use the FPLS, and U.S. agents or U.S. attorneys who have the authority to act in parental kidnaping and child-restraint cases.

Parents or their lawyers can also petition a court to have the FPLS locate the fugitive and child. Or they can file a request with police and have them submit it to the district attorney, who will forward it first to the state parent-locator service and then to the government computer. A parent must pay ten to fifteen dollars for a location request. Sometimes a federal agent or federal lawyer will agree to add a missing parent's name into the FPLS. A parent should contact the U.S. Attorney's office or the FBI to find out how to apply.

Each state child-support enforcement agency has a parent-locator service that can search within the state. State parent-locator services can ask other state locator services to help find the suspect. Parents follow the same procedure they use for hooking into the FPLS to access the state computer system.

If either service does turn up the offender, it will provide the person's most recent address and place of employment. But it does not have the authority to arrest the alleged criminal. Parents must then go through the courts to retrieve their children. Some parents simply steal them back. While parents may be disappointed that the parent-locator service cannot apprehend the snatcher, its potential ability to locate is useful. Usually finding the thief is the hardest part.

So is finding a good lawyer, who can make the difference between recovering the kids and never seeing them again. The most effective attorneys are well connected and may be able to pull strings. They may be able to obtain a warrant for the abductor, because they know the mayor, chief of police, or governor. A lawyer with less clout might get turned away at the door. It is not enough to hire high-powered counsel. He or she should also have experience in child-stealing cases, or at the very least, in family law.

Parents can call the local chapter of the American Bar Association, which provides lists of ABA attorneys and their credentials. Prospective clients should always stick with family-law specialists. Mothers and fathers could also ask the dean of a nearby law school or a domestic-relations professor to recommend a lawyer. Sometimes an attorney suggests that the parent engage a private detective; an experienced lawyer can recommend a reliable detective. This is an expensive and risky route. Most child-stealing authorities contend investigators should be hired only as a last resort—if police won't help, and if the mom or dad has no leads or thinks a former spouse has changed his or her name and the child's.

Lawyers will advise left-behind parents on their legal options. They may either try to obtain a criminal complaint or file a civil suit against their former spouses for violating a custody or visitation decree. The criminal course entails filing charges against the kidnaper—the crime is usually a misdemeanor or a felony, depending upon the law of the state in which the abduction

218

occurred. Then the searching parent must get an arrest warrant, and have the police hunt and apprehend the suspect.

The civil route involves going to court and obtaining a contempt-of-court citation against the snatcher. Any parent who violates the provisions of a custody order can be slapped with this charge. As a penalty for contempt, a kidnaper can either be jailed or fined. A contempt-of-court citation is only binding within the court's jurisdiction, and therefore is somewhat ineffective, since many childsnatchers leave the state, and there is no guarantee the citation will be honored by other judges elsewhere. But this document may just convince a judge in the asylum state to enforce the original decree—or at least not to exercise jurisdiction and start a new custody contest there.

Victim parents should pursue both the civil and the criminal paths simultaneously: procure an arrest warrant *and* request a contempt-of-court citation. The offender may be absolved of criminal charges—custodial interference or parental kidnaping—but can still be held for contempt.

With the help of a lawyer, parents can put pressure on the kidnaper's family and friends in an attempt to make them divulge the child's location. An attorney can subpoena relatives or acquaintances of the abducting parent and force them to reveal what they know about the snatcher's whereabouts. If they refuse to answer, a court can order them to talk. Those who still refuse to cooperate can be held in contempt of court and fined and/or jailed until they do. They may be intimidated enough by the legal assault to tell what they know.

Another possibility: parents can sue their ex-in-laws—or others believed to have helped carry off the crime—for false imprisonment, infliction of emotional distress, unlawful enticement, or other similar torts available under state law. Parents who want to bring these kinds of actions must have some belief that the friend or relative has either aided and abetted or conspired with the kidnaper. Plaintiffs should sue for the amount it will cost to retrieve the kids, from detectives' and lawyers' fees to plane fare and hotel tabs. A left-behind adult may be able to recover even more for the emotional toll the abduction has taken. Even if the plaintiff does not collect any money, a lawsuit may cause a conspirator to reveal the whereabouts of the child, rather than face the annoyance and expense of defending a legal proceeding. The Uniform Child Custody Jurisdiction Act (see Chapter 6) also stipulates that a parent can sue a thieving ex-mate for expenses incurred during the search. Under the act, mothers and fathers must first retrieve their children before initiating this action.

An adult can always sue former in-laws or the ex-spouse's associates, since their whereabouts are usually known. But since a summons and complaint must be served on a defendant in order to initiate a lawsuit, an ex-husband or wife can't be sued if the victim parent does not know where he or she is. An adult may try and lure the snatcher home by attaching property (real estate holdings, such as the house, if it is in the kidnaper's name) or a bank account in the jurisdiction from which the ex-spouse fled. With this attachment in place, the searching parent may obtain a judgment against the ex up to and including the value of the property.* Seeing these assets given away may make him or her hightail it home. Once the abductor is back, he or she is subject to the jurisdiction of the courts of the home state, and can be held liable to the full extent of the assets.

These "hardball" tactics should only be considered if the kidnaper's family and friends remain hostile and uncooperative. Parents should give them a chance to reveal the hideout voluntarily. If these people continue to resist inquiries, they can always be forced to talk under oath.

Staying on the good side of the snatcher's family is crucial.

---

* This method of obtaining jurisdiction of an absent parent may not be available in all instances because of recent Supreme Court cases that call into question the constitutionality of this procedure.

It is unusual, but not unheard-of, for relatives to inform on their own flesh and blood. Sometimes grandparents believe their child is an unstable parent and, out of concern for the grandchild, may tell where the fugitive is hiding. Other relatives may talk because they simply don't approve of the kidnaping.

Parents should grill everyone who knows the abductor: siblings; neighbors; bowling buddies; business associates; boyfriends and girlfriends—*everyone*. A boss may reveal where he forwarded the last paycheck, or, if a new employer has requested a reference, he may say where it was sent. Present lovers might not cooperate now, but they may later if they have a tiff with the snatcher and want to hurt the person.

Mothers and fathers must never reveal where they have looked or plan to look. They must be as devious as their former spouses, assuming that everything they say will be repeated and reported. If their former in-laws or the kidnaper's friends give them quick or unprompted answers about where the children might be, searchers should think twice about their accuracy. They may have been rehearsed about what to say to throw the other parent off the track. Or the sources may not even know the full extent of the snatcher's scheme. It is possible that the abductor never leveled with them, and told them, for instance, that he or she was just going away on a short trip with the children. The source may know the location of this "vacation" spot and divulge it freely, not realizing the import of the disclosure.

Parents would be prudent to ask these people to ask the snatcher to phone or write. This tactic serves three purposes. It gets third parties involved and makes them feel obligated to help. If they relay the message, the absent parent may hear from the ex-spouse. Most important, the call the informant makes to the abductor may lead the victim to the child. It confirms that the person knows where the snatcher is hiding, and the custodial parent may be able to obtain the caller's phone records and trace the number to the kidnaper.

If the abductor calls and makes demands, a parent must pretend to comply. Say, for instance, it is the mother and she asks for a reconciliation in exchange for the kids. The father should tell her he would love to try again, even if the thought is abhorrent. It may just bring her back with the children, and then, if he wants, he can take her to court. If she writes, the postmark on the envelope may reveal her hiding place. One father inadvertently disclosed his Canadian retreat when he sent his stepson a birthday card. The man mailed the card in one envelope to his girlfriend in the United States and she re-mailed it in another to confuse the custodial parent. But when the child received the card, his mother noticed the name of the manufacturer on the back, and "made in Canada" written in both English and French. The woman phoned the manufacturer's headquarters in Toronto. The card had to have been purchased in one of three Canadian provinces—Nova Scotia, Quebec, or Ontario—because of the French, they told her. It turned out the fugitive had settled with his sons in Nova Scotia.

Mothers and fathers must decide how the kidnaper is likely to support the children, and search with economics in mind. If a father is a professional scuba diver, he may move near the ocean. Perhaps he has fled to Florida or California. House-wives who steal might get a job, but they might also run to relatives and live off them. Parents should know the addresses of these aunts and uncles, cousins and siblings. Abductors who don't work may be easier to find than those who are employed. They must get their money from someone. Amateur sleuths must discover who this sugar daddy is.

Some snatchers change professions to avoid detection. Assuming this may have occurred, parents should consider what a former mate might do to produce income. If a man always has been handy around the house, he might be a carpenter. If a woman had worked for an advertising agency, she might have landed a job with her client's company on the sales side. Even the most elusive thieves who change their names usually find jobs in the fields in which they were trained, or in related lines of work.

Generally, they stay in contact with their families. Watching them carefully is smart strategy, especially around holidays when the kidnaper is most likely to contact relatives. "Trashing" is one method victim parents (and detectives) use to determine if the snatching dad or mom is communicating with relatives or friends. This maneuver entails rifling through the garbage of a possible conspirator to see if there are letters or telephone messages from the abductor. Trashing is carried out the night before a garbage pickup, when the household is asleep. Parents call the local town dump to find out which day the garbage is collected. Usually raiders will remove the trash from the cans and drive to a secluded spot to sort out pertinent information. Then they repackage the garbage in identical bags and cart the debris back where it belongs. When the owner awakens, it will appear untouched.

Trashing is one way to keep tabs on sympathizers. Some parents prefer a more direct—and illegal—approach. They burglarize suspects' homes, scouring desk drawers for letters or telephone bills that might lead them to their former mates. Bolder parents hire professionals to do the dirty work for them —tapping telephones, or breaking into houses or mailboxes to swipe suspicious correspondence.

Since telephone bills are one of the best ways to track a fugitive, victim parents have been known to bribe telephone company employees to read them the long-distance numbers on the bill of a relative or friend of the snatcher, or to hire detectives to find an insider at Ma Bell.

Parents concoct ruses to obtain these records. One woman posed as three people—the kidnaper's first wife, his mother, and his sister. Every month she would call, pretending to be one of these three women, and ask to have long-distance charges on her bill verified. She procured a partial monthly record of their statements, which revealed a new out-of-state number on the sister's bill. These digits belonged to the childsnatcher.

More legitimate ways exist to obtain records. If a criminal investigation is pending, police or the district attorney may order the telephone company, or banks or credit card offices, to hand over the snatcher's records. If there is no criminal investigation but a civil suit has been filed against the abductor or the sympathizer, an attorney can subpoena a large variety of documents from any person who may have been in contact with the kidnaper. The problem with this procedure is that the snatcher might be tipped off by the person whose records have been subpoenaed, and run once he realizes he has been spotted. Depending upon local law, however, a victim parent may be able to gain access to these records without the knowledge of the subpoenaed party. Then the kidnaper would have no idea he had been located.

Parents must figure out what final business the fugitive conducted before leaving town. How? By deciding whom *they* would notify if they planned to vanish. They might close a bank account, or ask the post office to forward mail, or advise credit card companies, insurance brokers, or magazine distributors of their new location. Searching adults should assume their ex-partners did some or all of these things and ask the abductor's bank if he or she closed an account or changed to a new branch. If the answer is no, they may be able to find out if the person has written any checks since the kidnaping and from where. A kidnaper might be sending in the mortgage payments on the house so his or her credit record will be clean. In that case, a custodial parent could learn the return address. Banks are more likely to help if parents maintained a joint account. Yet this rarely happens, unless a couple is still married; separated or divorced parents would not share the same checkbook. Banks that refuse to cooperate voluntarily can be forced to divulge their records to police or a plaintiff in a civil action in response to a subpoena.

It may be expensive, but is often expedient for victim parents to leave their joint accounts open, in the hope that the snatcher will draw on them. Returned checks may indicate where she has settled, or at least the route she is following. The same is true with charge cards. Credit card companies may help, and can be forced to do so with subpoenas. Again, they will probably be more receptive if there are two names on the account. Perhaps the bank or credit card company will show the searching parent the letter of cancellation, which may contain a new address.

Post office officials may reveal the kidnaper's forwarding address, if she or he has left one. So might employees of magazines and newspapers to which the childsnatcher subscribed. Most likely, the fugitive owns an insurance policy on his or her car, house, or life. Parents should ask the company if the premiums are being paid, and from where the checks are issued, or if the policy was canceled. Searchers can see if the absconding parent renewed a driver's license. What address was given on the application form?

Possibly the abductor has stopped doing business with the gas and electric companies, or has asked them to send the bills elsewhere. If the account has been closed, the final bill may have been forwarded to a different city or state. While they may not tell, utility companies might cooperate if the snatcher has opened an account in a new place—provided the new place is known.

Successful searchers report trapping their former mates through a variety of creative methods, from press exposure to "wanted" posters. Many find their offspring through publicity. Parents should try to get their stories into print or onto the screen via newspapers, magazines, or television. Photographs of the child and of the snatcher that would accompany the piece can be enormously effective, since a viewer may recognize the youngster and contact the hunting parent. Publicity may also embarrass the abductor or his or her family and force the person home. A write-up in a national magazine is preferable to coverage in a local tabloid—although both would be ideal—since the circulation of a national magazine is likely to be larger. The larger the audience, the greater the chance of someone's spotting the parent or child. On the other hand, local papers have the advantage of ensuring that the kidnaper will hear about the piece from family and friends. Of course, there is always the risk that the exposure may drive her or him even further underground.

The press can be powerful. In April 1981, the *Ladies' Home Journal* published an article on childsnatching, which featured the photographs of several youngsters. As a result of that story, one child, missing more than two years, was located twelve days after the issue hit the newsstands. When the magazine ran a follow-up piece with still more pictures of kids, many of them, too, met their parents again.

A more unorthodox approach, which works for some parents, is to offer a financial reward for the return of the children. John H. of Ohio explains how this strategy paid off for him:

I posted a five-hundred-dollar reward for my daughter. My ex-wife had also fled with her boyfriend Rick, who, luckily for me, had just served a jail term for aiding in an armed robbery. He had escaped from a halfway house, so the police were willing to help—that is, they were willing to pick him up if I found him. That meant I still had to track him down. I made sure that I got in touch with his friends, so they knew about the reward, as I had with my ex-wife's family. A couple of months after I offered the reward, I got an anonymous call at the garage where I work. This guy said, "Have you heard from your ex-wife?" He asked if the five hundred dollars were still up for grabs, and then said, "I'm not very good at this, but I know where she is, and I need the money." He told me to meet him at a park thirty minutes away in an hour, and made me promise to go alone. He refused to tell me what he looked like. After I described what I was wearing, he said, "I'll find you," and hung up.

I was terrified. My ex-wife's boyfriend was known to be armed. I thought maybe he had hired a friend to blow me away because the reward angered him. I decided not to involve the police, though, because they would scare off the caller and I would never know where my daughter Cindy was. I met this guy on a park bench. He said that while he needed the money, he was also telling me because he couldn't see Cindy being with Rick if there were someone who really wanted her. He told me where to find her and what kind of car they had. I gave him two hundred and fifty dollars. He said, "I'll call you after the weekend, and if you haven't found your daughter, I'll return the money. If you do find her, you owe me two fifty." I followed his instructions and drove sixty miles to a brown, two-family house. Their car was in the driveway. I wrote down the license plate number and went to the nearest phone booth to call police. I told them I knew where Rick was, and if they didn't come in five minutes, I would go in by myself.

They met me immediately. My ex-wife gave the sheriff a fake name for herself and Cindy and told my daughter to say her name was Susan. I asked the police to take me into their house and let me verify that Susan was really Cindy. They brought me up the back stairs and told me I was only allowed to say yes or no when identifying them. Cindy was in the hallway, and when I spotted her, I jumped up and down and screamed, "Cindy, baby, it's daddy!" At this point the deputy grabbed me and took me outside. I heard Cindy sob as I was leaving. When the police first arrived, they didn't have a search warrant and Rick was hiding. They could look for him but were barred from moving around any furniture. Shortly after, more police appeared with a search warrant and found Rick hiding in the bedroom between two mattresses.

Besides reward money, many parents draw up "wanted" posters. These are handmade, mimeographed or Xeroxed sheets of paper written to resemble FBI fugitive posters. Usually the child-stealing version says "WANTED" or "KIDNAPED CHILD" at the top of the page, and lists the abductor's name, date of birth, aliases, Social Security number, driver's license, professional training, and physical description. If there is an arrest warrant for him or her, it is also mentioned. At least one photograph of the kidnaper is printed on the poster. Generally a description and picture of the child are included. At the bottom of the page are the searching parent's name and telephone number, with "Call collect" written after the digits. Like press articles, posters may put enough pressure on the snatcher and his or her family to make him or her return the child.

Posters should be plastered near the home and business of an abductor's parents, siblings, and associates, where they will be certain to see them. One woman traveled three hundred miles to her husband's parents' hometown in upstate New York. She tacked "wanted" posters to the wall of her in-laws' country club, their grocery store, and neighborhood clothing shop. The couple was sufficiently mortified to get in touch with their son, who was hiding in Florida. A friend of the family phoned the mother to inform her about the Florida call. The mother then sent more signs to places she thought her husband might be in that state. She contacted hospitals, because her son had recurrent ear infections that required constant treatment. She wrote to florists throughout the state, since her husband had worked in a flower shop before absconding with their boy. On the hunch that her son was enrolled in a day-care center, she phoned hundreds of them and followed up the calls by mailing them posters. Her instincts were correct. She found her boy attending school under an assumed name. The mother procured the names and addresses of the hospitals, flower shops, and child-care facilities by flipping through a Florida telephone book. Most local libraries stock out-of-state directories.

Some determined parents undertake the exhaustive task of mailing these posters to every public and private school in the country—more than 120,000. Occasionally a mother or father will get lucky and receive a call from a teacher who recognizes the youngster's picture. On the other hand, a school principal may relegate the poster to the junk-mail pile and never read it. It can take months to send notices to thousands of schools. By the time the job is completed, the child may have moved again. While this method is potentially effective, a left-behind adult may not be able to afford the time or the money, a couple of thousands dollars in stamps alone.

To obtain the names and addresses of public schools, a parent should ask a local librarian for the proper resource books. Private, licensed schools are listed by state, and can be found by writing or calling the school licensing division of the state education department in the state's capital.

There may be a far more efficient way to track a child through the school, provided the snatcher has requested that the youngster's school transcripts be transferred. According to the federal Family Educational Rights and Privacy Act (FERPA), both parents have the right to know if the other parent has asked that school records be sent to a new school, or if that parent applies for copies of the records. Both mother and father are also entitled to know from school officials at either end the name of the child's new school, as well as his or her address and telephone number, unless there is a provision in the custody order denying the other parent access to this information. If a mother or father had the foresight to put this clause in the order, and advises the child's school of this stipulation, the request for transcripts will be denied. Many schools require school records before admitting the youngster, so the snatcher may be forced into the open in order to get the child enrolled in the new hometown. At the very least, the searcher can obtain from the old school the address from which the transcript request came, a vital clue in locating the fugitive.

An absent parent should ask the old school if a request has been made by a former spouse for these transcripts, where the request came from, and where the records were sent. The FERPA provides that the institution can lose its federal funding if it fails to comply with a request for this information. An attorney can also subpoena the school if it is not forthcoming. This is a costly and slow alternative. Each school district has its own policy on how it will grant these requests. Lawyers or parents should ask local school officials for a copy of their guidelines.

Pediatricians can also notify a custodial parent if an ex-partner writes away for the child's health records. Youngsters who require ongoing medical attention may possibly be tracked down through hospitals or specialists. These names are found through telephone directories, but the hunting party must know the child's general location.

Support groups for parental kidnaping victims (see Appendix A) may be a first-rate source of information on how to be an effective sleuth. The more established organizations have had enough members recover their kids that they can provide tips and shortcuts for locating youngsters or, if necessary, introduce a parent to a reputable detective. At the very least, meeting others in similar straits should be comforting.

How do parents recover their children? Once the parent has spotted them, she or he may hire private investigators to watch the kids while going to court in the refuge state to win them back. Detectives should ensure that the abducting parent does not flee the new state before court proceedings are resolved. Some attorneys and child-stealing support groups advise a custodial parent to first file an out-of-state custody order with the court in the new state and then resteal the offspring rather than risk an uncertain outcome from another judge—and a hefty legal bill, too. If a custodial parent does snatch back, there is a chance that he or she could be charged with child stealing and prosecuted if the former spouse has managed to obtain a new custody decree in the asylum state—even if the snatching parent has a valid order from his or her state. It is wise to check to see if there is a conflicting order in the new state. An attorney can find out.

The proper approach to retrieving the child is through the courts. The victim parent shows the custody papers to a judge in the new state, then asks the judge to serve a writ of habeas corpus on the absconding parent. This writ orders the kidnaper to hand over the child to the petitioning parent. If the judge agrees to issue the writ, a sheriff may fetch the kids and give them back to the lawful guardian.

The UCCJA and the PKPA (see Appendixes B and C) request, but do not demand, judges in the new state to honor custody orders from the original state. The UCCJA is designed to stop noncustodial mothers and fathers from grabbing the children and running to a new state in order to receive a more favorable custody verdict. But sometimes a scheming abductor sneaks through the system. In the past, kidnapers have been able to get conflicting custody decrees in states which did not sign the UCCJA, and thus did not honor other states' custody orders. The new federal statute aims to eliminate the incentive to flee to non-UCCJA states by requiring that both signatories and nonsignatories honor one another's decrees. Although judges have the discretion under the UCCJA and PKPA to decide if they will award custody to the snatcher, they often will return the child to the original custodian.

A parent who traces a child to a different state can present a foreign decree to the local courts in the new state and ask them to enforce it. This is done by filing a certified copy of the original order with the clerk of a court in the new state. The parent may then march into court with the custody decree, tell the judge it has been filed in that court, and demand the child.

Even if the abductor is picked up by police on a criminal arrest warrant and tossed in jail, the custodial parent still needs to go through the courts and obtain a writ of habeas corpus in order to legally recover the children. Lawful guardians should make sure they are in close contact with state and local officials, so that as soon as their former mate is apprehended, they can race to the refuge state and retrieve their kids. Sometimes out-of-state police neglect to notify the parent's attorney that an ex-spouse is about to be arrested. Since the arrest applies to the suspect and not to the children, they are not necessarily brought along to the police station. It can take no time for an abductor to post bail, be back with the children, and run off with them again.

Once out on bail, the offender may await an extradition hearing to determine if he or she will be sent to another state to stand trial on criminal charges. It is up to the governor in the asylum state to decide whether to deny or approve an extradition request. In the meantime, the kids will be back home.

· 14 ·

How to Help Returned Kids Cope

B E I N G S T O L E N has alarming long-term effects, yet there are ways to mitigate the damage so that returned children can mend quickly. This advice on how to help kids cope is culled from professionals, parents, and the victims themselves, abducted boys and girls. Knowing what to say and what not to say, what will be comforting and what will cause pain, is crucial for the child's recovery. Experts queried agree that a strong support system is essential immediately upon the youngster's return. They urge prompt psychiatric help as well as tender loving care, both at home and at school.

Parents must prepare for the reunion itself. If they do their homework well, this initial encounter can set the tone for the children's homecoming and subsequent adjustment. Seasoned parents say that, as with blind dates or job interviews, first impressions are important. Parents may be nervous about the meeting, but the kids will be, too. Gaining their confidence is essential.

Specialists suggest that parents take to the meeting familiar objects from the youngsters' past: a favorite stuffed animal or toy, or even the children's puppy (perhaps now a greying old-timer), to calm them down and remind them of the old days. Photographs of long-ago hugs and smiles might bring back memories of closeness and belonging. Authorities agree that parents should explain to the kids how difficult it was to trace them, and if they are old enough, to show them detectives' bills and lawyers' correspondence as evidence of their efforts. After all, gullible children often believe the snatcher, who claims the missing parent did not want them, or was not searching for them. Reassuring confused children that, if they like, they can maintain a relationship with the abductor is also prudent. Frequently youngsters are attached to their thieving parents and do not want to cut off contact. A reappearing parent should consider bringing along a psychologist or social worker to treat any acute trauma on the scene for kids who may be excessively scarred—those gone for years, or told the absent grownup is dead.

Counseling is crucial after the reunion, too. "Run, don't walk, to a therapist," advises one father, whose three children are in treatment after eight months in captivity. Kids return with grudges against both their kidnaping *and* searching parents. They need to vent their feelings of anger and betrayal, their concern for their abductors, and their overwhelming sadness because of the Mom-against-Dad, no-win situation. Youngsters caught up in conflicts of divided loyalty may not be able to talk about one parent to the other. Often, too, the custodial parent cannot bear to hear about the abductor's good qualities. A neutral, skilled therapist lets children admit their feelings of ambivalence and work through these emotions. Few professionals specialize in parental kidnaping, so parents should consult a reputable child psychiatrist, social worker, or psychologist who is recommended by school officials, pediatricians, or child-stealing support groups.

Social worker Peg Edwards treats returned kids for an average of six months to one year. "When I first see a child, I can find out within two sessions what kind of information he has been fed by how he plays. If his father stole him, he might take the female doll and say, 'You didn't love me, you let Daddy take me. You never tried to find me.' There is a lot of anger and questioning. Sometimes kids will say, 'You're dead, you're not really my mommy, the other woman is my mommy.' They will act out their emotions of anger and pain through dolls, Play-Doh, and paint."

For older patients, Edwards prefers talk to play. But her goal for all ages is the same: to rid kids of their hurt feelings and to build new relationships of trust. Edwards urges parents to seek therapy, too, not only to help their offspring, but also to expunge their own feelings of guilt for a messy divorce. "A lot of times children will slap and kick the custodial parent and say, 'I'm mad at you. I don't like you,'" explains Edwards. "Therapy helps a parent learn to handle these outbursts and encourages the child to express his anger. That does not mean a parent will allow his youngster to hurt him; but that he should tell the child he understands his feelings, and that it is acceptable to feel that way."

Anger is not necessarily unhealthy. It can be cathartic for kids to feel furious, but then they need to know that Mom or Dad did not abandon them but, in fact, hunted frantically. Says social worker Judith Nadeau: "If the child acts mad, a parent should say, 'It looks as if you're still pretty angry at me,' and acknowledge that the kid blames him or her for the steal. The first thing a parent must do is to let the child be angry, and then let the child understand that there was nothing he or she could do, and detail how much that parent missed him. The problem is, a child does not like to view a parent as unable to protect him or her, so presenting oneself as helpless is also frightening to a child. It is very complicated, and that is why so many people need professional guidance."

Talk, talk, talk, say child therapists. Getting kids together with other snatch victims can be medicinal. Knowing that they have suffered and survived may make children feel less freakish and alone. Peers in similar straits allow kids to be candid—perhaps more than with a parent or a therapist. Nonabducted friends may still make excellent confidants, and reinforce the child's sense of self-worth. "My friends were more helpful than my mom or my shrink," claims Howie, who had felt terribly different when returned. "I thought they'd want to know everything. We spoke about the abduction a bit, but they acted as if it didn't matter. So I was a kid again, instead of some kind of animal, like before."

Youngsters may want to speak about their experiences, but keep quiet because of cues received from their reunited parents. "I have not brought up the kidnaping, and feel there is no reason to," says a custodial father, whose son was hidden abroad. "I want to downplay the experience with Marc, as if he went away on vacation, and therefore it wasn't any big deal. My attitude is, it happened, and I don't talk about it at all. I'm trying to shield Marc from it, to minimize the ordeal and not discuss it, so it will slowly drift out of his consciousness."

Wrong. Keeping secrets can be disastrous, intensifying trauma instead of dissipating it. The assumption that a problem will mysteriously disappear by not discussing it is naive. Contends Judith Nadeau: "It is awful not to mention the experience to the child, because it tells the youngster he does not have permission to express his feelings, which would somehow support in the child's mind that the kidnaping was his fault." Psychologist Dr. Daniel O'Leary has a different notion: "I don't think there needs to be a great amount of discussion about the ordeal. Unless the child was blindfolded, he knows what happened. I instruct parents to listen intently when the child brings up the topic, but I do not think there is any need for the parent to initiate the conversation. Unless, of course, the child does not seem to be adjusting well."

What to say when the subject comes up? When kids beg for the truth—why they were stolen—should parents spill all? Grownups need not be vindictive to be honest. It is natural to want to disparage a former mate, but when a parent indulges this urge, the child suffers even more. This tit-for-tat mentality is destructive. One parent is still berating the other. The custodial parent is taking out her or his anger on the child. A retaliatory mother or father is acting as immaturely and as inappropriately as the abductor. And parents know how kids cope—or don't cope—when brainwashed. Says one Ph.D. candidate in psychology, whose former partner fled to San Juan with their kids: "I have been careful not to say bad things about their father. Still, I wanted to share a little bit. I told them that prior to my sending them to San Juan for a visit with their father, he and I had made an agreement that he would have them for two months and would return them in time for school. My son said, 'Daddy loved us so much, he couldn't send us back.' I said, 'You're right, he does love you, but when you promise someone something, you have to stick by it.' I was angry at my ex, but did not want to bad-mouth him." "If a child is operating on the premise that Daddy said he loved me, and that's why he took me," says psychologist Eugene Evans, "and the new parent says, 'No, he took you because he wanted to get back at me,' the child won't understand."

One New Jersey mother did the opposite. Her son was grabbed for spite and eventually abandoned by his father. The boy's mother would not lie about motives: "I told Mike that his father and I could not live together anymore, and because Mommy asked Daddy for a divorce, he became very upset. To hurt me he took him away. I could not say the man loved him, because the man would not have treated Mike that way if he did."

Most older youngsters claim they want the truth. They are used to being lied to while on the lam by one parent. Farfetched explanations from the other side will convince them that neither grownup is trustworthy. Kids who cannot trust cannot heal. A Long Island, New York, mother waited several months before leveling with her six-year-old daughter: "We were in the car one day, and finally I told Jennifer the truth—that her father took her without my knowing it and that I wanted to see her, but my ex-husband would not let me. She was relieved and shot back, 'But Mommy, why didn't you tell me?' She had wanted to know."

Obviously, there should be a balance between being straight and being too straight. Parents must tone down a lurid tale, and talk without attacking, letting kids know they understand the difficulties of being stolen and of being recovered.

Adults should empathize without infantilizing. Usually youngsters return with an array of fears, and need to be cuddled and comforted. But parents must also urge them to cut the clinginess and carry on with their lives. "I can't pat the boy on the head for the rest of his life," says one woman, whose son was dragged to three states, "because John had a rough time. He would like to stay home from school with Mommy and shut out the world. His therapist told me I should treat John like any other eleven-year-old boy, keeping in mind the fact that he has some problems. The way to rid him of these problems is to make life as normal as possible."

Most professionals concur with John's psychologist, who discourages the special-treatment approach. Parents should be warm and loving, and build back trust, but not spoil Sonny, or he may never be well adjusted. Frequently adults act over-indulgent because they want to compensate for their kids' terrible time away. They feel guilty for "allowing" the abduction and want to make it up to their children. Grownups may be so delighted the kids are back that they fail to discipline them. Also, Mom and Dad may be terrified that their offspring will reject them if they set limits. Parents are wrong. Being a pushover is hurtful, not helpful. Often children behave like bandits, tormenting the custodial parent to test him. These youngsters may welcome authority. A no-nonsense adult may make them straighten up, and show them that being kidnaped does not entitle them to be brats. "Don't make the mistake I did," wails the mother of three wild boys. "I was so anxious to see my sons, I let them get away with a lot. I was scared to discipline them. Now they are unruly and disrespectful."

More is needed than boxing gloves. Often kids will calm down when they stop worrying about being restolen. Children cannot feel secure unless they know how to ward off another abduction attempt. Even when the chances are negligible, the greatest fear returned kids have is of a repeat snatch. Being prepared will reassure them that they *can* control events, that they *can* slip away in the event the kidnaper tries to grab them again. Parents must provide tips and tactics: what to do; where to go; how to go. They must rehearse children on telephone numbers, area codes, credit cards, taxis, buses, and twenty-cent stamps. Adults must be diplomatic—ready the kids for Round Two, while not seeming too nervous about its actually happening. This is a tough task for a parent with justifiable fears. Says one woman whose child was returned more than two years ago: "There isn't a day that goes by that I don't wonder where Jim is when he is outside. But I don't want him to be a scared sissy, either. I have taught him how to use the phone if his father comes for him again. He knows how to escape."

Parents may think it is worth shaking up kids to keep them safe. Experts suggest that schools help parents prepare a disaster plan, pointing out where the children will run if the kidnaper shows up in class. The purpose: to let children know adults will protect them. It is a sound exercise for both sides: teachers will be sensitive to pupils' fears, and youngsters will learn how to flee. This system worked well for one boy from Maryland. "The school was terrific to my son," says Billy's father. "His teachers made certain he felt safe, and assigned him a 'buddy' who walked around with him to make sure he wasn't snatched from the schoolyard. His friend was instructed to run to the teacher if Billy's mother reappeared. He knew he had this backup. Slowly he relaxed. After a while, Billy didn't need the 'buddy' anymore."

Unexpected meetings with kidnapers may spook recovered boys and girls, but what about approved rendezvous? Kids often cower when they see their abductors during scheduled visitations, haunted by memories of captivity, or by the thought of more days away. "Please," they beg, "don't force me to see Daddy," or, "Make Mommy leave me alone."

Parents often think that visitation is destructive, that it invites their former mates to steal again. Having the kidnaper come to their home is somewhat safer, but is still not snatcher-proof. Yet lawful guardians must defer to judges, who usually uphold a thieving parent's visitation rights, ordering supervised reunions even after he or she has been convicted of child stealing. The parent who disregards the visitation decree can be held in contempt of court, fined, or even thrown in jail! Only after an abductor makes off with his or her mark will visits be curtailed. Then, of course, it is too late. Jurists are willing to risk a repeat to ensure that both sides have access to the child. After all, it is "in the child's best interests" to have two parents, the argument goes. But kids traumatized by an abductor and uninterested in a relationship are forced into one. The question becomes: Whose best interests are served—the child's or the kidnaper's?

The issue is not that clear-cut, say some therapists and jurists. Youngsters may not *want* to be with the snatcher, but may actually be better off with their part-time company. Dr. Jeannette Minkoff, who has treated recovered children for almost twenty years, believes that they should see their captors at least once, so that they do not fantasize or distort their days on the run. "My own theory is that when kids are returned, they are told, either verbally or through people's behavior, 'The abductor was a bad guy, he did terrible things to you, he's a monster.' If children are not given the opportunity to see their fathers and mothers and remember what actually happened, their minds can play games, because they think that the custodial parent wants to hear they were mistreated. But if you are able to get this kid to look at his abductor, and you can say, 'You told me that your father tied you to a bedpost when he went out to buy groceries, and that you cried and screamed and nobody came. But I saw your father today. Is he the kind of person who would tie you to a bedpost?' The child will realize he has been exaggerating, and get back in touch with reality. If the child does not back down, at least you are getting your facts straight."

Therapists agree that in certain situations—where a child has been sexually molested, or becomes hysterical at the sight of the snatcher, for example—she or he should not be subjected to visits from the kidnaper. When courts disagree, meetings must always be supervised until the child feels safe enough to see the parent alone. Dr. Minkoff describes one instance in which the judge erred and insisted on enforcing the father's rights at the expense of the child.

The first visit between the returned boy and his father was unbelievable. He had been back for two months. I said, "You should at least see your dad. Maybe it will make you feel better." He threw a fit, but finally agreed after a series of questions: "Can I sit with you behind your desk?" "Can I sit with you off to the other side?" "Do I have to look at my father?" "Do I have to touch him?" "Will he be allowed to touch me?" "Where am I going to be in the room?" "Will he be able to take me again?" I explained to him that my office was in the courthouse and there was a deputy sheriff in the hallway, so he did not have to worry. I got him into the office and this ten-year-old literally crawled under my desk. He would not look at his father, and kept saying, "I hate him, I hate him. He's going to take me." The father said, "You know we had a good time when we were away," and the boy replied, "But we didn't, we didn't." He was a mess and kept whimpering.

Four months later he came in again and I had him pretty well assured that his father would not take him again, and he sat on a chair behind the desk, but he was still not willing to talk to his father. Now, two years later, he sees him once a month in my office. He puts all the responsibility for starting the conversation on his father. I speak with the boy alone after their meetings, and he asks me why he has to waste his time seeing him. I tell him that the court feels it is important for him, and he says, "But I don't want to see my father. It still hurts me. I don't trust him. I never trusted him."

Some kids yearn to be with their parents, but the abductor never comes calling. Children are devastated and bewildered by being abruptly dropped. If the parent who stole them *really* loved them while away, why should that change when they come back? Often it isn't until the kidnaper cuts off contact that youngsters begin to fathom their complicated part as pawns. Sometimes they are still not sure why the snatcher doesn't visit. "I don't see my dad now, even though he has reservations [sic] to see me," weeps an eleven-year-old California boy, home for more than a year. "He doesn't want to see me. I don't know why. I'm just so sad."

Special occasions, like birthdays and holidays, can make depressed kids even bluer. Those who seem to be coping well may suddenly fall apart—the absence of a card or call reinforcing their feelings of unimportance. "I have more trouble with my sons around their birthdays," says a woman whose former husband has not gotten in touch with her three boys since their return. "When my ex doesn't write, the kids get wild and temperamental. The other two will wait for the birthday boy to get a card, and when he doesn't, they all get disturbed. They don't understand why he took them for three and a half years, and does not even bother to write now."

Parents should except that holidays may trigger problems.

(Of course, understanding and anticipating these outbursts won't tame a snarly, whiny child!) The mood swings of the Carter kids have been trying for their father and his new wife. Even though they have been back for three years, the two girls and boy still act up on schedule. "We know they saw their mother for the last time in June of 1979," declares their stepmother, Anne. "For the past two years in June, the thirteen-year-old is strange the whole month. She is grumpy and absolutely unbearable to live with. For the youngest, it's December. Christmas is his last memory of his mother. For the past two Christmases, he has gone on a hunger strike for two weeks, and will eat only cereal, practically the only food he was fed on the run. This Christmas is coming up soon and we won't panic. We'll give him all the cereal he wants." Ordinarily composed, the middle child slumps into a deep depression every four months —the amount of time she spent away—and goes on crying jags for three or four days. "We're due for another episode in three weeks," the stepmother sighs wearily.

Why do kids want to see a parent whom they allegedly hate? Though they may detest a mother or father for whisking them away, children still need to believe that person cares, atrocities notwithstanding. Admits twelve-year-old Penny of Chicago, who has not seen her dad in the two years she has been back, "Part of me still hates him for what he did, but the other part says he's my father and that will never change." Legal guardians can ease the pain for children by providing insight into the kidnapers' absence, explaining that their not visiting does not mean they do not love the youngsters. Reassuring them that the abductor misses them and is thinking of them, but may be ashamed or embarrassed by his or her prior actions, may also be soothing. Parents can say, too, that sporadic contact with the kids may be too difficult for adults accustomed to uninterrupted (though illegal) time with their offspring. Grown-ups may not be lying, either.

Studies on why noncustodians do not visit after a divorce

show that often the loss of children is so devastating, and the mourning for them so great, that seeing them only intermittently is intolerable. Ironically, it is the parent who cares the most for his or her child who may not be able to visit. Such a parent may feel that the only way he or she can cope with the reduced role is to completely exclude the youngster. The same reasoning may apply for parents denied regular access to their children after a kidnaping. Judges do not allow most convicted snatchers to see their kids without a third party present. Parents may find this condition insulting and intrusive, and decide that if they can't have quality time alone, they would rather have no time.

Supportive. Kind. Patient. Loving. These words may sound like a boy scout's pledge, but they are intended to explain the qualities that parents should hone to hasten their children's recovery. Being understanding may be trying and exhausting— but it will help kids cope.

V

THE FUTURE

· 15 ·

Suggestions and Solutions

PARENTS INTENT on abducting their offspring will succeed, regardless of the penalty. Not even the threat of fifty years behind bars or a five-hundred-thousand-dollar fine would dissuade the more determined mothers and fathers. Yet many grownups would pause before running off with their kids if there were more stringent laws and stiff sentences imposed for their crimes.

Parental kidnaping can be curbed. What if there were no incentive to steal? What if divorced spouses were satisfied with their custody arrangements, and worked out their hostility through counseling—not through the kids? Or what if an adult did abduct a child, and found the consequences exquisitely unpleasant? It is possible to reduce the epidemic, both through prophylactic and post-abduction treatment. None of these remedies alone will cure the problem, but in combination they may provide a potent antidote.

Snatching will never totally cease, but it may subside once

adults realize that they will be slapped with swift and severe punishment, rather than the present obligatory reprimand for the record. Through its penal statutes, the system must tell thieves that if they dare kidnap, the children will be returned, and they will be dealt with as criminals—not as loving mothers or fathers.

Putting tough laws on the books for the purpose of inhibiting would-be snatchers is not enough. Officers must enforce these laws by arresting, extraditing, and prosecuting offenders. No longer can police and prosecutors, attorneys and judges dismiss kidsnatching as a low-priority problem. Parental victims, too, have reinforced its insignificance by filing charges and then withdrawing them, thereby condoning the actions of former spouses. If mothers and fathers want results, they must follow through on their complaints.

Child stealing will be treated as a weighty crime only if there is cooperation on all levels—from the FBI to the local cop on the beat. Abductors who knew they would be intercepted at airports or highway tollbooths by a national network of lawmen might reconsider their schemes. Typically, law-enforcement officials are slow when it comes to answering an anguished parent's pleas for help—if they intervene at all. Acting fast may make the difference between a short stay away and a permanent "vacation."

The government must aid grownups in locating and returning kidnaped children, so that searching parents need not resort to "self-help," or have to stop hunting because they are broke. Child Find suggests that the government organize a task force of investigators attached to the FBI, who would be assigned exclusively to missing-children cases. Most parents do not hold detective licenses, and do not know where, or how, to find their thieving ex-mates.

Since snatchers almost always relocate to a new city, officials must exchange information ungrudgingly, offer to extradite new residents, and honor one another's custody decrees. The Uniform Child Custody Jurisdiction Act urges, but does not require, each signatory state to abide by the order of the court in the home state. If he or she chooses, a local trial judge may still award control of the child to the violating party. The states that have not enacted the UCCJA are not compelled to recognize prior custody rulings. They have become havens for abductors. These refuge states must sign the UCCJA, too, so that this "uniform" act is really uniform.

To discourage custody shopping, a central computer could store all custody decisions and tell a judge if a parent who applies for custody has already been through a contest in another state. (Of course, a crafty parent could always change his or her name so it would not appear in the data bank.)

State and federal legislation is so new, poorly disseminated, ambiguously worded, and open to interpretation that confusion abounds. Authorities who should know how to handle a parental kidnaping case often don't. Frequently mothers and fathers find themselves giving the police crash courses in family law—instead of the other way around. Lawyers and judges, too, are not always up to date on child-stealing statutes. In fact, the average attorney has probably never heard of the UCCJA or the federal Parental Kidnapping Prevention Act of 1980 (PKPA). How can he or she be expected to advise the client well? Mandatory education seminars for those who deal regularly with custody matters would ensure that authorities keep current on statutes and the remedies available to victimized parents.

For years, child advocates pushed for federal legislation, touting it as *the* way to deter abductions. But since its arrival, the PKPA has proven relatively ineffective, mostly because it is not enforced universally, and because it does not make snatching a federal offense. Since the Lindbergh Act specifically excludes parents, no federal law prohibits the crime. Either the

249

Lindbergh Act or the PKPA must be amended so that parents are charged with a federal misdemeanor for stealing a child across state lines, or a new law should be created to fill the gap.

Advocates of stricter statutes believe there should be federal legislation not only to protect a parent whose child is stolen, but also to police visitation rights in cases where the lawful guardian denies a former spouse access to the children. The federal government prefers that states handle child-stealing matters internally—even when it is instructed to intervene under the terms of the PKPA. It is unlikely, then, that the national government would ever address the more cumbersome problem of enforcing visitation rights. Yet snatchers cite denial of visitation as the chief reason for their actions. A law that insists upon honoring visitation privileges on the state, if not the federal, level might well make custodial mothers and fathers abide by their agreements, and thus eliminate the need to abduct.

Parents who run off with their kids *before* there is a custody order should also be subject to penalties. Under current statutes, only parents who steal after a decree has been issued have violated the law.

Along with federal legislation, each state must make parental kidnaping a felony. Only forty-two states do so now. That designation will increase the chances of extradition if an abductor flees the home state, and also allows the government to intervene, should it choose. Making the stealing or concealment of a child within the state an offense would also discourage this behavior. In some states, both the taking *and* hiding of a youngster must occur within one state in order for any law to be broken. Thus, a child could be stolen in one state and concealed in another, and no crime would be committed.

To discourage childsnatchers from getting help, states should consider making it a felony to aid and abet a thieving parent. An aunt or fraternity brother who knew she or he could become a convicted felon for harboring an abductor would be less likely to be a gracious host.

Stealing might be significantly reduced, it has been suggested, if kidnapers-to-be knew they would not be allowed to spend any time with their youngsters if they absconded with them and were later found. On the run, abductors fear that they will lose the right to see their children if they are caught. Their anxiety is unfounded, since as things now stand usually even convicted child stealers who request visitation privileges are granted them. While this punishment might deter some snatchers, however, it ultimately victimizes the children, because they would be denied any access to one of their parents.

Of course, it is crucial to close up the loopholes in existing laws, and to incorporate new provisions that ban the taking of the child under any conditions. However, unless the U.S. policy on international abductions is overhauled, too, more and more parents frustrated by restrictions here will escape abroad.

Once parents grab a son or daughter, they must expect severe repercussions. Yet a no-nonsense policy should not put the child's return in jeopardy. Kidnaping moms and dads must be encouraged to bring back their "hostages" and even be rewarded for prompt compliance. In a few states, adults who return their children unharmed within a reasonable time period receive special deferential treatment from prosecutors and judges. This is a diplomatic remedy that should be instituted by every state. The point is to effectuate a speedy homecoming, not to punish needlessly.

On the other hand, child stealers who do not voluntarily return their offspring should be treated harshly. Lengthy jail sentences just may frighten off potential robbers. The threat of doing time does not scare snatchers at the present time, since they know their abducting brethren rarely wind up in prison. The few who are unlucky enough to get caught, convicted, and sentenced almost never spend a day behind bars. Even those few offenders who are given hefty jail terms are put on probation. Some authorities would be uncomfortable incarcerating a parent. Instead of doling out traditional punishment, such as prison or steep fines, these jurists should consider making kidnaping parents pay the consequences creatively. As it stands now, the custodial parent—the victim—must finance the hunting expedition. This does not seem fair. While snatchers should help reimburse their ex-mates, a custodial mother or father could conceivably purchase a policy for kidnaping and ransom insurance, which would cover the costs of retrieving the child. This type of policy is traditionally reserved for stranger abductions, but could possibly be expanded to include parent kidnaping. Ordering abductors to pick up the tab for fees incurred by their searching spouses—for detectives, attorneys, psychiatrists, and traveling—would prove painfully expensive. Judges could demand such monetary reparations in lieu of a stay in jail or the imposition of a fine, or use all three sanctions on more heinous fugitives. Recently a California judge condemned a child stealer to twenty-one days in jail and three years' probation. The judge also ordered him to dish out $6,250 in fines, and $7,000 in fees for his ex-wife's lawyers. His Honor insisted upon supervised visitation, mandatory psychotherapy, and a bond secured by the defendant's home, in case he tries to kidnap his boys again.

Another alternative to criminal penalties is a civil tort action—an effective legal deterrent that punishes an abductor through the pocketbook. The custodial parent can sue the snatcher for mental anguish and emotional suffering caused by the abduction, and recover damages—as well as be reimbursed for the costs of recovering the child. Money judgments are easier to win than a conviction for kidnaping.

In a landmark decision handed down on August 30, 1978, a New York federal judge fined Queens jeweler Fabian Kajtazi $181,340 for child abduction and false imprisonment of his then three-year-old son, Biter. His ex-wife Olyvia, a TWA flight attendant, also filed suit against Fabian's brother and father, who lied about Biter's and Fabian's whereabouts, giving them time to flee to Yugoslavia. Besides awarding one hundred thousand dollars in punitive damages to Biter and Olyvia, the judge also charged them twenty dollars a day for false imprisonment and fifty dollars a day for child abduction for each additional day the child was concealed. No money was actually paid, since the case was eventually settled. On September 28, 1979, Olyvia was reunited with her son after nearly two years. There was no question that the judge's get-tough sentence imposed not only on the father, but also on his relatives who conspired with him, put pressure on Fabian to return his son. Apparently the word reached the father all the way across the ocean.

While potential abductors must be warned about the consequences of child stealing, boys and girls must be informed that parental kidnaping is a possibility. They should be instructed on how to proceed if it occurs. A massive education job is imperative. Trusted teachers or PTA representatives could explain the issue to students and offer advice on how to escape a grabbing mom or dad. Signs and brochures, book reports and lectures, advertisements on prime-time television or during Saturday cartoons could acquaint kids with the topic.

Gloria Yerkovich, head of the support group Child Find, estimates that it will take three years for youngsters to become familiar enough with the subject to know to call home. Periodically, Yerkovich's group runs public-service announcements on local radio stations urging children who think they have been stolen to telephone Child Find's toll-free number. For an hour and a half after these commercials air, Child Find's telephone rings continuously with calls from kids who want to be reunited with parents, reports Yerkovich. Child Find also mails posters to public and private schools that read: "Some parents are sad because they don't know where their children are. Child Find helps children and parents find each other. Can Child

Find help you? Ask your librarian or teacher." The number of the nonprofit organization's hot line is listed at the bottom.

It is not enough to make kids aware of the problem. School principals must refuse to admit youngsters who don't have proper records from previous schools, as well as report them to police if a situation looks suspicious. Teachers should try to verify custody stories on their own when it is feasible.

School officials and students are not the only ones who must be educated. Judges, too, must be brought up to date on the latest psychological and legal studies on the effects of divorce and various custody arrangements on kids and their parents. Stuck on stereotypes such as "Men are men and women are mothers," many jurists routinely award children to females without probing the merits of the particular case. Parents are at the mercy of judges. It is a matter of luck whether His Honor is enlightened or Neanderthal. This needn't be the case, however. There can be standard guidelines for judges to follow that would make the outcome of custody contests more predictable and just, while still taking into consideration the unique circumstances of each case.

Most judges have a narrow orientation. They are familiar with local statutes, but untrained in child psychology. Yet they must weigh a variety of nonlegal factors when deciding with whom a child should live. Sometimes they resent or ignore the opinions of psychotherapists. Admits a candid New York Court of Appeals judge: "A former district attorney who becomes a supreme court judge probably isn't going to have the expertise or the sensitivity to make a custody determination, and that determination often becomes the final one."

Some jurists are so insensitive to children's feelings following divorce that critics of the legal system question whether they are even qualified to determine custody. Experts agree that the adversary approach—where attorneys pit clients against each other and a judge determines the "best man"—is an ineffective and callous way to deal with children's lives. The best interests of a child are often sabotaged by a system which demands that attorneys fight for their clients, even if they know their clients should not receive the kids. Custody is often determined on the basis of which parent has hired the better lawyer. Frequently parents who part amiably are dragged into bitter courtroom battles by overzealous attorneys.

Even the terminology in custody suits reflects the children-as-chattel attitude of the courts: mothers and fathers "win" or "lose" custody; the victor is "awarded" the offspring, while the noncustodial parent is granted "visitation."

Is there any alternative to this trial-by-combat approach to custody? A panel system, in which a team of mental health professionals dispense justice, rather than a jurist, is one option being bandied about. At the very least, family court judges need intensive training from custody experts so these umpires can make more intelligent placement decisions. They must also draw on the talents of social scientists and rely more on their sophisticated investigative techniques. Courts need to clear their back-logged calendars and attend to the issue of custody immediately after a couple files for divorce. Currently all aspects of the breakup—from property to money to custody—may be settled at the same time. Getting a court date can take as long as two years, and some sparring mates may be forced to stay in the same house awaiting the trial. Caught in the middle, a child may be the center of vicious feuding.

Proving popular among some parents are alternatives to this father-against-mother system, such as mediation, conciliation, and arbitration. Instead of having lawyers dig up dirt to prove the unfitness of the other side, skilled negotiators sit down with warring parents and help them work out custody conflicts peacefully. These intermediaries are usually child psychologists, social workers, or marriage counselors. Proponents of these nonadversary approaches claim that mothers and fathers who

255

have a say in their arrangements will feel satisfied, and that satisfied parents rarely return to court. Nor do they steal their children.

Some lawyers and judges oppose challenges to the adversary system for less than altruistic reasons. Attorneys know that their fees will shrink, sometimes by one-third, if their clients opt for the settlement route. A mediated divorce, for example, costs fifteen hundred dollars on the average, and of that, only four hundred or so goes to the lawyer. On the other hand, an adversarial procedure ordinarily nets an attorney at least three thousand dollars, and can soar to forty thousand in more messy battles. Judges have partially honorable and partially personal motives for favoring the adversary method. They contend that they have presided over enough cases to be able to decide who is more fit to parent. At the same time, many jurists are impressed with their power and resent any intrusion on their turf.

Despite protests, courts are discovering that conciliation and mediation services help promote better relationships by mitigating the trauma of a breakup. Seventeen states now have court-connected programs in which pre- or post-divorce parents and their children receive counseling from psychiatrists, psychologists, or social workers. Therapists help parents draft custody agreements, arbitrate hassles, recommend custody arrangements, or tell children what to expect after the split. The staff usually issues a report and makes a recommendation to the judge on which parent should be awarded custody.

Unlike conciliation services, mediators are not necessarily attached to the courts. (A California law however, effective January 1981, mandates mediation in all contested cases. It is the first such law in the country.) Mediators assist couples in reaching and drafting their own agreements. When signed by the referring judge, the agreement becomes an order of the court. Top-notch negotiators, these mediators concentrate on coming up with a satisfactory arrangement, rather than on the psychological or legal aspects of the issue.

Parents who prefer to step even further outside the courtroom can choose arbitration. Instead of judges or attorneys, specially trained arbitrators make legally binding decisions for parents. Arbitrators also assist them in drawing up agreements and negotiating settlements. When ex-partners can't agree on an issue—whether it be apportionment of property or child support or custody—the third-party arbitrator decides for them. Couples must contact the American Arbitration Association (the AAA has an office in most large cities) and consent to incorporate the arbitrator's decision into their separation agreements.

Another solution to custody squabbles, and thus to the child-stealing problem, is to make counseling mandatory for all parents who have children and file for divorce. Mothers and fathers could pay on a sliding scale, or perhaps the courts could pick up the costs if specialists in family court provided the therapy. In the long run, offering counseling would be a smart investment for courts. Content with custody arrangements, parents would not return to court for additional, contested proceedings, and congested dockets would be cleared for other matters.

In especially bitter battles, therapy might be ordered after the divorce has been granted. Emotions don't automatically abate just because parents receive a piece of paper telling them the relationship is over. Therapy helps diffuse potentially volatile confrontations that could hurt or anger an ex-spouse and cause retaliation.

Parents are beginning to rebel. No longer do mothers and fathers blindly follow the winner-take-all system. No longer will all fathers accept being relegated to once-a-month, noncustodial visitors. Instead, a number of "zoo daddies" are pushing for more rewarding custody arrangements, like joint custody. In this setup, parents share the decision making and assume equal responsibility for their children after a separation or divorce. The child may live with one parent at a time on a fifty-

fifty or a split-time basis. At least twenty-seven states authorize joint custody; some create a presumption of joint custody, so that a judge has to divide custody unless one side can prove the other is unfit.

This setup offers both mother and father continued contact with the offspring. Neither side feels excluded or neglected. Child-custody advocates claim this alternative reduces parental kidnaping, because grownups who have access to their children and feel important to them don't feel the need to abduct. A joint-custody dad, who is also a lawyer, agrees: "Put yourself in the position of a father who pays child support and alimony and does not have the kids. He has been kicked out of his house, without even getting the dog, and is only allowed to see his children every other weekend for three hours. The minute his ex-wife looks at him cross-eyed, he is in family court on an assault charge. After he has had enough, he takes off with the kids. Joint custody eliminates a lot of potential problems."

Dual-parenting critics contend that if a mother or father with shared custody abducts the children, it will be hard to prosecute him or her, because both sides are legally entitled to the offspring. Those who object say a joint-custody award is an easy out for judges too lazy to decide which parent is more fit to take charge of the kids. The opposition maintains that youngsters become disoriented shuttling between houses, that children need the security of one place they can call their own.

The most hotly debated aspect of joint custody is whether it works when parents are feuding. "There are people who are out to slaughter each other after marriage," says eminent child psychologist Dr. Lee Salk, "and if you gave them joint custody, those children would become the target. I think sometimes a child is better off with one parent. That doesn't mean he shouldn't have a good relationship with the other parent. But there is no conflict over decisions with sole custody, because one person makes them all."

Some joint-custody veterans counter that their arrangement

forces them to cooperate, and that if both Mom and Dad are concerned with their children's best interests, the kids will not become the center of their animosity. Instead, proponents maintain that when both sides share the responsibility for decision making, they make it a point to negotiate their differences.

Obviously joint custody will only work under certain conditions. Couples must be able to afford this arrangement. Because of expenses, shared parenting remains a middle-class phenomenon. One joint custody expert estimates that 25 percent more income is needed to support two houses—not to mention the two sets of Atari games, Chatty Cathy dolls, and school clothes. It can only work, too, if parents live near enough each other so the kids can attend one school and keep the same friends, if mothers and fathers agree to share the children, and the kids want to be shared.

Says Dr. Mel Roman, co-author with William Haddad of *The Disposable Parent,* a book that advocates this divided plan: "In my view, there is just no question that kids are better off with joint rather than sole custody. Whatever logistical difficulties there are are far outweighed by having meaningful, ongoing contact with both parents. Staying in touch with both sides is probably the most important issue in divorce. Therapists are seeing that the loss of a parent traumatizes a child like nothing else. It is very rare in the mental health field when there is a single thing you can do—like instituting joint custody—that will help kids. This is one of those times."

Divided parenting, claim some social scientists, aids mothers and fathers as well—not just the children. "The family is an organic system," states Dr. Roman. "You can't have a destructive arrangement with one individual in the family without its having negative repercussions throughout the system." If children are not happy, parents suffer, and vice versa.

Although still scarce, research is emerging on the effects of divorce on families, specifically on the noncustodial parent. One study of forty legally separated or divorced New York fathers claims that sole custody can harm parents and children. Conducted by Judith Brown Greif, a social worker at the Albert Einstein College of Medicine, the study found that the less fathers were allowed to visit their children, the less they wanted to, because it was too painful seeing them sporadically. "With few exceptions, the trauma of divorce can be minimized by the child's continuous open and easy access to both parents," the study concluded. "One clear way of doing that is through joint custody arrangements."

Ultimately it does not matter whether parents elect joint custody over sole custody, or the adversary system over an alternative approach. What is important is that parents who part be civil to each other—at least for the sake of the kids. Staying civil means being gracious about sharing the children with a former spouse. Yet parents cannot give ungrudgingly until they come to terms with their breakup, and understand that the death of a marriage need not mean the death of fatherhood or motherhood. When parents cannot accept the end of the marriage, when bitterness lingers, snatching can occur. Child stealing is often the final statement, the continuation of an unresolved conflict.

How do couples learn to accept that the party is *really* over? Besides counseling, separating spouses are now finding more unorthodox ways to make their split-ups final. Divorce cards are chic proclamations of a couple's new marital status: "I am pleased to announce that Lucy and I are no longer married . . ." Trendy, too, are divorce ceremonies. Frivolous though they may sound, they force parents to officially admit that their marriage is over, but that their parental responsibilities are not. Rabbi Earl Grollman of Belmont, Massachusetts, conducts divorce ceremonies, which take place in the sanctuary of his temple—where many of the same couples were wed. "You have come together now to say goodbye to your marriage," he tells the former husband and wife, and their friends and family who gather to "celebrate." "You haven't succeeded as man and wife, but you must succeed still as mother and father of these children."

These ceremonies are not magical panaceas for curing bad feelings that arise out of divorce. Failed marriages are never happy affairs. Misery spawns child stealing. Proposing solutions to the snatching epidemic may deter the more mature marital casualties. But human nature, which cries "revenge" rather than "conciliation," promises to prevail.

Sadly, the future of childsnatching is more certain than the future of children. Parental abductions are guaranteed to grow because of the rampant rate of divorce, the ineffective laws, and the current "It's not my problem" attitude of police and prosecutors. Even if everything possible were done to wipe out the problem—if stealing became a federal offense, if every state raised the penalty to a felony, if an international treaty were enacted, and if judges made fairer custody decisions—snatching would never completely cease. Not at least until men and women realize that parents must be allowed to be parents forever, and that children must be given the chance to be children. Without that insight, boys and girls will continue to get caught in the crossfire of their mother and father's battles. For the kidnaping parent, these spoils of war are a perverse victory indeed.

Appendix A
Support Groups

Child Custody Project
American Bar Association
1800 M St. NW
Washington, DC 20036
(202) 331-2250

Provides literature on child custody and kidnaping laws.

Child Find, Inc.
P.O. Box 277
New Paltz, NY 12561
Attention: Gloria Yerkovich
(914) 255-1848
(800) 431-5005 (toll-free number for searching children and those identifying them only; hot line open 8 A.M.–8 P.M., seven days a week.)

Annual registration fee: $50 per child; $25 each additional child. Matches missing children and registered parents. Directory with children's pictures sent to 3,000 schools, hospitals, social service agencies, etc. Publicizes parents' plights through media exposure.

Children's Rights of Florida
P.O. Box 173
Pinellas Park, FLA 33565
Attention: Kathy Rosenthal

Children's Rights of New York, Inc.
19 Maple Ave.
Stony Brook, NY 11790
Attention: John Gill
(516)751-7840

Counsels parents, offers referral lists of lawyers and investigators. Monthly support meetings on Long Island, N.Y., provide "how to" tips and introduce parental victims to one another. Publishes newsletter.

Family and Friends of Missing Persons
P.O. Box 21444
Seattle, WA 98111
Attention: Mary Miller
(206)782-8306

Missing Persons Bureau
Bergen County Sheriff's Office
One Court Street
Hackensack, NJ 07601
Attention: Sgt. Richard Ruffino
(201)646-2192

Data bank for unidentified bodies. Parents should send a letter including the date the child was last seen and a physical description of the child (especially outstanding features), along with a recent photograph.

Mothers Without Custody, Inc.
P.O. Box 76
Sudbury, MA 01776

Chapters in 112 cities and towns throughout the United States; their addresses available by writing Massachusetts group. For women living apart from their children. Will put female parental victims in touch with others in similar straits. Offers lawyer referral services, publishes newsletter. Dues are $18 a year.

National Missing Children's Locate Center
201 Yamhill Law Center
1123 SW Yamhill Street
Portland, OR 97205

Operates on an at cost basis to help parents locate their kids. Publishes newsletter.

National Runaway Switchboard
(800)621-4000 (toll-free)
(800)972-6004 (toll-free in Illinois—service is called Illinois Youth Switchboard)

Advises parents and children.

Parents Against Child-Snatching
5311A Williams Road
Norcross, GA 30093
(404)921-8526 (Kimberly Willis)
(404)928-1831 (Cathy Frederic)

Atlanta area group. Counsels parents, lobbies for local child-stealing legislation. Monthly meetings.

Parents Helping Parents—Child Abductions
Route 1, Box 406D
Myakka City, FL 33551
Attention: Cindy Teel
(813)322-2082

Local group that introduces parental victims to one another.

The Roberta Joe Society
P.O. Box 124
Circleville, OH 43113
Attention: Robin Steely
(614)474-5020

SEARCH
560 Sylvan Ave.
Englewood Cliffs, NJ 07832
Attention: Charles A. Sutherland
(800)526-4603 (toll-free)
(201)567-4040 (in New Jersey)

Concentrates on abductions by strangers but may be helpful for parental kidnaping cases. Sends its publication to 14,000 law-enforcement agencies and 6,000 other agencies, with pictures and descriptions of missing children. Takes two to four months to appear. First insertion costs $90; each additional one, $45.

Stolen Children Information Exchange
210½ Main St., Suite 1
Huntington Beach, CA 92648
Attention: Laurie Cancellara, Barbara Freeman
(714) 847-2676

Counsels searching parents. Provides referrals for lawyers and investigators. Also operates KIDS (Karing Individuals Dealing with Stealing) for parents in California.

United Parents Against Child Stealing, Inc. (UPACS)
P.O. Box 35428
Tucson, AZ 85740
Attention: Helen Hombosky
(602) 749-9303 (24-hour service)

Advises parents, but only those who have legal custody. Educates public about problem and legislates for child-stealing laws. Annual dues, $10.

Appendix B
Uniform Child Custody
Jurisdiction Act

Section 1. [Purposes of Act; Construction of Provisions.]

(a) The general purposes of this act are to:

(1) Avoid jurisdictional competition and conflict with courts of other states in matters of child custody which have in the past resulted in the shifting of children from state to state with harmful effects on their well-being;

(2) Promote cooperation with the courts of other states to the end that a custody decree is rendered in that state which can best decide the case in the interest of the child;

(3) Assure that litigation concerning the custody of a child take place ordinarily in the state with which the child and his family have the closest connection and where significant evidence concerning his care, protection, training, and personal relationships is most readily available, and that the courts of this state decline the exercise of jurisdiction when the child and his family have a closer connection with another state;

(4) Discourage continuing controversies over child custody in the interest of greater stability of home environment and of secure family relationships for the child;

(5) Deter abductions and other unilateral removals of children undertaken to obtain custody awards;

(6) Avoid relitigation of custody decisions of other states in this state insofar as feasible;

(7) Facilitate the enforcement of custody decrees of other states;

(8) Promote and expand the exchange of information and other forms of mutual assistance between the courts of this state and those of other states concerned with the same child; and

(9) Make uniform the law of those states which enact it.

(b) This act shall be construed to promote the general purposes stated in this section.

Section 2. [Definitions.]

As used in this act:

(1) "Contestant" means a person, including a parent, who claims a right to custody or visitation rights with respect to a child;

(2) "Custody determination" means a court decision and court orders and instructions providing for the custody of a child, including visitation rights; it does not include a decision relating to child support or any other monetary obligation of any person;

(3) "Custody proceeding" includes proceedings in which a custody determination is one of several issues, such as an action for divorce or separation, and includes child neglect and dependency proceedings;

(4) "Decree" or "custody decree" means a custody determination contained in a judicial decree or order made in a custody proceeding, and includes an initial decree and a modification decree;

(5) "Home state" means the state in which the child immediately preceding the time involved lived with his parents, a parent, or a person acting as parent, for at least six consecutive months, and in the case of a child less than six months old the state in which the child lived from birth with any of the persons mentioned. Periods of temporary absence of any of the named persons are counted as part of the six-month or other period;

(6) "Initial decree" means the first custody decree concerning a particular child;

(7) "Modification decree" means a custody decree which modifies or replaces a prior decree, whether made by the court which rendered the prior decree or by another court;

(8) "Physical custody" means actual possession and control of a child;

(9) "Person acting as parent" means a person, other than a parent, who has physical custody of a child and who has either been awarded custody by a court or claims a right to custody; and

(10) "State" means any state, territory, or possession of the United States, the Commonwealth of Puerto Rico, and the District of Columbia.

Section 3. [Jurisdiction.]

(a) A court of this state which is competent to decide child custody matters has jurisdiction to make a child custody determination by initial or modification decree if:

(1) This state (i) is the home state of the child at the time of commencement of the proceeding, or (ii) had been the child's home state within six months before commencement of the proceeding and the child is absent from this state because of his removal or retention by a person claiming his custody or for other reasons, and a person or person acting as parent continues to live in this state; or

(2) It is in the best interest of the child that a court of this state assume jurisdiction because (i) the child and his parents, or the child and at least one contestant, have a significant connection with this state, and (ii) there is available in this state substantial evidence concerning the child's present or future care, protection, training, and personal relationships; or

(3) The child is physically present in this state and (i) the child has been abandoned or (ii) it is necessary in an emergency to protect the child because he has been subjected to or threatened with mistreatment or abuse or is otherwise neglected [or dependent]; or

(4) (i) It appears that no other state would have jurisdiction under prerequisites substantially in accordance with Paragraphs (1), (2), or (3), or another state has declined to exercise jurisdiction on the ground that this state is the more appropriate forum to determine the custody of the child, and (ii) it is in the best interest of the child that this court assume jurisdiction.

(b) Except under Paragraphs (3) and (4) of Subsection (a), physical presence in this state of the child, or of the child and one of the contestants, is not alone sufficient to confer jurisdiction on a court of this state to make a child custody determination.

(c) Physical presence of the child, while desirable, is not a prerequisite for jurisdiction to determine his custody.

Section 4. [Notice and Opportunity to Be Heard.]

Before making a decree under this act, reasonable notice and opportunity to be heard shall be given to the contestants, any parent whose parental rights have not been previously terminated, and any person who has physical custody of the child. If any of these persons is outside this state, notice and opportunity to be heard shall be given pursuant to Section 5.

Section 5. [Notice to Persons Outside This State; Submission to Jurisdiction.]

(a) Notice required for the exercise of jurisdiction over a person outside this state shall be given in a manner reasonably calculated to give actual notice, and may be:

(1) By personal delivery outside this state in the manner prescribed for service of process within this state;

(2) In the manner prescribed by the law of the place in which the service is made for service of process in that place in an action in any of its courts of general jurisdiction;

(3) By any form of mail addressed to the person to be served and requesting a receipt; or

(4) As directed by the court [including publication, if other means of notification are ineffective].

(b) Notice under this section shall be served, mailed, or delivered, [or last published] at least [ten, twenty] days before any hearing in this state.

(c) Proof of service outside this state may be made by affidavit of the individual who made the service, or in the manner prescribed by the law of this state, the order pursuant to which the service is made, or the law of the place in which the service is made. If service is made by mail, proof may be a receipt signed by the addressee or other evidence of delivery to the addressee.

(d) Notice is not required if a person submits to the jurisdiction of the court.

Section 6. [Simultaneous Proceedings in Other States.]

(a) A court of this state shall not exercise its jurisdiction under this act if at the time of filing the petition a proceeding concerning the custody of the child was pending in a court of another state exercising jurisdiction substantially in conformity with this act, unless the proceeding is stayed by the court on the other state because this state is a more appropriate forum or for other reasons.

(b) Before hearing the petition in a custody proceeding, the court shall examine the pleadings and other information supplied by the parties under Section 9 and shall consult the child custody registry established under Section 16 concerning the pendency of proceedings with respect to the child in other states. If the court has reason to believe that proceedings may be pending in another state, it shall direct an inquiry to the state court administrator or other appropriate official of the other state.

(c) If the court is informed during the course of the proceeding that a proceeding concerning the custody of the child was pending in another state before the court assumed jurisdiction, it shall stay the proceeding and communicate with the court in which the other proceeding is pending to the end that the issue may be litigated in the more appropriate forum and that information be exchanged in accordance with Sections 19 through 22. If a court of this state has made a custody decree before being informed of a pending proceeding in a court of another state it shall immediately inform that court of the fact. If the court is informed that a proceeding was commenced in another state after it assumed jurisdiction it shall likewise inform the other court to the end that the issues may be litigated in the more appropriate forum.

Section 7. [Inconvenient Forum.]

(a) A court which has jurisdiction under this act to make an initial or modification decree may decline to exercise its jurisdiction any time before making a decree if it finds that it is an inconvenient forum to make a custody determination under the circumstances of the case and that a court of another state is a more appropriate forum.

(b) A finding of inconvenient forum may be made upon the court's own motion or upon motion of a party or a guardian ad litem or other representative of the child.

(c) In determining if it is an inconvenient forum, the court shall consider if it is in the interest of the child that another state assume jurisdiction. For this purpose, it may take into account the following factors, among others:

(1) If another state is or recently was the child's home state;

(2) If another state has a closer connection with the child and his family or with the child and one or more of the contestants;

(3) If substantial evidence concerning the child's present or future care, protection, training, and personal relationships is more readily available in another state;

(4) If the parties have agreed on another forum which is no less appropriate; and

(5) If the exercise of jurisdiction by a court of this state would contravene any of the purposes stated in Section 1.

(d) Before determining whether to decline or retain jurisdiction, the court may communicate with a court of another state and exchange information pertinent to the assumption of jurisdiction by either court with a view to assuring that jurisdiction will be exercised by the more appropriate court and that a forum will be available to the parties.

(e) If the court finds that it is an inconvenient forum and that a court of another state is a more appropriate forum, it may dismiss the proceedings, or it may stay the proceedings upon condition that a custody proceeding be promptly commenced in another named state or upon any other conditions which may be just and proper, including the condition that a moving party stipulate his consent and submission to the jurisdiction of the other forum.

(f) The court may decline to exercise its jurisdiction under this act if a custody determination is incidental to an action for divorce or another proceeding, while retaining jurisdiction over the divorce or other proceeding.

(g) If it appears to the court that it is clearly an inappropriate forum, it may require the party who commenced the proceedings to pay, in addition to the costs of the proceedings in this state, necessary travel and other expenses, including attorneys' fees, incurred by other parties or their witnesses. Payment is to be made to the clerk of the court for remittance to the proper party.

(h) Upon dismissal or stay of proceedings under this section, the court shall inform the court found to be the more appropriate forum of this fact, or if the court which would have jurisdiction in the other state is not certainly known, shall transmit the information to the court administrator or other appropriate official for forwarding to the appropriate court.

(i) Any communication received from another state informing this state of a finding of inconvenient forum because a court of this state is the more appropriate forum shall be filed in the custody registry of the appropriate court. Upon assuming jurisdiction, the court of this state shall inform the original court of this fact.

Section 8. [Jurisdiction Declined by Reason of Conduct.]

(a) If the petitioner for an initial decree has wrongfully taken the child from another state or has engaged in similar reprehensible conduct, the court may decline to exercise jurisdiction if this is just and proper under the circumstances.

(b) Unless required in the interest of the child, the court shall not exercise its jurisdiction to modify a custody decree of another state if the petitioner, without consent of the person entitled to custody, has improperly removed the child from the physical custody of the person entitled to custody or has improperly retained the child after a visit or other temporary relinquishment of physical custody. If the petitioner has violated any other provision of a custody decree of another state, the court may decline to exercise its jurisdiction if this is just and proper under the circumstances.

(c) In appropriate cases a court dismissing a petition under this section may charge the petitioner with necessary travel and other expenses, including attorneys' fees, incurred by other parties or their witnesses.

Section 9. [Information Under Oath to Be Submitted to the Court.]

(a) Every party in a custody proceeding in his first pleading, or in an affidavit attached to that pleading, shall give information under oath as to the child's present address, the places where the child has lived within the last five years, and the names and present addresses of the persons with whom the child has lived during that period. In this pleading or affidavit, every party shall further declare under oath whether:

(1) He has participated (as a party, witness, or in any other capacity) in any other litigation concerning the custody of the same child in this or any other state;

(2) He has information of any custody proceeding concerning the child pending in a court of this or any other state; and

(3) He knows of any person not a party to the proceedings who has physical custody of the child or claims to have custody or visitation rights with respect to the child.

(b) If the declaration as to any of the above items is in the affirmative, the declarant shall give additional information under oath as required by the court. The court may examine the parties under oath as to details of the information furnished and as to other matters pertinent to the court's jursdiction and the disposition of the case.

(c) Each party has a continuing duty to inform the court of any custody proceeding concerning the child in this or any other state of which he obtained information during this proceeding.

Section 10. [Additional Parties.]

If the court learns from information furnished by the parties pursuant to Section 9 or from other sources that a person not a party to the custody proceeding has physical custody of the child or claims to have custody or visitation rights with respect to the child, it shall order that person to be joined as a party and to be duly notified of the pendency of the proceeding and of his joinder as a party. If the person joined as a party is outside this state, he shall be served with process or otherwise notified in accordance with Section 5.

Section 11. [Appearance of Parties and the Child.]

(a) The court may order any party to the proceeding who is in this state to appear personally before the court. If that party has physical custody of the child, the court may order that he appear personally with the child.

(b) If a party to the proceeding whose presence is desired by the court is outside this state with or without the child, the court may order that the notice given under Section 5 include a statement directing that party to appear personally with or without the child and declaring that failure to appear may result in a decision adverse to that party.

(c) If a party to the proceeding who is outside this state is directed to appear under Subsection (b) or desires to appear personally before the court with or without the child, the court may require another party to pay to the clerk of the court travel and other necessary expenses of the party so appearing and of the child if this is just and proper under the circumstances.

Section 12. [Binding Force and Res Judicata Effect of Custody Decree.]

A custody decree rendered by a court of this state which had jurisdiction under Section 3 binds all parties who have been served in this state or notified in accordance with Section 5 or who have submitted to the jurisdiction of the court, and who have been given an opportunity to be heard. As to these parties the custody decree is conclusive as to all issues of law and fact decided and as to the custody determination made unless and until that determination is modified pursuant to law, including the provisions of this act.

Section 13. [Recognition of Out-of-State Custody Decrees.]
The courts of this state shall recognize and enforce an initial or modification decree of a court of another state which had assumed jurisdiction under statutory provisions substantially in accordance with this act or which was made under factual circumstances meeting the jurisdictional standards of the act, so long as this decree has not been modified in accordance with jurisdictional standards substantially similar to those of this act.

Section 14. [Modification of Custody Decree of Another State.]
(a) If a court of another state has made a custody decree, a court of this state shall not modify that decree unless: (1) it appears to the court of this state that the court which rendered the decree does not now have jurisdiction under jurisdictional prerequisites substantially in accordance with this act or has declined to assume jurisdiction to modify the decree, and (2) the court of this state has jurisdiction.

(b) If a court of this state is authorized under Subsection (a) and Section 8 to modify a custody decree of another state, it shall give due consideration to the transcript of the record and other documents of all previous proceedings submitted to it in accordance with Section 22.

Section 15. [Filing and Enforcement of Custody Decree of Another State.]
(a) A certified copy of a custody decree of another state may be filed in the office of the clerk of any [district court, family court] of this state. The clerk shall treat the decree in the same manner as a custody decree of the [district court, family court] of this state. A custody decree so filed has the same effect and shall be enforced in like manner as a custody decree rendered by a court of this state.

(b) A person violating a custody decree of another state which makes it necessary to enforce the decree in this state may be required to pay necessary travel and other expenses, including attorneys' fees, incurred by the party entitled to the custody or his witnesses.

Section 16. [Registry of Out-of-State Custody Decrees and Proceedings.]

The clerk of each [district court, family court] shall maintain a registry in which he shall enter the following:

(1) Certified copies of custody decrees of other states received for filing;

(2) Communications as to the pendency of custody proceedings in other states;

(3) Communications concerning a finding of inconvenient forum by a court of another state; and

(4) Other communications or documents concerning custody proceedings in another state which may affect the jurisdiction of a court of this state or the disposition to be made by it in a custody proceeding.

Section 17. [Certified Copies of Custody Decree.]

The clerk of the [district court, family court] of this state, at the request of the court of another state or at the request of any person who is affected by or has a legitimate interest in a custody decree, shall certify and forward a copy of the decree to that court or person.

Section 18. [Taking Testimony in Another State.]

In addition to other procedural devices available to a party, any party to the proceeding or a guardian ad litem or other representative of the child may adduce testimony of witnesses, including parties and the child, by deposition or otherwise, in another state. The court on its own motion may direct that the testimony of a person be taken in another state and may prescribe the manner in which and the terms upon which the testimony shall be taken.

Section 19. [Hearings and Studies in Another State; Orders to Appear.]

(a) A court of this state may request the appropriate court of another state to hold a hearing to adduce evidence, to order a party to produce or give evidence under other procedures of that state, or to have social studies made with respect to the custody of a child involved in proceedings pending in the court of this state; and to forward to the court of this state certified copies of the transcript of the record of the hearing, the evidence otherwise adduced, or any social studies prepared in compliance with the request. The cost of the services may be assessed against the parties or, if necessary, ordered paid by the [county, state].

(b) A court of this state may request the appropriate court of another state to order a party to custody proceedings pending in the court of this state to appear in the proceedings, and if that party has physical custody of the child, to appear with the child. The request may state that travel and other necessary expenses of the party and of the child whose appearance is desired will be assessed against another party or will otherwise be paid.

Section 20. [Assistance to the Courts of Other States.]

(a) Upon request of the court of another state the courts of this state which are competent to hear custody matters may order a person in this state to appear at a hearing to adduce evidence or to produce or give evidence under other procedures available in this state [or may order social studies to be made for use in a custody proceeding in another state]. A certified copy of the transcript of the record of the hearing or the evidence otherwise adduced [and any social studies prepared] shall be forwarded by the clerk of the court to the requesting court.

(b) A person within this state may voluntarily give his testimony or statement in this state for use in a custody proceeding outside this state.

(c) Upon request of the court of another state a competent court of this state may order a person in this state to appear alone or with the child in a custody proceeding in another state. The court may condition compliance with the request upon assurance by the other state that state travel and other necessary expenses will be advanced or reimbursed.

Section 21. [Preservation of Documents for Use in Other States.]

In any custody proceeding in this state the court shall preserve the pleadings, orders and decrees, any record that has been made of its hearings, social studies, and other pertinent documents until the child reaches [eighteen, twenty-one] years of age. Upon appropriate request of the court of another state the court shall forward to the other court certified copies of any or all of such documents.

Section 22. [*Request for Court Records of Another State.*]
If a custody decree has been rendered in another state concerning a child involved in a custody proceeding pending in a court of this state, the court of this state upon taking jurisdiction of the case shall request of the court of the other state a certified copy of the transcript of any court record and other documents mentioned in Section 21.

Section 23. [*International Application.*]
The general policies of this act extend to the international area. The provisions of this act relating to the recognition and enforcement of custody decrees of other states apply to custody decrees and decrees involving legal institutions similar in nature to custody institutions rendered by appropriate authorities of other nations if reasonable notice and opportunity to be heard were given to all affected persons.

Section 24. [*Priority.*]
[Upon the request of a party to a custody proceeding which raises a question of existence or exercise of jurisdiction under this act the case shall be given calendar priority and handled expeditiously.]

Section 25. [*Severability.*]
If any provision of this act or the application thereof to any person or circumstances is held invalid, its invalidity does not affect other provisions or applications of the act which can be given effect without the invalid provision or application, and to this end the provisions of this act are severable.

Appendix C
Parental Kidnaping
Prevention Act of 1980*

[*Findings and Purposes.*]
Section 7.

(a) The Congress finds that:

(1) There is a large and growing number of cases annually involving disputes between persons claiming rights of custody and visitation of children under the laws, and in the courts, of different states, the District of Columbia, the Commonwealth of Puerto Rico, and the territories and possessions of the United States;

(2) The laws and practices by which the courts of those jurisdictions determine their jurisdiction to decide such disputes, and the effect to be given the decisions of such disputes by the courts of other jurisdictions, are often inconsistent and conflicting;

(3) Those characteristics of the law and practice in such cases, along with the limits imposed by a federal system on the authority of each such jurisdiction to conduct investigations and take other actions outside its own boundaries, contribute to a tendency of parties involved in such disputes to frequently resort to the seizure, restraint, concealment, and interstate transportation of children, the disregard of court orders, excessive relitigation of cases, obtaining

* Public Law 96–611—December 28, 1980.

of conflicting orders by the courts of various jurisdictions, and interstate travel and communication that is so expensive and time-consuming as to disrupt their occupations and commercial activities; and

(4) Among the results of those conditions and activities are the failure of the courts of such jurisdictions to give full faith and credit to the judicial proceedings of the other jurisdictions, the deprivation of rights of liberty and property without due process of law, burdens on commerce among such jurisdictions and with foreign nations, and harm to the welfare of children and their parents and other custodians.

(b) For those reasons it is necessary to establish a national system for locating parents and children who travel from one such jurisdiction to another and are concealed in connection with such disputes, and to establish national standards under which the courts of such jurisdictions will determine their jurisdiction to decide such disputes and the effect to be given by each such jurisdiction to such decisions by the courts of other such jurisdictions.

(c) The general purposes of Sections 6 to 10 of this act are to:

(1) Promote cooperation between state courts to the end that a determination of custody and visitation is rendered in the state which can best decide the case in the interest of the child;

(2) Promote and expand the exchange of information and other forms of mutual assistance between states which are concerned with the same child;

(3) Facilitate the enforcement of custody and visitation decrees of sister states;

(4) Discourage continuing interstate controversies over child custody in the interest of greater stability of home environment and of secure family relationships for the child;

(5) Avoid jurisdictional competition and conflict between state courts in matters of child custody and visitation which have in the past resulted in the shifting of children from state to state with harmful effects on their well-being; and

(6) Deter interstate abductions and other unilateral removals of children undertaken to obtain custody and visitation awards.

[*Full Faith and Credit Given to Child Custody Determinations.*]
Section 8.

(a) Chapter 115 of title 28, United States Code, is amended by adding immediately after section 1738 the following new section:

279

"*§1738A. [Full faith and credit given to child custody determinations.]*

"(a) The appropriate authorities of every state shall enforce according to its terms, and shall not modify except as provided in Subsection (f) of this section, any child custody determination made consistently with the provisions of this section by a court of another state.

"(b) As used in this section, the term:

"(1) 'Child' means a person under the age of eighteen;

"(2) 'Contestant' means a person, including a parent, who claims a right to custody or visitation of a child;

"(3) 'Custody determination' means a judgment, decree, or other order of a court providing for the custody or visitation of a child, and includes permanent and temporary orders, and initial orders and modifications;

"(4) 'Home state' means the state in which, immediately preceding the time involved, the child lived with his parents, a parent, or a person acting as parent, for at least six consecutive months, and in the case of a child less than six months old, the state in which the child lived from birth with any of such persons. Periods of temporary absence of any of such persons are counted as part of the six-month or other period;

"(5) 'Modification' and 'modify' refer to a custody determination which modifies, replaces, supersedes, or otherwise is made subsequent to, a prior custody determination concerning the same child, whether made by the same court or not;

"(6) 'Person acting as a parent' means a person, other than a parent, who has physical custody of a child and who has either been awarded custody by a court or claims a right to custody;

"(7) 'Physical custody' means actual possession and control of a child; and

"(8) 'State' means a state of the United States, the District of Columbia, the Commonwealth of Puerto Rico, or a territory or possession of the United States.

"(c) A child custody determination made by a court of a state is consistent with the provisions of this section only if:

"(1) Such court has jurisdiction under the law of such state; and

"(2) One of the following conditions is met:

"(A) such state (i) is the home state of the child on the date of the commencement of the proceeding, or (ii) had been the child's home state within six months before the date of the commencement of the proceeding and the child is absent from such state because of his removal or retention by a contestant or for other reasons, and a contestant continues to live in such state;

"(B)(i) it appears that no other state would have jurisdiction under Subparagraph (A), and (ii) it is in the best interest of the child that a court of such state assume jurisdiction because (I) the child and his parents, or the child and at least one contestant, have a significant connection with such state other than mere physical presence in such state, and (II) there is available in such state substantial evidence concerning the child's present or future care, protection, training, and personal relationships;

"(C) The child is physically present in such state and (i) the child has been abandoned, or (ii) it is necessary in an emergency to protect the child because he has been subjected to or threatened with mistreatment or abuse;

"(D)(i) it appears that no other state would have jurisdiction under Subparagraph (A), (B), (C), or (E), or another state has declined to exercise jurisdiction on the ground that the state whose jurisdiction is in issue is the more appropriate forum to determine the custody of the child, and (ii) it is in the best interest of the child that such court assume jurisdiction; or

"(E) The court has continuing jurisdiction pursuant to Subsection (d) of this section.

"(d) The jurisdiction of a court of a state which has made a child custody determination consistently with the provisions of this section continues as long as the requirement of Subsection (c)(1) of this section continues to be met and such state remains the residence of the child or of any contestant.

"(e) Before a child custody determination is made, reasonable notice and opportunity to be heard shall be given to the contestants, any parent whose parental rights have not been previously terminated, and any person who has physical custody of a child.

"(f) A court of a state may modify a determination of the custody of the same child made by a court of another state, if:

"(1) It has jurisdiction to make such a child custody determination; and

"(2) The court of the other state no longer has jurisdiction, or it has declined to exercise such jurisdiction to modify such determination.

"(g) A court of a state shall not exercise jurisdiction in any proceeding for a custody determination commenced during the pendency of a proceeding in a court of another state where such court of that other state is exercising jurisdiction consistently with the provisions of this section to make a custody determination."

(b) The table of sections at the beginning of Chapter 115 of Title 28, United States Code, is amended by inserting after the item relating to section 1738 the following new item:

"1738A. [Full faith and credit given to child custody determinations.]"

(c) In furtherance of the purposes of Section 1738A of Title 28, United States Code, as added by Subsection (a) of this section, state courts are encouraged to:

(1) Afford priority to proceedings for custody determinations; and

(2) Award to the person entitled to custody or visitation pursuant to a custody determination which is consistent with the provisions of such Section 1738A, necessary travel expenses, attorneys' fees, costs of private investigations, witness fees or expenses, and other expenses incurred in connection with such custody determination in any case in which:

(A) A contestant has, without the consent of the person entitled to custody or visitation pursuant to a custody determination which is consistent with the provisions of such Section 1738A, (i) wrongfully removed the child from the physical custody of such person, or (ii) wrongfully retained the child after a visit or other temporary relinquishment of physical custody; or

(B) The court determines it is appropriate.

[*Use of Federal Parent Locator Service in Connection with the Enforcement or Determination of Child Custody and in Cases of Parental Kidnaping of a Child.*]
Section 9.

(a) Section 454 of the Social Security Act is amended:

(1) By striking out "and" at the end of Paragraph (15);

(2) By striking out the period at the end of Paragraph (16) and inserting in lieu thereof "; and"; and

(3) By inserting after Paragraph (16) the following new paragraph:

"(17) in the case of a state which has in effect an agreement with the secretary entered into pursuant to Section 463 for the use of the Parent Locator Service established under Section 453, to accept and transmit to the secretary requests for information authorized under the provisions of the agreement to be furnished by such service to authorized persons, and to impose and collect (in accordance with regulations of the secretary) a fee sufficient to cover the costs to the state and to the secretary incurred by reason of such requests, to transmit to the secretary from time to time (in accordance with such regulations) so much of the fees collected as are attributable to such costs to the secretary so incurred, and during the period that such agreement is in effect, otherwise to comply with such agreement and regulations of the secretary with respect thereto."

(b) Part D of Title IV of the Social Security Act is amended by adding at the end thereof the following new section:

"[Use of Federal Parent Locator Service in Connection with the Enforcement or Determination of Child Custody and in Cases of Parental Kidnaping of a Child.]
"Section 463.

"(a) The secretary shall enter into an agreement with any state which is able and willing to do so, under which the services of the Parent Locator Service established under Section 453 shall be made available to such state for the purpose of determining the whereabouts of any absent parent or child when such information is to be used to locate such parent or child for the purpose of:

"(1) Enforcing any state or federal law with respect to the unlawful taking or restraint of a child; or

"(2) Making or enforcing a child custody determination.

"(b) An agreement entered into under this section shall provide that the state agency described in Section 454 will, under procedures prescribed by the secretary in regulations, receive and transmit to the secretary requests from authorized persons for information as to (or useful in determining) the whereabouts of any absent parent or child when such information is to be used to locate such parent or child for the purpose of:

"(1) Enforcing any state or federal law with respect to the unlawful taking or restraint of a child; or

"(2) Making or enforcing a child custody determination.

"(c) Information authorized to be provided by the secretary under this section shall be subject to the same conditions with respect to disclosure as information authorized to be provided under Section 453, and a request for information by the secretary under this section shall be considered to be a request for information under Section 453 which is authorized to be provided under such section. Only information as to the most recent address and place of employment of any absent parent or child shall be provided under this section.

"(d) For purposes of this section:

"(1) The term 'custody determination' means a judgment, decree, or other order of a court providing for the custody or visitation of a child, and includes permanent and temporary orders, and initial orders and modification;

"(2) The term 'authorized person' means:

"(A) Any agent or attorney of any state having an agreement under this section, who has the duty or authority under the law of such state to enforce a child custody determination;

"(B) Any court having jurisdiction to make or enforce such a child custody determination, or any agent of such court; and

"(C) Any agent or attorney of the United States, or of a state having an agreement under this section, who has the duty or authority to investigate, enforce, or bring a prosecution with respect to the unlawful taking or restraint of a child."

(c) Section 455(a) of such act is amended by adding after paragraph (3) the following: "Except that no amount shall be paid to any state on account of amounts expended to carry out an agreement which it has entered into pursuant to Section 463."

(d) No agreement entered into under Section 463 of the Social Security Act shall become effective before the date on which Section 1738A of Title 28, United States Code (as added by this title) becomes effective.

[Parental Kidnaping.]
Section 10.

(a) In view of the findings of the Congress and the purposes of Sections 6 to 10 of this act set forth in Section 302, the Congress hereby expressly declares its intent that Section 1073 of Title 18, United States Code, apply to cases involving parental kidnaping and interstate or international flight to avoid prosecution under applicable state felony statutes.

(b) The Attorney General of the United States, not later than 120 days after the date of the enactment of this section (and once every six months during the three-year period following such 120-day period), shall submit a report to the Congress with respect to steps taken to comply with the intent of the Congress set forth in Subsection (a). Each such report shall include:

(1) Data relating to the number of applications for complaints under Section 1073 of Title 18, United States Code, in cases involving parental kidnaping.

(2) Data relating to the number of complaints issued in such cases; and

(3) Such other information as may assist in describing the activities of the Department of Justice in conformance with such intent.

Suggested Reading

Abrahms, Sally. "The Joint Custody Controversy." *New York*, June 18, 1979, p. 56.

————. "Kidnap!" *New York Daily News Sunday Magazine*, December 9, 1979, p. 60.

————, and Joseph N. Bell. "Have You Seen These Children?" *Ladies' Home Journal*, April 1981, p. 77.

Agopian, Michael W. *Parental Child-Stealing*. Lexington, Mass.: D. C. Heath & Co., 1981.

Baum, Charlotte. "The Best of Both Parents." *New York Times Magazine*, October 31, 1976, p. 44.

Black, Bonnie Lee. *Somewhere Child*. New York: The Viking Press, 1981.

Bodenheimer, Brigitte M. "Progress Under the Uniform Child Custody Jurisdiction Act and Remaining Problems: Punitive Decrees, Joint Custody and Excessive Modifications." *California Law Review* 65 (1977).

Demeter, Anna. *Legal Kidnaping*. Boston: Beacon Press, 1977.

Downey, Sue. "Child Stealing: The Custody Tug-of-War." *Tucson Citizen*, October 13, 1979, p. 8.

Dullea, Georgia. "The Battle Over Custody: Where the Rights of Children and Parents Clash." *New York Times*, July 23, 1981, p. 1.

————. "Parental Kidnaping: Boundaries Widen." *New York Times*, January 29, 1980, p. 14.

Fenyvesi, Charles. "The Hostages: Re-Entry Problems Ahead." *Psychology Today*, November 10, 1980, p. 35.

Fielding, Joy. *Kiss Mommy Goodbye*. New York: Doubleday & Co., 1981.

Fox, Catherine. "Tearing the Ties That Bind." *Maclean's*, July 7, 1980, p. 27.

Francke, Linda Bird, et al. "The Children of Divorce." *Newsweek*, February 11, 1980, p. 58.

"From Hostages to Heroes—The Trauma of Coming Home." *U.S. News & World Report*, November 10, 1980, p. 35.

Galper, Miriam. *Co-Parenting*. Philadelphia: Running Press, 1978.

Gill, John Edward. *Stolen Children*. New York: Seaview Books, 1981.

Goldstein, Joseph, Anna Freud, and Albert J. Solnit. *Beyond the Best Interests of the Child*. New York: The Free Press, 1973.

Grossman, John. "Hostage Psychology: The Science of Necessity." *Family Health*, November/December 1980, p. 10.

Harden, Blaine. "Young, Wealthy . . . And Mixed Up." *Boston Globe*, September 18, 1981, p. 43.

Haskett, Mary Ellen. "Divorced Fathers Want Their Kids, Too." *Philadelphia Bulletin*, Focus section, July 22, 1979, p. 1.

Interstate and International Child Custody Disputes. Washington: The American Bar Association, 1981.

Jares, Susan Ellen. "A Victim and a Childnapper Describe the Agonizing Problem of the 'Stolen' Kids of Divorce." *People*, February 9, 1981, p. 40.

Katz, Sanford N. *Child Snatching: The Legal Response to the Abduction of Children*. Chicago: American Bar Association Press, 1981.

"Kidnaping: A Family Affair." *Newsweek*, October 18, 1976, p. 24.

Leo, John. "Kidnaped by Mom or Dad." *Time*, July 14, 1980, p. 41.

Moore, Beverly J. "Parental Child Stealing Takes Its Toll." *Los Angeles Times*, View section, September 13, 1981, p. 1.

"Moving to Stop Child Snatching." *Time*, February 27, 1978, p. 85.

Olsen, Jack. *Have You Seen My Son?* New York: Atheneum Publishers, 1982.

Ramos, Suzanne. *The Complete Book of Child Custody.* New York: G. P. Putnam's Sons, 1979.

Rofes, Eric R., ed. *The Kids' Book of Divorce.* Lexington, Mass.: The Lewis Publishing Company, 1981.

Roman, Mel, and William Haddad. *The Disposable Parent.* New York: Holt, Rinehart & Winston, 1978.

Salk, Lee. *What Every Child Would Like Parents to Know About Divorce.* New York: Harper & Row Publishers, 1978.

Silver, Gerald A., and Myrna Silver. *Weekend Fathers.* Los Angeles: Stratford Press, 1981.

Strickland, Margaret. *Child-Snatched.* Moore Haven, N.J.: Rainbow Books, 1979.

Van Gelder, Lindsy. "Beyond Custody: When Parents Steal Their Own Children." *Ms.*, May 1978, p. 52.

Wallop, Malcolm. "Child Snatchers: Concerned Parents or Criminals?" *Law Enforcement Communications*, June 1980, p. 26.

Zipser, Andrew. "Childsnatching—A Tangled Web of Family Ties." *Phoenix Gazette*, Today's Living section, February 29, 1980, p. 6.

Index

Index

SALLY ABRAHMS has written extensively on family law issues for *New York, Ladies' Home Journal, McCall's,* the *New York Daily News,* and other periodicals. In 1981, one of her articles on childsnatching resulted in the reunion of a stolen child and mother; a segment on childsnatching which Abrahms reported and helped produce for the ABC News Program *20/20* won an Emmy Award nomination in 1980. She has also served as the legal consultant for the Columbia Pictures film *And Justice for All.* Sally Abrahms lives with her husband, David Rosenthal, and her daughter, Anna, in Boston, where she is a contributing writer at *Boston Magazine.*